DEVELOPING CAPACITY THROUGH TECHNICAL COOPERATION

DEVELOPING CAPACITY THROUGH TECHNICAL COOPERATION

COUNTRY EXPERIENCES

Edited by: Stephen Browne

Earthscan Publications Ltd
London and Sterling, Virginia

First published in the UK and USA in 2002
by Earthscan Publications Ltd

Copyright © 2002
United Nations Development Programme
One United Nations Plaza
New York, NY, 10017

ISBN: 1 85383 969 8 paperback
            1 85383 974 4 hardback

DISCLAIMER
The responsibility for opinions in this book rests solely with its authors. Publication does not consti-
tute an endorsement by the United Nations Development Programme or the institutions of the
United Nations system.

Design and layout by Karin Hug
Printed in the UK by The Bath Press

A catalogue record for this book is available from the British Library.

Library of Congress Cataloging-in-Publication Data

Developing capacity through technical cooperation : country experiences / edited by Stephen
Browne.
        p. cm.
    ISBN 1-85383-969-8 (pbk.) -- ISBN 1-85383-974-4 (hard)
      1. Technology--Developing countries--International cooperation. 2. Technology transfer--
Developing countries. 3. Technical assistance--Developing countries. 4. Research,
Industrial--Developing countries. I. Browne, Stephen.

  T49.5.D478 2002
  338'.01--dc21
                                                            2002013268

Earthscan Publications Ltd
120 Pentonville Road, London, N1 9JN, UK
Tel: +44 (0)20 7278 0433. Fax: +44 (0)20 7278 1142
Email: earthinfo@earthscan.co.uk. Web: www.earthscan.co.uk

22883 Quicksilver Drive, Sterling, VA 20166-2012, USA

Earthscan is an editorially independent subsidiary of Kogan Page Ltd and publishes in association
with WWF-UK and the International Institute for Environment and Development.

This book is printed on elemental chlorine-free paper.

CONTENTS

Foreword

These are pivotal times for foreign aid. For 10 years following the end of the Cold War, total assistance flows were in decline. The poorest countries in Africa were doubly jeopardized, for as the assistance ebbed, aid was being switched away from that continent and in favor of Europe and Central Asia. Technical cooperation – defined here as free-standing technical assistance provided by multilateral and bilateral donors – went down with aid, with the declines even faster in the poorest countries.

Although a few bilateral donors successfully maintained their previous levels of assistance, the general fall demonstrated the extent to which aid had become strategic as well as developmental. There were also genuine concerns about aid effectiveness, a debate UNDP helped to spark with its 1993 book *Rethinking Technical Cooperation*. Important questions were posed about the nature of the assistance and the productiveness of its use.

But as the millennium turned, so did the debate. Vociferous civil society campaigning helped to remind the international community of the growing rift between rich and poor countries. There was progress at last on reducing the unpayable external debt of the poorest countries. At the UN's Millennium Summit of 2000, the international community rededicated itself to the Millennium Development Goals. With the goals came a determination to find more resources to meet them, and at the International Conference on Financing for Development in Monterrey in March 2002, several major donors resolved to halt and significantly reverse the decline in aid.

Within aid, technical cooperation now begins to assume growing importance. Concessional flows of capital are expected to increase in the coming years. As the health of the global economy is restored, there also will be renewed flows of private capital and foreign direct investment. Technical cooperation will be the indispensable complement of finance, developing capacity to absorb and manage resources within the broader development process.

This book provides some concrete inputs to the new thinking about the contribution of technical cooperation to capacity development on the basis of very practical examples. It is about the experience over the last decade of developing management capacities through technical cooperation in 6 countries: Bangladesh, Bolivia, Egypt, Kyrgyz Republic, Philippines and Uganda.

The records have been mixed, but two clear underlying themes have emerged. On one hand, building capacity has not usually been a conscious and clearly defined objective of the development process; on the other, technical cooperation – by its very nature and origins – is motivated and driven by considerations other than support to capacity development.

This is the second book to emerge from a research programme on *Reforming Technical Cooperation for Capacity Development,* which UNDP has been undertaking with the support of the Government of The Netherlands. The first book, *Capacity for Development: New solutions to old problems,* launched at the Monterrey Conference, was a debate and dialogue around the issue of improving effective capacity development, to which a number of practitioners, academics and policy makers within and outside UNDP have contributed. This volume is anchored in specific country experiences and distils the work of teams of researchers based in those countries. It is important to note that the two books demonstrate a remarkable convergence of views about what has gone right and wrong in the conceptualization of capacity development and the application of technical cooperation – and what future steps should be taken to make it more effective in helping catalyse efforts to achieve the Millennium Development Goals.

MARK MALLOCH BROWN
Administrator
United Nations Development Programme

Preface

The last decade has seen a continuing scrutiny of aid levels and effectiveness. But these discussions have not just been a deconstructive process of endless debating and debunking. This heightened awareness of the urgent stakes attached to improved performance comes with unprecedented movement towards beneficial change. This book provides many intimations of this movement at the country level.

It is complemented by progress at the global level as well. In February 2002, as part of its continuing work to review the contribution of technical cooperation to capacity development, UNDP organized a high-level Round Table in Accra, Ghana. The meeting brought together ministerial-level representatives of developing and donor governments, international organizations, civil society organizations and academia. A key outcome of the meeting was the Accra Statement, which follows.

The statement encompasses an emerging consensus on how national capacity development can best be supported by technical cooperation, and how the traditional donor-recipient relationship can evolve into more even-handed partnerships.

CARLOS LOPES
Deputy Director
Bureau for Development Policy, UNDP

Accra Outcomes Statement

DEFINING THE CAPACITY DEVELOPMENT AGENDA

This statement is an outcome of the High-Level Round Table, "Towards a capacity development agenda," held in Accra on 11-12 February 2002. While not having any formal status, the document captures the spirit and key messages emerging from the discussions.

Context

There is a new spirit of global partnership. It is manifested in the growing consensus around a common development agenda and a universal set of development goals agreed to by the Millennium Declaration in September 2000. There is now a need to help countries achieve these goals on a sustainable basis, for which national poverty reduction strategies can provide a focus.

A growing global consciousness has also developed as a result of the increasingly global market for skilled labour, as well as access to information by people all over the world through new technologies.

In the new global partnership, developing countries will determine their own needs for capacity development, for which technical cooperation provides indispensable support.

Action points

1. Focus on capacity development to determine the role of technical cooperation.

The subject has been viewed through the wrong end of the telescope – the technical cooperation (TC) end. We need to look through the capacity development (CD) end to determine what needs to be done, and how TC can support the process. In short, a supply-driven process needs to be replaced by one that is demand-driven. This means:

- Identifying inadequacies and obstacles to CD. It implies examining factors affecting the use, retention, and continuous upgrading of capacities.

- CD should not only be considered in the public sector but should embrace capacities in all sectors of society: academia, the private sector and civil society. This requires engagement of these non-state actors in dialogue with government in determining needs and priorities.

- Effective CD builds on a clear vision of human resource development with particular regard to education systems and labour markets.

2. Knowledge should be acquired and not merely transferred.

TC has been operating under an assumption that knowledge mainly resides in the donor countries and needs to be transferred. But there is knowledge everywhere, and true partnership implies an equitable sharing of it. Information and communications technology opens up new opportunities for sharing. Thus:

- Available indigenous knowledge and expertise must be acknowledged in responding to the challenges of CD.

- Expertise brought in from outside should be in response to country demand and should be fully compatible with the local institutional context.

- The need for expatriate expertise is reduced because of the facilitation of access to information and communications technologies.

- 'Scan globally, reinvent locally.'

3. Reform of technical cooperation has been too slow.

Progress in the implementation of TC reforms endorsed in the early 1990s has been slow, and much more has to be done by all multilateral and bilateral partners if TC is to serve CD more effectively. Areas requiring urgent action are:

- Harmonization of procedures and accountability requirements as part of ongoing OECD/DAC discussions.

- Placing projects within coordinated frameworks determined by developing country governments to reduce the burden on their administrative capacities.

- Working through national structures instead of setting up parallel structures.

- Increasing efforts to promote and utilize local and other developing country expertise and procurement in the interests of seeking cost-effective and appropriate inputs whenever available.

- Promotion of TC practices which support national processes for priority-setting and public expenditure management.

4. Capacity development has to be guided by clear strategies that are nationally-owned.

Ownership of the development process is both a means and an end in itself, articulated in an interactive manner through effective participation of all stakeholders, and sustained by genuine partnerships.

- It is important for countries to develop clear strategic frameworks, as well as the capacity to formulate them. This implies strategic planning capacity in the country.

Truly country-owned PRSPs are an example, and can be used as a mechanism for focusing and coordinating donor assistance.

- National ownership implies a fully participatory process of engagement with citizens, civil society, academia, trade unions, the private sector, etc., in addition to different government agencies.

5. Distortions in public sector employment are major obstacles to CD.

Ultimate responsibility for public policy and its implementation reside in governments and require an effective and motivated civil service. In many countries, the failure to implement civil service and fiscal reforms impedes progress by making it impossible to attract and retain scarce human resources. This is especially important in view of the increasingly global skills market.

- The issue of improving the incentive structure for public services in developing countries must be addressed so that capacity is available and nurtured.

- Civil service and fiscal reforms must be addressed as a matter of priority.

- Attempts by donors to offer salary supplements and other inducements can never be more than temporary palliatives; they introduce distortions into the local labour markets and should be brought to an end.

6. "Poor performers" present particular CD challenges and require flexible responses.

Since many "poor performers" with the weakest capacities are Least Developed Countries, it is important that donors do not abandon them, and instead seek appropriate entry points for supporting positive elements that may exist, particularly at the local level.

While support to civil society may be the most appropriate route, it should not be at the expense of dialogue with the state.

7. Governments and external partners must be primarily accountable to the people they serve.

New accountability frameworks are needed for both donors and recipients that satisfy constituencies on both sides, and in each case involve full civic engagement. Accountability is also a reciprocal condition, implying responsibilities of donor to recipient as well as recipient to donor.

- The ultimate intended beneficiaries – the people most affected – should be fully engaged and have a decisive voice in determining priorities, taking action and judging actual progress. Appropriate instruments and criteria need to be urgently developed for measuring impact and outcomes of capacity development.

8. Change the terms of the North-South dialogue.

Partnership implies an end to the preponderant 'North-South' axis of dialogue. And transparency, frank dialogue and genuine engagement should be demonstrated by all development partners.

- Forums for the exchange of experience and information on TC and CD practices among developing countries are needed and should be initiated and owned by the countries concerned

9. Action is urgently required now.

Steps should be taken as soon as possible to begin implementing practices and principles of capacity development.

Acknowledgements

This book is a product of the combined efforts of a large team whose members reside in every region.

The Bangladesh, Bolivia, Egypt, Kyrgyz Republic, Philippines and Uganda country chapters are based on the collaborative work of country teams that have undertaken original research over several months. (See About the Authors.) The country studies were directed and managed by Mary Hilderbrand of Harvard University, in close collaboration with Thomas Theisohn, Project Coordinator of UNDP's Reforming Technical Cooperation initiative. Paul Matthews and Lina Hamadeh-Banerjee, along with UNDP colleagues in the Country Offices of the six countries, provided important support to the research teams.

Particular thanks go to the peer reviewers who contributed many clarifications and improvements to the text and presentation, in particular Carlos Lopes, Leelananda de Silva, Sakiko Fukuda-Parr, Bob Griffin, Terence Jones, Ngila Mwase and Christopher J. Ronald. The production and editing team also included Marixie Mercado, Fe Conway and Bozena Blix. Logistical support was provided by Arleen Verendia.

This volume is part of the larger initiative on Reforming Technical Cooperation for Capacity Development at UNDP, and benefits from an immense body of work already undertaken, including electronic discussions, workshops and roundtables. The book also draws on the outcomes of a series of country deliberations on capacity development and technical cooperation that were held in Cameroon, China, Egypt, Ghana, Kenya and Turkey. The data, analyses and insights that came out of all these undertakings are invaluable and the whole process involved contributions from many individuals, including colleagues from the project's Advisory and Facilitation Group, the World Bank, UNDP, the European Center for Development Policy Management, Harvard University and the African Capacity Building Foundation. Many thanks in particular are due to: Niloy Banerjee, Pierre Baris, Heather Baser, Ghada Jiha, Pim de Keizer, Carlos del Castillo, Gus Edgren, Tony Land, Albert Ondo Ossa, Nadia Rasheed, Michael Sarris and Maki Suzuki. Last, but not least, many thanks to the Government of The Netherlands, for funding the initiative.

With much gratitude for all the support received, the editor and the contributing authors assume full responsibility for the opinions expressed in the study.

STEPHEN BROWNE
Principal Advisor on Capacity Development
Bureau for Development Policy, UNDP

1 Introduction[1]

RETHINKING CAPACITY DEVELOPMENT FOR TODAY'S CHALLENGES

While financial aid was intended to close the domestic and external resource gaps of developing countries, the original objective of technical cooperation (TC)[2] was to compensate for skills. We have long known that this 'skills gap' was much too narrow a concept. For while TC has over many years successfully purveyed training and expertise across the full range of lacking skills, there has been limited impact on the ability of countries to sustainably manage their own development processes, and thus enable them to become more independent of aid. Development management is a much broader and deeper process, subtly differentiated country by country, which TC can only partially assist.

This chapter sets out to examine the real target of TC: the development of the capacity to manage. What does this really mean? What is the nature of capacity development? Against what do we measure progress? How much can TC assist, and in what ways?

The three-dimensional nature of capacity development

Among development practitioners, capacity has traditionally been conceived in two dimensions: human resources and organizational functions. "Capacity building"[3] – as

---

[1] This chapter was prepared by Stephen Browne, Principal Advisor on Capacity Development, Bureau for Development Policy, UNDP.
[2] In this book technical cooperation refers to free-standing (as opposed to investment project-related) technical assistance.
[3] In this book, there is a preference for the use of "capacity development" over "capacity building". The former connotes a long-term process that covers many crucial stages, including building capacities and ensuring national ownership and sustainability.

it has most commonly been referred to – therefore involved human resource development and organizational engineering, or "institution building", with particular reference to the public sector. The organizational dimension significantly extended that of human resource development, since it implied the need for management skills that reached beyond the technical (ECOSOC 2000).

It has become apparent that institution building, as a basis for development capacity, also needs to expand beyond the formal functions of organizations in the public sector, for at least two reasons. In the first place, the functioning of the public sector is itself influenced by non-organizational factors, including what might be termed the "state of governance": the legitimacy and independence of the various organs of state, the relevance and quality of public policy, and so on. Secondly, capacity for development increasingly encompasses organizations and institutions that lie entirely outside the public sector – private enterprise and civil society organizations in particular.

In the companion volume to this book, UNDP defines capacity as "the ability to perform functions, solve problems, and set and achieve objectives". This generic definition builds on an earlier one drawn up by UNDP and UNICEF[4], but is a significant departure from the previous focus on human resource development and institution building. Encompassing individual and institutional levels previously addressed, UNDP emphasizes the importance of a third, societal level of capacity development that involves "capacities in the society as a whole" (Fukuda-Parr et al and UNDP, 2002).

The first level is that of the individual. The second, the institutional, merits an interpretation beyond the merely organizational. Institutional capacity involves laws, procedures, systems and customs. As a symptom of the importance of these institutional factors, some of the country papers allude to the problems of corruption and the misuse of power and resources, which impede capacity development. Two other indispensable facets suggested by the book are policies and leadership.

The policy environment is critical to capacity development. But the mere enunciation of "good" policy is not enough. It must be consistently and transparently enacted, for which there need to be capacities for planning and implementation, and mechanisms of objective inspection and auditing.

Policies are determined in large part by the qualities and commitments of leaders, and recent development history is replete with examples. Leadership is important for another reason. Development is a process of transformation, and capacities are continually needing to change and adapt. Strong leadership – and the strategic vision that goes with it – is necessary to anticipate change and adjust to it.

The third dimension, the societal, encompasses the facilitatory processes which lie at the heart of human development: the opening and widening of opportunities that enable people to use and expand their capacities to the fullest. Social capital and cohesion are at the core of societal capacity and apply both nationally and locally. Capacity development cannot ignore the critical importance of decentralized village and

---

4 A UNDP/UNICEF study in 1999 described capacity as "the ability to define and realize goals effectively". See references.

community-based organizations and units, right down to the individual household, where the empowerment – or "capacitation" – of women is an important consideration.

Capacity development also needs to take account of the global environment, which increasingly impinges on the capacity of countries, at all three of these levels, to address the challenges of development. People, goods, finance, technology and information are moving across the globe in unprecedented quantities and frequencies. The ramifications of globalization can be positive or negative, but they cannot be ignored. The globalization of the skilled labour market, the opportunities and adversities of more open external markets, and the impact of the digital divide, all have important consequences for the development of capacity.

In sum, capacity is both easy and hard to define. A generic definition, at its simplest, includes both the attainment of skills and the capabilities to use them. But the answers to the questions "which skills?" and "whose capabilities?" are much more complex because each development context is unique, and none is static. It is the very particularized circumstances of countries and communities that make capacity development such an inexact science. A flavour of these particularities is provided by the six country studies in this book.

Achieving the Millennium Development Goals: Not Just Resources But Capacities

The answer to the question "for what?" may be somewhat easier to determine. In September 2000, a large majority of the world's heads of government met in New York at the Millennium Summit and agreed to the Millennium Declaration, the most comprehensive development agenda ever endorsed at that level. The Millennium Development Goals (MDGs) have brought a much clearer focus to the global development task, together with the target date of 2015 (see box). The MDGs represent the internationalization of global norms and standards. Their realization is a task to which all countries – aid recipients and donors alike – must contribute.

For the developing countries, these goals are clustered around four development domains: economic governance, health, education and the environment. The UN system – led by its UN Development Group (principally UNDP, UNICEF, UNFPA, WFP) – has begun to monitor the status and progress of the MDGs through a series of regular country reports. These reports are an essential frame for the massive two-fold development challenge of marshalling the resources and developing the country capacities to meet the goals.

Resources. After a long and barren period, the development resources picture has begun to change. The Heavily Indebted Poor Countries (HIPC) Initiative of 1996, and its enhanced version two years later, heralded the beginning. Although very slow to work through, lower debt servicing obligations have begun to make significant sums available to certain HIPC countries for spending on poverty-related programmes. HIPC relief comes partially from existing official development assistance (ODA) allocations.

A more significant watershed was reached at the International Conference on Financing for Development at Monterrey, Mexico, in March 2002. Many European donors renewed their determination to advance ODA contributions towards the 0.7% of GNP target level, and the United States promised to increase its aid through a new Millennium Challenge Account. The combined new commitments are expected to lead to an immediate reversal in the downward ODA trend, and could help aid levels rise by up to 25% by the middle of this decade. For many donors, the financing of the MDGs has provided the principal rationale for the aid increase. Although the projected increases fall far short of the 50-100% additional aid resources which some have estimated to be needed to meet the MDGs (Zedillo 2001, World Bank 2002, OXFAM 2002), these new commitments will put significant new funding at the disposal of many poor countries.

Capacities. New resources – large or small – will not be sufficient. How they are applied and managed, the commitment of leaders, the ability of the organizational structures to deliver benefits, and the wider policy and institutional environment of facilitation and enablement will all be of primordial importance to the achievement or non-achievement of the goals. These are critical concerns of capacity development.

For every goal, there are at least 10 kinds of national capacity to be developed:

> **The capacity to set objectives:** based on an understanding of the national and local contexts, requires sound data and information about current needs and targets vulnerable groups;

> **The capacity to develop strategies:** requires a clear prioritization of needs, an understanding of the processes which can contribute to meeting them, and the development of meaningful benchmarks to determine progress;

> **The capacity to draw up action plans:** based on an agreed strategy, requires a detailed listing of required actions, identification of the parties involved in carrying them out, and a clear timetable;

> **The capacity to develop and implement appropriate policies:** requires design of policies and methodologies for effective and accountable policy implementation;

> **The capacity to develop regulatory and legal frameworks:** requires adapting national laws and regulations for compatibility with relevant global conventions;

> **The capacity to build and manage partnerships:** requires full and constructive consultation among key stakeholders (based on appropriate incentives), to secure commitments by the organizations and entities to be involved in the implementation of the action plan;

> **The capacity to foster an enabling environment for civil society:** the success and sustainability of development initiatives require the participation of all relevant stakeholders, particularly the more vulnerable;

MILLENNIUM DEVELOPMENT GOALS AND TARGETS

Goal 1:	Eradicate extreme poverty and hunger
Target 1:	Halve, between 1990 and 2015, the proportion of people whose income is less than one dollar a day
Target 2:	Halve, between 1990 and 2015, the proportion of people who suffer from hunger
Goal 2:	Achieve universal primary education
Target 3:	Ensure that, by 2015, children everywhere, boys and girls alike, will be able to complete a full course of primary schooling
Goal 3:	Promote gender equality and empower women
Target 4:	Eliminate gender disparity in primary and secondary education preferably by 2005 and to all levels of education no later than 2015
Goal 4:	Reduce child mortality
Target 5:	Reduce by two-thirds, between 1990 and 2015, the under-five mortality rate
Goal 5:	Improve maternal health
Target 6:	Reduce by three-quarters, between 1990 and 2015, the maternal mortality ratio
Goal 6:	Combat HIV/AIDS, malaria and other diseases
Target 7:	Have halted by 2015, and begun to reverse, the spread of HIV/AIDS
Target 8:	Have halted by 2015, and begun to reverse, the incidence of malaria and other major diseases
Goal 7:	Ensure environmental sustainability
Target 9:	Integrate the principles of sustainable development into country policies and programmes and reverse the loss of environmental resources
Target 10:	Halve, by 2015, the proportion of people without sustainable access to safe drinking water
Target 11:	By 2020, to have achieved a significant improvement in the lives of at least 100 million slum dwellers
Goal 8:	Develop a Global Partnership for Development
Target 12:	Develop further an open, rule-based, predictable, non-discriminatory trading and financial system that deals with a reduction in debt to sustainable levels
Target 13:	Address the Special Needs of the Least Developed Countries
Target 14:	Address the Special Needs of landlocked countries and small island developing states
Target 15:	In cooperation with developing countries, develop and implement strategies for decent and productive work for youth
Target 16:	In cooperation with pharmaceutical companies, provide access to affordable medicines
Target 17:	In cooperation with the private sector, make available the benefits of new technologies, especially information and communications

The capacity to mobilize and manage resources: requires a quantification of the resources (human, financial and other) that are needed for implementation, and requires that these resources be mobilized and put at the service of the plan;

The capacity to implement action plans: requires that those responsible for carrying out every part of the plan be appropriately selected, that they be aware of their responsibilities, and know to whom they are accountable for performance;

The capacity to monitor progress: requires that people and mechanisms be put in place to enable the measurement of agreed benchmarks and indicators; provides for feedback to ensure that objectives and strategies are adjusted so that progress is realized and sustained.

The Lessons of History

In numerous ways, and over long periods of time, societies have been adapting and transforming. They have done so through complex processes of cumulative learning, combining different actors, and in ways specific to local circumstances. These processes are virtually impenetrable to the outside eye. Local self-reliance and grassroots initiatives – discussed as optional paradigms in the development literature – have always been the basis of human advance for most of the world.

In some countries, change has been sponsored and abetted by strong public administration. Two millennia ago, China wedded literacy and political culture and developed an efficient, merit-based civil service founded on the institutional and moral precepts of Confucianism. For a thousand years, the civil service performed a critical and unifying role, compiling regular censuses and land registers, and collecting taxes.

The modern equivalent might be the emergence of the Indian Administrative Service, formerly the Indian Civil Service, in the 20th century. The strength of the IAS lies in its recruitment, transfer and promotion systems, its assured place within the Indian Constitution and its relative autonomy from political pressures. The prestige of IAS service derives from the respect accorded to it by Indian society, and helps to compensate for the modesty of the pay and conditions (de Silva, 2002). The origins of public service in what are now the world's two largest countries are a reminder that these foundations for development capacity in public administration were laid down well before the era of aid and TC.

There are some obvious lessons to be drawn from history; here are three. First, capacity is an indigenous phenomenon and its development has always been largely an endogenous process. It follows, secondly, that capacity development is inherently idiosyncratic, being substantially determined by local contexts. It resists rigour and blueprinting. Third, capacity development occurs as a result of interactions among different parties and at different levels: from metropolitan-based public administrations to distant rural communities; between the public sector and civil society; between politics and administration.

Capacity development can also be quickened and broadened in response to outside stimuli. Throughout history, there have been numerous instances of countries turning to foreign sources for technical cooperation. In the 18th century, Russia brought in experts and technology in substantial quantities from Western Europe for its own modernization. In the second half of the 19th century, it was Japan. After the Second World War, a devastated Europe was rebuilt with the help of American capital and technical aid. Also in the 20th century, China has acquired technical assistance, partly through the aid window. In all these cases, the importations were transformative, as the countries concerned strove to catch up with their richer suppliers.

These were just a few of the many successful examples of how countries, over the centuries, have benefited from international partnership. Leaders with a clear vision of the direction they wanted to take perceived the gaps in their country's capacities, and sought to procure the help and expertise they needed from wherever it was available. History, therefore, yields us lessons four and five: the importance of enlightened leadership and the need for the demands for assistance to be self-determined. Post-war TC, however, has altered the parameters.

When the aid era arrived after World War II, the concept of 'gap-filling' became enshrined in development theory, to a degree which encouraged the idea that aid was synonymous with development (Browne 1990). Technical cooperation – skills and know-how – was the means to fill the third gap characterizing developing countries (along with the two financial gaps represented by the budget deficit and the imbalance of external payments)[5]. The concept was convenient, for as independence progressed, the rich countries sought to extend post-colonial patronage through transfers of capital and skills into the gaps that appeared to hamper development progress.

In contrast to the historical process of countries purchasing skills and know-how from suppliers, the relationship now appears very different (Morgan 2001):

- **Control:** Demand was manufactured, not self-generated. The capacity gaps came to be perceived and funded by donor country governments, not the recipients, and control of the transfer arrangements shifted accordingly. The recipient countries owned neither the gaps nor the resources put up to fill them. For as long as there has been aid, there have been concerns about country ownership.

- **Public sector bias:** The reversal of control was facilitated by the fact that aid was in the public funding domain of the donors. This had various consequences:

o technical cooperation became the preserve of bureaucratic minds and processes in the donor countries, with an often limited comprehension of the character and context of the recipient countries;

o each donor bureaucracy devised its own set of procedures and practices for administering TC, resulting in a proliferation of administrative paperwork;

---

[5] There have been many exponents of gap-filling, among which Rostow (1960) and Chenery and Strout (1966).

o   "projectization" became a feature. Technical cooperation was conceived in time- and money-bound segments, a configuration which best suited public spending patterns.

- **Accountability:** Aid had key stakeholders in the donor countries, but beneficiaries elsewhere, setting up a potential tension between two sets of objectives. The stakeholders had expectations of how aid should "perform", and the criteria of success were often commercial, political or in other ways strategically significant, rather than developmental.

Donor-driven, public sector-managed and internally accountable TC has yielded very mixed results. There have been numerous micro-successes. Millions throughout the developing world have benefited from better infrastructure, health care, education, housing and improved means of productive livelihoods in agriculture and industry, as a result of projects underwritten by aid. These micro-successes have been confirmed by the results of evaluations conducted by development agencies, showing that the proportion of "effective" projects is usually over 60%, and rising over time.

But the macro failure of aid has been the inability to render itself redundant. Half a century has witnessed over one million TC projects. Many of them have been strung end-to-end, repeating the same objectives, and targeting the same countries and beneficiary organizations. The most aided countries have generally remained so.

The outputs of aid projects have abounded and these are manifestations of development. But they are also in part a substitute for it, to the extent that many countries have not been able to use TC as a tool to build sustainable capacities and manage their development independently. The word sustainable is important. Inappropriate TC, far from building sustainability, may undermine it. An example is provided by the exodus of skilled personnel from the organizations in which they have been trained ("brain drain"), often under TC programmes.

The six country studies that form the basis of this book reveal that there have been positive changes in donor-recipient relationships. Asymmetry is being corrected as patronage yields to more country ownership as a basis for partnership (Browne 1999). Countries have begun to strengthen their resolve to align TC more closely to their strategic development interests – which they are defining more purposefully. Many donors are also showing a new willingness to support stronger central management of aid by recipient governments and organizations.

But if sustainable capacity is to be developed, then the lessons of history should be heeded. A clearer understanding of the nature of capacity development is indispensable to increasing the effectiveness of TC. This calls for a new paradigm.

A new paradigm for capacity development as the target for technical cooperation.

In the first volume, Capacity for Development: New solutions to old problems, UNDP outlined a paradigm of capacity development set in the broader context of transformative development. This framework is reproduced in Table 1.1.

TABLE 1.1: A NEW PARADIGM FOR CAPACITY DEVELOPMENT

	Current paradigm	New paradigm
Nature of development	Improvements in economic and social conditions	Societal transformation, including building of "right" capacities
Conditions for effective development cooperation	Good policies that can be externally prescribed	Good policies that have to be home-grown
The asymmetric donor-recipient relationship	Should be countered generally through a spirit of partnership and mutual respect	Should be specifically addressed as a problem by taking countervailing measures
Capacity development	Human resource development, combined with stronger institutions	Three cross-linked layers of capacity: individual, institutional and societal
Acquisition of knowledge	Knowledge can be transferred	Knowledge has to be acquired
Most important forms of knowledge	Knowledge developed in North for export to South	Local knowledge combined with knowledge acquired from other countries – in the South and North

In the present book, we begin to take that analytical framework a practical step further. Drawing on country experience — of which the six country studies in this book are representative examples — we have disaggregated some of the key elements of capacity development and knowledge acquisition (the last three categories in the above table) in terms of the current and new paradigms, and illustrated these by reference to specific examples of TC support. In terms of the CD/TC relationship, the "current paradigm" is a slightly exaggerated caricature of capacity development *driven by TC in an asymmetric donor-recipient relationship*. The "new paradigm" is characterized as nationally-owned and country-driven capacity development *supported by TC*.

The terms "current" and "new" may seem awkward. The latter paradigm contains the modern features of change, but is based on principles of capacity development that are redolent of the historical, indigenous processes of adaptation and transformation: self-determined, organic and participatory.

In this new paradigm, we have outlined six facets of capacity development.

Knowledge acquisition: Human resource development has long been perceived as the core of capacity development, and pursued through formal training schemes that aim to transfer knowledge in a vertical (top-down) mode. In the new paradigm, knowledge acquisition is understood as a much more subjective process, fostering an environment of interactive learning that is able to respond more readily to the demands of learners. Rather than formal training events and courses, it relies more on group and on-the-job learning. New information and communication technologies are helping to vastly expand individualized and organizational learning opportunities.

TABLE 1.2: CAPACITY DEVELOPMENT: TRADITIONAL AND NEW PERSPECTIVES AND PRACTICES

	Traditional perspective and practices	New perspective and practices
Knowledge acquisition	**HRD approach/knowledge transfer** • Formal training • Scholarships • Reliance on expatriate experts	**Knowledge acquisition** • Knowledge networks • South-South, South-everywhere exchange • Interactive training • Reliance on national experts • Demand-driven
Country study examples	**Bangladesh:** Use of donor consultancy firms **Egypt:** US-sponsored Ph.D. scholarships **Kyrgyz Rep:** Valuable training abroad, but use of expatriate experts with inappropriate skills; short-term training valued for foreign travel opportunities **Uganda:** Use of inadequately qualified foreign consultants despite training of senior civil servants under past TC programmes	**Kyrgyz Rep:** Donor support for higher education; in-country training and consultancy services; international and regional research linkages; and Internet access **Philippines:** Growing use of local consultants, consulting and research institutes and universities; wide use of information technology in public service **Uganda:** South-South exchanges under UN auspices **Bangladesh:** Use of Bangladeshis residing and working abroad
Institution building	**Organisational strengthening** • Public sector emphasis • Imported "best practices" • Top-down reform • Reinventing the wheel: each TC project starting afresh	**Transformation/change management processes** • Organisations and institutions viewed in broader national context • Nurturing of existing capacity • Change management process from within • Attention to incentive systems and sustainability
Country study examples	**Bangladesh, Kyrgyz Rep, Uganda:** Heavy TC emphasis on public sector **Uganda:** Failure to take past capacity development into account	**Philippines:** Use of national execution of TC projects by some donors
Institutional environment and partnerships	**Narrow view** • Each organisation considered separately and in isolation • No overview of capacity development needs	**Broad view** • Consideration of all relevant organisations and institutions, at national/local levels • Concern with institutional environment within which organizations and individuals work • Importance of inter-organisational partnerships
Country study examples	**Kyrgyz Rep:** Donors implementing parallel projects with favoured target organizations **Uganda:** Donors not undertaking adequate inventory of in-country capacity; no manpower survey since 1989	**Bolivia, Philippines:** Growing involvement of municipal and provincial level institutions **Egypt:** Heavy emphasis of USAID TC on support to the private sector **Bolivia, Kyrgyz Rep:** Incresing emphasis on institutional reforms that may better support capacity development

Policy environment	**Viewed as neutral** • Policy environment not considered in most TC, except when projects specifically aim at policy reform • Incentive systems not factored in	**Viewed as integral to, and compatible with, change process** • Development of alternative policy scenarios • Piloting and feedback to demonstrate impact
Country study examples	**All countries:** TC projects tended to ignore policy environments, although policies influence capacities and incentives of individuals and organizations to change	**Bangladesh:** TC bringing more transparency to customs procedures **Philippines:** Supportive policy environment for NGOs; TC support for policy analysis **Uganda, Bolivia, Kyrgyz Rep:** Strong influence of TC on design of economic reforms
Country commitment and autonomy	**Weak and subjective** • Donor domination of the TC agenda • Expressions of interest by immediate TC recipients • Use of externally-funded project implementation units (PIUs)	**Objective, nationally owned and developmentally strategic** • Commitment by leadership at all levels • Driven by national development frameworks
Country study examples	**Egypt:** Autonomous PIUs (e.g in Central Bank) **Kyrgyz Rep:** Out-of-control supply of TC **Bolivia, Philippines:** Distortions due to patronage-based public service sector **All countries:** Unharmonised and complex donor procedures and practices	**Bangladesh, Uganda:** Donors encouraged to provide central budget support, some use of SWAps **Philippines, Uganda:** Strong central TC management by Government **Philippines:** "Organic" project implementation units compatible with public sector structure **Bolivia:** Management of TC and other aid as part of overall public investment, but also growing weight of donors in policy making, e.g. poverty reduction strategies
Results and accountability	**Organisationally specific** • Donor-recipient "closed loop" dialogue • Output-related	**Impact on beneficiaries** • Beneficiary impact evaluation • Development outcome-oriented (e.g. MDGs)
Country study examples	**Bolivia:** Strong donor emphasis on donor accountability	**Philippines:** NGOs and beneficiary groups actively monitor government projects; 'Social Weather Stations' surveys

Institution building: Organizational strengthening has been perceived as a technocratic add-on process. Technical cooperation has sponsored imported "best practices" that were often applied in piecemeal fashion. But institution building eschews facile prescription. Every organization is unique because of the particularity of the institutional environment. In the new paradigm, capacity development is a more organic process. It starts with an assessment of each organization's capabilities, and builds on them in a manner that respects continuity and fosters sustainability. In every organization, change has to start from within. Leaders need to be committed to change, and key change-agents must be identified within the organization to help develop and pursue the agreed new direction. Concern with capacity retention has to be built in, which means paying more attention to the factors and conditions that motivate or de-motivate people.

Institutional environment and partnerships: Capacity development has traditionally tended to focus on individuals and organizations within the state sector. This focus has been too narrow, because it leaves out the many agents of developmental transformation that lie outside the state sector. As the role of the state changes – e.g. by doing less, and by facilitating and regulating more – it is even more imperative to conceptualize capacity in a holistic sense, and capacity development as a process which encompasses a range of different stakeholders in the public, private and civic domains, and at central and at local levels.

Thus, while institution building is pursued at the level of individual organizations, there must be cognizance of the relevance of each organization within a wider institutional framework. The benefits of collaboration and interaction among different organizations need to be sought out, leading to the forging of public-public and public-private partnerships.

Policy environment: The hitherto more technocratic approaches to capacity development have tended to leave the policy environment out of account. The new paradigm recognizes that a conducive policy environment is fundamental to the concept of capacity development. Policies can both hinder and facilitate the ability of individuals and organizational entities to perform functions, and can prevent or ensure that these functions enhance the collective good.

Country commitment: Under the traditional paradigm, governments manifested commitment by contributing counterpart resources to TC projects, whether in cash or in kind. This is tantamount to the obverse of the TC-for-CD process. Countries must take charge. They should make their own determination of capacity development needs as part of a coherent development strategy. Strategies need a clear focus on development goals, and they should identify how TC can be used in support.

Strong and legitimate leadership is fundamental to country commitment. Leadership is required to ensure beneficial change and adaptation, whether at the level of the individual organization or the polity.

Results and accountability: Each country determines its own development goals, and these are enshrined in periodic development plans, longer-term vision statements and poverty reduction strategies. An important focus is now provided by the Millennium Development Goals, which codify the basic human indicators that have long been considered critical outcomes of the development process. Capacity development, therefore, should no longer be focused exclusively on externally-prescribed criteria such as "sound" economic governance and "efficient" public institutions. These "means" need to be seen in relationship to the broader "ends" of income poverty reduction, better education, health and other targets. Capacity development objectives need to be framed by the task of ultimately reaching these human development outcomes.

A more "macro" or holistic orientation of capacity development implies major changes in how accountability is perceived and practiced. To date, with the focus on training and institutional strengthening, trainees and their organizations have been considered the "beneficiaries" of traditional capacity development. The true beneficiaries, however, are not usually even conscious of – let alone involved in conceiving – the capacity development programmes that are ultimately designed to benefit them. Effective capacity development needs to involve the real beneficiaries in the conception, design and evaluation of programmes.

References

Baser, Heather and Peter Morgan. 2001. "The pooling of technical assistance." A study for the Netherlands Ministry of Foreign Affairs.

Browne, Stephen. 1990. *Foreign Aid in Practice*. London: Pinter Publishers.

_____. 1999. *Beyond Aid: From Patronage to Partnership*. Aldershot: Ashgate.

Chenery, Hollis and A.M. Strout. 1966. "Foreign assistance and economic development." *American Economic Review*.

De Silva, Leelananda. 2002. "Capacities for development: the role of technical cooperation." Background paper for the United Nations Development Programme.

Economic and Social Council. 2002. "United Nations system support to capacity building." New York.

Fukuda-Parr, Sakiko, Carlos Lopes and Khalid Malik (Eds.) and the United Nations Development Programme. 2002. *Capacity for Development: New solutions to old problems*. London: Earthscan.

Morgan, Peter. 2001. "Technical assistance." Background paper for the United Nations Development Programme.

Oxfam International. 2002. "Last Chance in Monterrey: Meeting the Challenge of Poverty Reduction." Briefing Paper. Oxford.

Rostow, W.W. 1960. *The Stages of Economic Growth*. Cambridge: Cambridge University Press.

United Nations Development Programme (UNDP). 2001. "Poverty Reduction Strategies: What Have we Learned?" Report of the Bergen Conference. New York.

United Nations Development Programme/United Nations Children's Fund (UNDP/UNICEF). 1999. "Capacity Development: an analysis and synthesis of its current conceptualisation and implications for practice." Harare.

Zedillo, Ernesto. 2001. "Financing for Development." Report of a High Level Panel on Financing for Development. New York.

World Bank, 2002. "Goals for Development: History, Prospects and Costs." Policy Research Working Paper 2819. Washington, DC.

2 *Overview*[1]

MEETING THE CAPACITY DEVELOPMENT CHALLENGE: LESSONS FOR IMPROVING TECHNICAL COOPERATION

The six country studies in this volume (Chapters 3-8) were conducted as part of a new review of technical cooperation (TC), almost 10 years after an earlier effort at reform.[2] They are an attempt to provide insight and evidence, based on actual country experience, for how TC can more effectively support national capacity development.

Case study research is critical for grounding reform proposals. The countries studied — Bangladesh, Bolivia, Egypt, the Kyrgyz Republic, the Philippines and Uganda — represent a broad, though certainly not exhaustive range of TC and capacity development experience.[3]

The studies were based mainly on in-depth interviews with informants involved in TC from government, donor agencies and other organizations. The research teams, based primarily in universities or research and policy analysis institutions in the countries studied, also utilized donor and government reports, secondary literature and quantitative data. In some countries, workshops brought together various stakeholders and provided insights, feedback and a forum for discussion.

---

[1] This chapter was written by Mary Hilderbrand, Adjunct Lecturer in Public Policy and a Fellow in Development at Harvard University's John F. Kennedy School of Government.
[2] Berg, Elliot and the United Nations Development Programme: *Rethinking Technical Cooperation: Reforms for Capacity Building in Africa*. See references.
[3] The six countries were selected to represent wide regional diversity and variation in level of income per capita. All are aid recipients, but with varying degrees of aid dependence. The set consciously excluded countries with extremely high levels of civil conflict. Other considerations included feasibility of carrying out the research, potential value-added, and the potential impact of the study in the country.

This chapter synthesizes key findings. Particular attention is given to the context and patterns of TC during the 1990s, its contributions to capacity, trends in donor practices and government management of TC, issues around personnel and working with existing institutions, and pressures for and against change.[4]

Several themes run throughout the studies:

- significant and increasing diversity among partner countries in the challenges for TC and how it is carried out;

- the importance of giving national priorities centre stage;

- the critical role of national TC management;

- the constraining role of weak institutions;

- the importance of using local expertise;

- the importance of mainstreaming TC and capacity development into partner countries' institutions.

Context During the 1990s

Whereas the critique of TC at the beginning of the 1990s was not just a reflection on the preceding decade, it was undoubtedly affected by the experience of the 1980s — an extremely difficult period for many developing countries, and one where the combination of economic crisis, greatly reduced resources, and dramatic changes in policy direction put capacity under stress. In many countries, existing capacity was challenged and sometimes seriously reduced. At the same time, there was a demand for new kinds of capacity, in government and in society more generally. Resource constraints and difficult economic and political conditions were not conducive to building capacity, however, and against such a backdrop, TC was similarly limited in its ability to contribute.

The 1990s provided a somewhat different context. Five out of the six countries studied experienced sustained economic growth throughout the decade. The Kyrgyz Republic, which had become independent only in 1991, experienced a 45% decline in its economy during the first half of the 1990s, as it began the transition from the Soviet command economy to a market system. By mid-decade, the trend was reversed and economic growth soared, at least for the period under consideration. Bolivia entered a serious recession as the 1990s came to a close, a change from its performance during most of the decade.

Despite the generally good economic performance, per capita economic growth rates were fairly low in almost all the countries. This was not a period of fast, transformative growth like that experienced in East Asia until recent years, although for most of the countries it did represent an important turnaround from poor economic

---

[4] Information on the countries for this chapter is drawn from Balihuta et al (2002); Cukrowski et al (2002); El-Refaie et al (2002); Gray Molina and Chávez (2002), Illo et al (2002), and Sobhan et al (2002). A shorter version of each is included in this volume, Chapters 3-8.

conditions, even crisis. Furthermore, resource constraints continued to plague the countries, and several continued to suffer from high levels of external debt that further limited resources. Conditions for capacity development were better than earlier, but still less than ideal.

The other notable characteristic of the decade was its continuation as a reform period, with an emphasis on the structural and institutional levels. Each of the six countries were carrying out reforms of various types. For some, the first generation stabilization reforms begun in the mid-1980s had already taken hold; the emphasis during the 1990s had shifted to structural reforms, and then to broader institutional reforms as the decade wore on. That pattern applied to Bolivia, Uganda and Bangladesh. Egypt and the Kyrgyz Republic both carried out a combination of stabilization and structural reforms during the 1990s. Egypt started in 1991, while the Kyrgyz Republic got serious about its reforms following the post-independence economic crisis, around 1995.

In the Philippines, the 1990s continued to be more about political reform and the consolidation of democracy than about the economy, though there was an effort during most of the decade to liberalize and make the economy more competitive. Indeed, like in the Philippines, political reform and democratic consolidation were also on the agenda in countries such as Bolivia, Uganda and the Kyrgyz Republic, where democratic transitions had occurred not too many years earlier.

The fact that the 1990s was a decade of reform is significant for understanding TC. Although TC is often discussed separately from other policy trends, it is strongly shaped by the priorities and concerns of the time. In the 1990s, those concerns were structural and institutional reforms. Whether in terms of money, emphasis or enthusiasm, much of the TC during this period was aimed at supporting reform efforts.

The increasing emphasis on institutional reform came along at roughly the same time as a new understanding of capacity development gained currency. As we saw in Chapter 1, this new understanding of capacity development went beyond human resource and organizational development to encompass larger institutional and societal frameworks. This amounts to a dovetailing, perhaps for the first time, of the direction of the larger reform programmes, on one hand, and priorities for capacity development on the other.

Trends in Technical Cooperation

The country studies attempted to document quantitative levels and patterns in TC during the 1990s. Several general observations can be made about trends in the six countries.

First, there is considerable variation in trends. Global data on official development assistance (ODA) and TC show that overall flows of ODA decreased during the 1990s, and that TC fell or stagnated starting about 1994, with poor countries and Sub-Saharan Africa especially experiencing declines. (A summary review of that data can be found in the Annex to this volume.) The data from individual countries studied here, however, make clear that macro-level trends only partially capture what is happening with TC, and that many countries' experiences may be quite different from the overall picture.

With regard to trends in development assistance generally, ODA has fallen in relation to economic indicators — GNP, revenue and exports — in Bangladesh, Egypt and the Philippines. In contrast, ODA levels have actually increased over the decade in the Kyrgyz Republic, Uganda and Bolivia (with some reduction at the very end of the decade in Bolivia).

Patterns in TC have been somewhat similar. Technical cooperation flows fell in Bangladesh and Egypt, but they rose in Bolivia, the Kyrgyz Republic and Uganda, whether measured in dollars or as a percentage of GNP or revenue.[5] The Philippines experienced an increase through the mid-1990s, after which TC declined.[6]

Second, for some countries, TC represents a substantial proportion of resources available for development. This is especially true in the countries where TC has been on the rise. By 1999, TC accounted for over 2% of GDP for Bolivia and the Kyrgyz Republic, and 5% of GDP for Uganda. In the Kyrgyz Republic, TC in that year equalled more than 18% of government revenue and 6% of exports. For Uganda, the levels were even higher, at 27% of revenue and 65% of exports.

For other countries, the figures are lower. For example, TC in Egypt averaged 1.4% of GDP and 5.0% of revenue. In the Philippines, TC represented only 0.3% of GDP and 1.3% of the budget for 1992-98. Technical cooperation in Bangladesh accounted for only 0.6% of GNP.

Third, in several countries, TC rose as a percentage of ODA during the 1990s, and is therefore an increasingly important part of the aid picture (see Table 2.1). This is the case in Bolivia and Uganda, but also in Egypt, where TC has fallen less than overall ODA. In the Philippines, the TC/ODA ratio increased to a high of 16.6% in 1996 and then fell back somewhat, but not to the level at the beginning of the 1990s. In Bangladesh and the Kyrgyz Republic, it is difficult to ascertain a clear trend, since the proportions have fluctuated.

Fourth, there is also considerable variation in the degree to which sources of TC funds are concentrated or diversified, and the type of donor. Egypt is the most highly concentrated, with 76% coming from the United States. For Uganda, the World Bank (IDA) is by far the largest source, accounting for 29%, while the next largest donor (the United States) provides about 16%. The Kyrgyz Republic and the Philippines both have many TC partners, but three in each country dominate: for Kyrgyzstan, the main providers are Germany, the Soros Foundation and Turkey; for the Philippines, they are Australia, the European Union and UNDP. Bolivia has a multiplicity of donors, bilateral, multilateral

---

[5] In Bolivia, TC rose in dollar terms. As a % of GNP, it rose and then fell somewhat, but not back to the levels of the early 1990s.

[6] All the data here need to be handled with caution. TC data overall are problematic, scarce and almost always partial; and there are conceptual problems related to how TC is defined and what is included. Furthermore, data from the different country studies are compiled from different sources that most likely are not entirely comparable. Therefore, they should not be assumed to be very accurate nor to provide very precise comparisons, but only to be indicative of general levels and trends.

TABLE 2.1: TECHNICAL COOPERATION (TC) AS A PROPORTION OF ODA (%)

Country	TC/ODA, 1990s average	TC/ODA, 1999	TC/ODA High (year)
Bangladesh	11.4	8.9	19.0 (1992)
Bolivia	28.0	33.8	33.8 (1999)
Egypt	28.3	48.6	48.6 (1999)
Kyrgyz Republic	38.0	26.0	88.3 (1992)
Philippines	9.6	8.2*	16.6 (1996)
Uganda	45.1	59.8	72.6 (1998)

Source: Data provided in country studies, and OECD/DAC data.
*1998

and non-governmental, but the United States, Germany, Japan and the World Bank play the largest roles.

Different patterns create different challenges. Countries dealing with a multiplicity of sources face the problems of fragmentation and competition among donors, and the need to find effective means of coordination. For countries dependent on single or very dominant partners, the issue is likely to be more one of the relative weight of the donor's priorities compared with those of the partner country, as well as the characteristics and procedural requirements of individual donors. Most countries have a mix of these challenges, but their relative importance varies. For instance, Bolivia's challenge is, above all, one of coordination and management, while in Egypt, the need for coordination is minor compared to the challenge of dealing with USAID's priorities and programmes. Uganda has a mixture of both. Whatever the challenges, they will be magnified if TC represents a large proportion of resources. In the Philippines, TC plays a smaller role and can be handled more easily than in most of the other countries.

Finally, across these countries there has been a move towards education and health as major sectors for TC (especially strong in Kyrgyzstan, the Philippines and Uganda), but also a strong showing for public service/public administration (Bangladesh, Kyrgyzstan and Uganda). In a number of countries, there has been a shift away from agriculture and rural development. In Egypt, agriculture received most support in the early 1990s, but was later replaced by support for private sector development; Egypt was the only country in which the private sector was a major focus. The trend towards greater emphasis on education and health is not surprising, given the current emphasis in the development community on poverty alleviation. The support for public administration reflects the new emphasis on institutional reform, including that of the civil service and the judiciary, which has characterized the latter half of the 1990s.

TC's Contributions to Capacity Development

The country studies credit TC for playing a role in developing some of the capacities that currently exist in the countries. For example, support for scholarships and universities in Uganda helped to create a base of well-educated professionals, many of whom are now leaders in government, the private sector and institutions of higher education in the country. During the past decade in the Kyrgyz Republic, TC played a substantial role in helping to develop new institutions for a market economy and a democratic government, and in training and acculturating the group of professionals needed to run those institutions. It also contributed to strengthening higher education in the country by supporting new institutions and helping to modernize teaching methods and curriculum in existing public institutions.

Reform programmes in Bolivia, including those essential to strengthening national capacity such as education and popular participation, were supported largely through TC. The blossoming of civil society and NGOs in the Philippines, while certainly not brought about by donors, was supported by their encouragement of participatory processes and institutions, and their openness to working with NGOs.

But these studies, like earlier ones, also found that TC has often failed to strengthen capacity, especially when considered in light of the amounts that have been invested over the years. Three major reasons for disappointing results were highlighted by the studies, and will be discussed in the following sections:

- institutional weaknesses in the recipient country;

- continuing TC practices that are not conducive to capacity development, although there are some promising changes; and

- the failure to mainstream capacity development.

As emphasized in Chapter 1, a country's capacity is first and foremost a result of its own history and social, economic, cultural and political processes, as well as its engagement with other countries and forces. Its development involves the creation, maintenance and upgrading of fundamental human and social capital. Technical cooperation's potential and actual contributions to capacity development should be viewed in this light. Weak capacity is not necessarily the fault of failed TC, and strong capacity, in most cases, will not be attributable in great degree to the successes of TC. Yet TC can and should be expected to contribute positively to existing capacity, and to support the larger forces that can transform a country's capacity.

The Importance of the Institutional Context

Poor institutional contexts in recipient countries — particularly adverse conditions in public administration, along with corruption — are a major factor in shaping and constraining the ability of TC (as well as that of domestic resources) to contribute to capacity development. These were repeatedly noted as reasons for frequent failure of efforts at the individual and organizational levels. Training and the provision of advisors do not always achieve the intended impact. They could also reduce the likelihood of fundamental TC reform.

In all the countries studied, certain characteristics and conditions in the civil service (and in the public administration more generally) represent capacity weaknesses and act as constraints on capacity development. With the partial exception of the Philippines, low public sector salaries hinder retention of qualified people and hurt morale.[7] Patronage systems prevail in most countries (including the Philippines) and politicization of positions means frequent turnover of large segments of the public service with every change of government (e.g. Bolivia and the Philippines). Lack of continuity and patronage-based recruitment systems and organizational cultures are extremely difficult environments for capacity development. Ironically, Bangladesh suffers from some of these problems, despite a highly institutionalized civil service. Frequent rotation without regard to expertise leads to a similar lack of continuity, and promotions based on seniority rather than performance serve as disincentives for either individual or organizational capacity development.

Corruption is also a problem in most, if not all, of the countries studied. High levels of corruption, along with weak public sector institutions, feed donors' doubts about whether funds will be used responsibly — an important factor behind donors' reluctance to cede control of TC. Improvement in these basic institutional frameworks is critical for more effective government, for TC (and other investments) that can have a real impact on capacity development, and for an environment that will enable fundamental change in TC itself.

Continuity and Change in Donor TC Practices

The UNDP-sponsored 1993 review of TC criticized many donor practices for hindering capacity development.[8] One of the questions the country studies set out to answer was whether, and to what extent, those practices still characterize TC. They found a mixed picture.

Continuity

There was evidence in all the country studies that many TC practices not supportive of capacity development persist. Many donors — especially but not only bilateral donors — still prefer to have their assistance carried out through individual projects, often reflecting their own priorities. Projects still tend to have short timeframes, limiting their ability to contribute effectively to longer-term processes of institutional change. Although some donors have moved away from requiring procurement of their own equipment and experts, others have not — persistent tying of aid and lack of transparency about costs lead to equally persistent inefficiencies and waste. Lack of coordination among donors and the resulting multiplicity of projects and accounting

---

[7] Despite general public sector salary increases, the Philippines still has the problem at senior levels, where salaries are not competitive with the private sector and there are difficulties attracting and keeping the best people.

[8] Berg, Elliot and the United Nations Development Programme: *Rethinking Technical Cooperation: Reforms for Capacity Building in Africa.* See bibliography.

systems place unmanageable burdens on already weak government ministries. Project implementation that bypasses normal institutions in favour of separate units misses opportunities for capacity development in core institutions, further increases fragmentation and distorts incentives.

Change

But there have also been significant changes in the direction of greater partnership and consultation in setting priorities, more focusing of TC efforts in line with national priorities, and processes of dialogue that extend participation to groups outside the government. Multilaterals have been in the lead in encouraging such changes, and TC is increasingly linked to comprehensive development frameworks, poverty reduction strategies, national dialogues, and other development consultations and strategies. Uganda and Bolivia provide good examples of these promising changes.

Even in the absence of broad strategies, many donors have been trying to move towards programme and sector-wide approaches (SWAps), at least as an umbrella for fitting otherwise discrete projects into a more coherent framework. Increasing use of programme and SWAps was reported in all the countries, particularly evident in health and education. Donor efforts to coordinate their activities were also reported. Evidence of donors working and cooperating more with NGOs and lower levels of government is notably prevalent in the Philippines. In Bolivia, there is an increasing effort to shift TC to the municipal and provincial levels, where it is needed to support capacity development in the context of the country's popular participation and decentralization reforms.

These are very recent shifts, and the jury will still be out for some time on whether they will really change the dynamics of TC. While they do not, at this point, represent fully participatory or nationally-led processes, these recent trends are also quite different from the traditionally piecemeal nature of TC.

Nevertheless, the Bolivian experience suggests that it is wise to be cautious in assuming that these new approaches will automatically solve all the problems with TC. Despite Bolivia being in many ways a test case for strategy- and dialogue-led TC, most process and development choices remain donor-driven. The Bolivia study found that the National Dialogue and the poverty reduction strategy processes, combined with donor efforts at self-coordination, have actually increased the weight of the donors in policy making and decisions about use of resources. The problem stems quite simply from the extreme asymmetry between the donors, with their resources, ideas and technical expertise, and the much weaker Bolivian state, which the new approaches to TC do not change.

One strand of thinking about improving TC emphasizes the need for coordination among donors, standardization of their processes and requirements, and harmonization of their goals. The evidence from the country studies suggest that these may be helpful in reducing some of the problems of fragmentation, competition, and the heavy administrative burden associated with donor funding that strain or even overwhelm partner country institutions. But they do not stand out as central or as complete solutions in themselves. Donor self-coordination and harmonization can make a significant difference only if they are carried out around locally-determined and accepted goals and priorities, rather than around donor goals. When there is a divergence between what the donors are trying to do and what the recipient government's self-determined priorities are, TC is unlikely to have a lasting impact on capacity.

The Bolivian experience noted above also suggests the importance of donor restraint. There needs to be space for countries to define their own goals, priorities and processes. In their enthusiasm, well-intentioned donors may fail to allow for that space. They are likely to have better results in capacity development if they stand back, let countries come to terms with their own challenges and how they want to deal with them, and then lend support in that context.

Growing Diversity

The country studies show that it is increasingly difficult to generalize about how TC is practiced because there are significant and increasing differences among recipient countries that shape their TC relationships. One major difference is between countries where the governments have asserted themselves and have taken the lead in shaping and managing TC, and those where TC continues to be much more donor-driven. In the former — the Philippines and Uganda, especially — the relationship is one of constructive partnership between the donors and the recipient country. In others, especially Egypt but to some extent the Kyrgyz Republic as well, TC still looks more like it did in the past.

Another key difference is in the existing level of human and social capital in the recipient country. In a country like the Philippines — with a highly educated population, a vibrant university and research sector, a large supply of well-qualified professionals, and an extensive and active NGO community — TC can draw heavily on local sources of knowledge and expertise. It can build on cooperation well beyond the central government. The Kyrgyz Republic, also with a high education level and a growing local capacity to provide professional, research and analytic services, provides another example of real strength that TC can utilize. In contrast, in countries with much lower levels of education and smaller pools of highly qualified professional and technical personnel, it will be harder to reorient TC as fully. In short, variations in existing levels of capacity help shape opportunities and constraints for TC reform.

Innovations in Donor Practices

The moves towards strategy-led TC, programme and sector-wide approaches, and emphasis on dialogue — both between donors and governments but also more broadly within countries — are innovations that are being tried by various donors and in collaboration with various partner countries. In addition to these fairly large-scale changes, a number of other innovations were reported in the country studies.

One set of innovations has to do with trying to increase the voice of NGOs and other domestic groups in donor projects and programmes. In the Philippines, where this has gone the furthest, some donors have created steering, advisory or management committees to involve NGOs in project management. This gives them a role in decisions about use of TC, selection of consultants and other project needs, broadens accountability and makes TC more responsive to community needs.

In Egypt, there have been efforts to make sure that decisions about the use of TC fit local needs. UNDP formed a think tank of leading intellectuals to provide input into the country programme, and a committee of donors invited the National Women's Association to be a member of the committee.

Also, in some countries including the Philippines and Bangladesh, donors have engaged in joint programming where funding needs are large.

In the Kyrgyz Republic, donors introduced interesting and valuable capacity development initiatives that were carried out on a regional scope. Kyrgyzstan's small size and shared contexts and needs with its neighbors in Central Asia made it appropriate to target some research training opportunities at the regional level – an innovative and flexible response to the needs of the country and region.

Partner Governments' Management of TC

The country studies suggest that there has been substantial change in the direction of more and better management on the part of the partner countries. It also indicates that this is an important trend and that more assertive and effective national management is essential to meaningful change in TC. As noted earlier, there is a striking difference between those countries in which the governments have asserted control over TC (and aid more generally) and those in which the donors operate freely. Furthermore, some of the most interesting and important innovations are found with reference to national management of TC.

In several countries including the Philippines, Uganda and Bolivia, there is a clearly stated government policy that all aid, including TC, is to be utilized in line with national priorities and policies. In some others, that clear statement of policy about TC is still missing. All the countries have put in place mechanisms to manage TC, or aid generally. In a number of countries, the recognition that managing aid was important came only at the end of the 1990s; for others, it was a longer step-wise process of improving systems.

There is also considerable difference in how effective these policies are. Uganda, the Philippines and Bolivia all have instituted relatively strong systems of TC/aid management; Bangladesh also works to get donors to support the national development plan through normal planning and budget allocation mechanisms.

Setting up an agency or unit within a central ministry that coordinates aid and integrates it with the national development planning process is a first step, but is not sufficient. The structure has to be credible, actively used for aid management, and closely linked with the institutions for economic development decision making and resource allocation. A number of countries including Egypt and the Kyrgyz Republic, have such structures but have not used them effectively in the past. Recent efforts in the latter to reorganize aid management and tie it more closely to central development decision making may make it more effective in the future. In Egypt, the role of the Ministry of International Cooperation is seen more in terms of negotiating agreements than of asserting national direction over TC's purposes and allocation.

The cases of Uganda and the Philippines, in particular, provide evidence that when governments have insisted on, and set up workable systems for TC management, donors have responded (although to varying degrees) to the changed framework for the relationship. In Uganda, some donors work fully within the system and now provide their TC as budgetary support; others continue to fund their own projects. But the study notes that even those donors who handle their funds separately increasingly do so in line with Ugandan priorities. Transparency of their projects and use of funds have also improved. In the Philippines, the donor-government relationship has evolved into much more of a partnership, with extensive, regular and institutionalized processes of consultation, and a high comfort level on both sides with the priorities, the process and the resulting allocation.

Managing TC Effectively

The cases provide examples of two approaches to national management. The first involves asking donors to provide TC as budgetary support, and to allow it to be fully integrated into the country's public investment and budget allocation processes, just as if it were a resource of domestic origin. Bangladesh and Uganda have followed this approach. The second is to use a framework that handles TC separately from other resources but closely linked with them. This approach uses nationally-defined priorities and goals as the basis for accepting or rejecting projects, analyzes projects as fully as possible in terms of their costs and benefits, and monitors and evaluates them. The Philippines and Bolivia have primarily used this approach. Various combinations of these approaches are possible.

What is important is that each approach inserts a level of national decision making between donors and their preferred projects and programmes, thereby reducing the donors' discretion in funding projects. At the same time, the evaluating, prioritizing and coordinating of demands and resources allows for better rationalization of TC use on the country's side.

At this point, it seems unlikely that a budgetary approach alone can be sufficient. Not all donors are willing to provide budgetary support. It is also unlikely that partner governments would reject all TC that does not come in as budgetary support. Indeed, this approach needs to be supplemented by a clear system for decision making with regard to other projects. The system will otherwise be limited in its coverage and effectiveness; donors can simply ignore it if they prefer. The experience of the health sector in Bangladesh illustrates this well. Bangladesh's preference was that donor funding earmarked for health be provided as budgetary support for a sector-wide umbrella programme under the development plan and budget. About half of total assistance and a third of TC was given as pooled, budgetary support for the programme. But that left the other half of ODA and two-thirds of TC under bilateral, donor-driven projects, with apparently little coordination and limited information available about how much money was being spent. A clear, institutionalized system for vetting and monitoring those projects would be a big step forward.

Building in flexibility to deal with different donors' TC practices and policies is clearly essential. Such flexibility is evident in all the countries' TC management. Whereas Uganda and the Philippines have asserted their TC framework more strongly, they still accommodate a range of donor approaches. In an important innovation, Uganda's budgeting system has mechanisms to compensate for donor funds that go directly to lower levels of government to avoid skewing allocations as a result of donor projects outside the framework of the national poverty plan and sectoral programmes. This is helpful in ensuring equity of resources among regions and ministries, and keeping overall allocation in line with government priorities.

Lack of adequate and independent data was cited as a limitation on effective aid management in the Kyrgyz Republic and Egypt, and it seems likely that that is typical. The experience of the teams that carried out the country research confirmed the weakness and absence of data. What were available were often of poor or uneven quality, and for many aspects of TC, little or no data existed. In many countries, UNDP was the main source. Of the six countries examined, Uganda provided the richest data available. But even so, the data were problematic and limited in coverage.[9]

Innovations in National TC Management

Having the capability to monitor performance of projects is essential to making any framework effective, but this capability is one of the pieces almost always missing from attempts at TC management. The Philippine government's system for monitoring implementation through annual reviews of project portfolios is an important innovation. The National Economic and Development Authority (NEDA) and the Department of Budget Management meet with project managers to review individual projects, and an annual review report is submitted to the NEDA board that oversees TC, including recommendations for improving implementation. In addition, the Philippines involves NGOs in monitoring projects, which improves accountability and responsiveness.

Bolivia has also been innovative in its relationship with donors. Against a history of freewheeling donors and non-existent country management of TC, Bolivia has recently been working to develop a framework that will allow it to coordinate and utilize TC (and ODA generally) more effectively. A major challenge was the sheer number of donors and the amount of time that went into dealing with each of them. The solution was to quit meeting with each donor individually, and instead provide the same information to all the donors at once. Competition and sensitivities between large and small donors, multilateral and bilateral, were dealt with by setting up joint committees to plan and design projects and programmes, even including donors not involved in funding a particular effort.

---

[9] Overall, the absence or unreliability of data limited the ability to ascertain or investigate trends and patterns and to carry out cross-national analysis of the data.

Bolivia also had to be innovative to meet the challenges of TC management posed by decentralization. The country is trying to redirect TC to the municipal level, where key decisions about investment for development are increasingly being made, and where capacity development is a critical need. Yet many municipalities lack the capacity to identify needs and formulate investment plans and programmes that would allow TC or other investments to be effective. The national TC management unit — the Vice Ministry of Public Investments and External Financing — is collecting TC demands from the municipalities and coordinating the relationship between municipalities and the donors. The Vice Ministry integrates the process with other public investment decisions, and works with the municipalities to develop the capacities needed to make rational resource allocation decisions, and to use TC effectively.

Uganda's system of adjusting the budget to compensate for donor projects at lower levels of government to keep the allocation in line with what was intended by the government is another important innovation that helps that country deal with the challenges of decentralization.

These examples of frameworks and innovations indicate that while some elements may be common across countries, each country will need to develop ways of managing TC and working with donors in accordance with its particular challenges and situations.

TC Personnel: The Question of Expertise

Personnel and hiring are among the most contentious and thorny issues in TC. Because TC has to do with knowledge and its sharing in various forms, people are central. It is also around this issue that some of the strongest vested interests gather. The traditional use of expatriate personnel is one of the most protected, but also the most strongly criticized and politicized issues in TC.

The country studies shed some light on this issue. First, they show that it is very complex and that black-and-white solutions — such as doing away with expatriate advisors altogether, or using only short-term and not long-term personnel — are not likely to be appropriate. There are situations in which even countries with the most highly developed human capital bases will need expertise that they do not have. As the Philippines report noted, expatriate advisors are appreciated when they bring knowledge and skills that are really needed. In Kyrgyzstan, during the first few years after independence, Western advisors played a critical role in bringing new ideas and approaches. But in the second half of the decade, as local experts began to return with new training, there was less need for expatriates. Highly qualified expatriate experts who speak Russian fluently and who have the technical expertise to fill specific needs are still greatly valued, but on a much more selective basis than before.

Furthermore, the time frame of tasks and the particular combination of requirements for technical skills and understanding of the local situation will vary. Different situations call for different solutions.

Nevertheless, the studies point to some serious problems with actual practice. They report that expatriates who do not know the language and cannot communicate (Kyrgyz Republic), and those who are not adequately qualified and use consultancies for on-the-job training for themselves (Uganda), continue to be supplied, even when appropriately qualified local professionals are available. Expatriate advisors are expensive relative to other forms of technical assistance, and donors tend not to be open about those costs. There are real issues of lack of transparency, which protects donors from pressures for greater efficiency in resource use. In most cases, it seems clear that if recipient countries have greater control over how resources are used, there will be less utilization of expatriates, as Uganda has demonstrated.

The limited data available on personnel suggests that in recent years, there has been a reduction in the number of expatriate advisors provided through TC, but that it is nevertheless still one of the ways in which TC is carried out. Furthermore, the Kyrgyzstan, Philippines and Bangladesh reports all note a recent trend among some donors of contracting out more TC to consulting firms in their own countries, and managing less in-house. The papers suggest that this shift may be leading to an increased reliance on expatriate consultants.

In several countries, there has been evolution towards greater use of local expertise, but with limits. Local professionals are now contracted to do most of the training in Kyrgyzstan. In the Philippines, local researchers carry out much of the analysis, but are rarely given the opportunity to serve as team leaders. In Uganda, earlier programmes in education and training of ministry staff (such as in economic policy and civil service reform) have reduced the need for consultants, whether expatriate or local; when needed, local professionals are increasingly hired. In most cases, however, the studies indicated that local expertise is under-utilized, including in the Philippines, Kyrgyzstan and Bangladesh, where there is substantial and evident capacity. In Egypt, there seems to be the least effort to use local consultants.

A strong and active research, analysis, education and consulting base are essential components of capacity and are necessary if a country is to be able to move away from excessive dependence on external expertise. The gap between the nature of TC in the Philippines where institutions are strong, and the nature of TC in the other countries studied, confirms the importance of strengthening the higher education, research and the consulting sectors. In the Kyrgyz Republic, support for these sector has helped shift TC away from almost complete dependence on expatriates to a greater reliance on local expertise, and towards a changing TC relationship.

An alternative to employing expatriates from the North, South-South (or East-East) TC is reported to have had good results and to be cost-effective. The Bangladesh study calls attention to the innovative use of Bangladeshi consultants working abroad and identified that as a way to get a combination of international-level qualifications and local knowledge.

Mainstreaming Capacity Development

Even when efforts to develop capacity have been successful in a narrow sense (as in developing the capacity within a project to carry out its work and achieve the desired results), often that capacity is neither sustained nor translated into meaningful capacity in existing organizations. This is partly because capacity development often is not "mainstreamed", but is kept parallel and apart. The issue of mainstreaming has two different components: the first relates to organizations such as government ministries directly involved in TC project and programmes, while the second covers the the country's learning institutions, whose purpose is to build human capital and provide knowledge services.

Mainstreaming TC in Implementing Organizations

The first component has received more attention in discussions of capacity development. There are a myriad of examples of how TC and capacity development efforts are kept distinct. Project management units that separate the project administratively from the regular institutions are perhaps the main example. While project management units have been widely criticized and there seems to be movement away from them, they are mentioned repeatedly in the country studies, and it is clear that they are still very much a part of how TC operates. Another form is to create new organizational units. In Egypt, for example, a project created a separate policy analysis unit in the Ministry of Finance, rather than strengthening and reorienting an advisory unit that was already there. In general, the very idea of the TC project, as something financed and carried out separately from regular government programmes, also contributes to the creation of parallel structures.

While all the country studies noted similar patterns, Bolivia is the most extreme example. Consultants (external and local) have been used so extensively and have become such an integral part of policy making that a completely parallel structure has developed, separate from the official bureaucracy, and paid for by donors with higher remuneration than government positions. It dominates the policy process at the analysis and formulation stages, while the "regular" bureaucracy is expected to implement the policies and programmes. Meanwhile, the official state organizations have continued to be governed by a political patronage system and have remained weak and ineffective. Short-run project goals can be served, and the administration's role in the patronage system may have helped to maintain political stability in a weak democracy where no one party had a broad enough base to govern alone. Nevertheless, this TC-linked bifurcation has not contributed to the strengthening of the government's capacity.

The Philippines study noted the presence of project management units that were organic to the implementing institution — that is, led by the head of the ministry or other unit, and staffed at least partly by the regular staff. Salaries for consultants who were brought in were the same as those of regular staff. Projects run in this way are more likely to be sustainable and to contribute to capacity in the larger organization, although the study did note the tradeoff between time and energy spent on the project and on regular responsibilities. Still, to the extent that project management units are neces-sary, this organic approach offers the potential of avoiding the problems of bypassing regular institutions.

Even so, thought needs to go into how to sustain capacity created within existing institutions. Bangladesh offered a pair of contrasting examples from its Finance Ministry: in one project, Ministry staff participated in a financial management project's technical work — an unusual occurrence in itself — and then remained posted in the Ministry and were able to use what they had learned in their regular jobs. In another project, personnel were tapped to participate in implementation and received training and expe-rience, but were then transferred immediately to unrelated positions in other ministries.

In the past, ineffectiveness and corruption of existing institutions have provided the rationale for donors to operate apart from them. With the emphasis on institu-tional reform, TC needs more than ever to be a part of an integrated effort to strengthen institutions, organizations and human resources. There is some movement in that direction. To the extent that countries are able to assert their own priorities and bring TC resources into the overall budget and resource allocation process, the possi-bility of TC operating separately will be reduced.

Mainstreaming Capacity Development in Educational and Research Institutions

The country studies call attention to another way in which capacity development has often not been mainstreamed, and which has limited its ability to contribute in a fun-damental and lasting way to capacity. Each country has institutions whose purpose is to build human capital and to engage in research and the creation and analysis of knowledge. These institutions — universities primarily, but also research institutes and NGOs involved in research and training — have a central role to play in capacity development in their own countries. They are critical in the long-term development of the essential human capital, and represent the sustained capacity to continue build-ing, regenerating and updating that human capital.

The Uganda study cited the isolation of TC from educational and research institutes as a failure to mainstream TC into the country's existing and authentic capacity develop-ment institutions. Instead, there was a general tendency to treat capacity development as something that agencies or their consultants did in connection with projects, rather than as a more basic contribution to the human and social capital in the country.

There has been some support to institutions of research and higher education, most substantially in the Kyrgyz Republic and in countries such as Bolivia, where some new universities have been created and existing ones strengthened. Despite the sup-port, in recent years, to primary education, the potentially catalytic role that higher education can play in mainstreaming capacity development remains to be explored.

Understanding Change, or Its Absence

A country study perspective only gives a partial view of the obstacles to change, but the studies did provide some insights into pressures operating at the country level. Not surprisingly, there was little direct evidence of the pressures on donors, although some factors were suggested. First, in the case of some donor-recipient relationships, there were strong strategic or political reasons for the donor to be involved, suggesting that there was an incentive to keep the aid flowing but less incentive to worry about how much real contribution its TC made to capacity development. United States aid to Egypt, and possibly German and Turkish involvement in the Kyrgyz Republic seem to fit this pattern, as well as multilateral assistance to Bolivia and Uganda, both portrayed as star models of reform. As reported in several studies, the tendency of donors to view projects positively and to keep extending them even when they were not working, may partly be driven by such political constraints.

Some donors have resisted allowing their TC to be put under a budgetary umbrella, as noted in the Bolivia, Philippines, Uganda and Bangladesh studies. Several different but related motivations were suggested: a concern about the level of corruption or inefficiency in the country, a desire for particular projects and results to be clearly identifiable as the donor's, and an unwillingness to allow donor priorities to be made subsidiary to those of the recipient country. All these are tied to concerns about accountability and support back home.

Budget constraints in recent years have also pushed several donors in the direction of cutting the size and involvement of country offices, resulting in more decisions being made in headquarters. The trend of relying more on consulting firms from the home country also distances decision making from the recipient country. Although not uniform, these trends may make it more difficult for the donor to respond to demands for change at the country level.

Resistance to change does not exist only on the donor side. Technical cooperation resources have sometimes become part of patronage systems. Ministries or other organizations (whether inside or outside government) have benefited from access to TC resources; individual managers can access opportunities such as training programmes as part of the system of rewards in an organization. This may be positive if it is tied to the organization's needs and used constructively to strengthen the organization. Evidence suggests that this is not often the case. As reported in the study of how TC has evolved in the Kyrgyz Republic, for instance, individuals value training opportunities for trips abroad, prestige and travel allowances, and often receive them regardless of the relation of the training's content to the person's need for training or ability to utilize it. Equipment and vehicles offer other possibilities for individual benefits not necessarily connected to developing capacity. Clearly, people who benefit in these ways from TC are not going to have an interest in upsetting the cozy relationship by increasing transparency, efficiency or effectiveness, and will be likely to drag their feet if asked to make changes.

With more attention to the broader institutional level and the linking of capacity development with institutional reforms, TC reformers, whether from the donor or the recipient side, are likely to meet even stronger resistance. Reform threatens established interests and ways of doing things. It tries to find ways to limit corruption and increase transparency, and it puts patronage systems at all levels under pressure. Bureaucratic and political barriers to such changes are therefore to be expected. Analyses of civil service and other institutional reforms in the country studies suggest that TC for such reform often does run into difficulty because of lack of support or active opposition from within the institutions.

Nevertheless, there were clear instances in the countries studied where political leaders or senior managers recognized that change was needed. In Uganda, for example, this was evident with the assertion of a new framework for TC governance. It seems to have come from a sincere commitment to the welfare of the country, and an unwillingness to continue wasting needed resources.

Political commitment from top leaders and their expression of such commitment to donors are important elements in making the TC management framework credible and effective. Too often, TC has been thought of as simply a bureaucratic matter. Yet TC involves fundamentally political relationships, and change requires the exercise of political leadership. A government that wants to make sure aid is used according to its priorities has to be prepared to go up against donors who may insist on their own ideas as well as against people in the bureaucracy who benefit personally or organizationally from the lack of direction and coordination. The management strategy needs to be accompanied by a political strategy to build support for change. Most important, though, is a clear message that the government intends to set priorities, and manage and monitor TC.

The Philippines is an example of a country where bringing new groups into the TC arena has been helpful in supporting change. Non-governmental organizations have been brought into discussions of priorities, planning of projects and programmes, and monitoring of TC. While some NGOs depend for their survival on donor projects and may have vested interests against change, cultivating civil society capacity and participation can build support for a more relevant, responsive and effective TC relationship.

Conclusions and Key Lessons

The analysis of the country studies brings out several major points that hold lessons for both donors and partner countries for improving TC.

The TC challenges that countries face are as varied as the countries' capacities and other characteristics.

> **Flexible responses.** Diversity among countries means it is extremely unlikely that a single blueprint for TC will meet all needs and settings. Instead, flexibility

to operate in ways that respond to individual countries' conditions is essential. The transferability of "best practices" should be viewed with caution.

Adjustment of approach to local capacity. Donors need to assess existing local capacities, and in countries where there is significant capacity, adjust their approaches to utilize and further strengthen it. In such cases, there needs to be more room for experimentation with approaches that reduce direct donor involvement. In countries with little capacity, donors should work to strengthen basic capacities.

National priorities of partner countries must be put front and centre if TC is to be more effective in supporting capacity development.

National priorities are the key for donor harmonization. While donor harmonization has a role to play in reducing the stresses from fragmentation, competition and administrative demands, it alone is not a solution. Donor harmonization will only result in real change if donors converge around national priorities and coordinate their activities in that context.

Importance of supporting national dialogues about development goals. Where partner countries have not established clear goals and priorities, donors can be helpful in supporting processes of dialogue about development goals to begin what is always going to be a prolonged and iterative process of defining goals and appropriate ways of going about meeting them.

Allowing space for national processes to work. It is important that donors do not overwhelm domestic interests and dialogue. Domestic processes, especially in countries with weak political and administrative institutions, need space to take place. There is a good case to be made for donors to stand back and allow for that space — whether in defining goals and strategies, or in carrying out TC.

Political commitment and effective national management are essential if TC is to contribute more to the capacity of partner countries.

Politics of TC reform. Highest level political commitment to managing TC resources in line with national priorities – expressed through a clearly articulated vision and strategy – is key to dealing with donor resistance to TC reform. But resistance to change does not exist only on the donor side. In some countries, strong vested interests among national policy makers and industry professionals continue to hinder reform. Recipient governments must also ensure that TC resources are not used in patronage systems still prevalent in some of the countries studied. Reform programmes need to be complemented with change management planning and a strategy for obtaining public support.

Policy framework for TC. If TC resources are to be used well and in support of national priorities, it is essential that recipient country governments establish a framework for making decisions about managing and monitoring TC. Effective management must include well defined, systematic and credible structures and processes that integrate TC as resource for meeting national goals, whether directly through the budget, or in a closely linked parallel system.

Donor assistance for building national TC management capacity. One of the most important things that donors, especially UN agencies and other multi-laterals, can do is to assist countries in establishing accountable and effective mechanisms for TC management. This would include helping to develop systems for the regular collection, analysis and utilization of TC data, and making data publicly available and meaningful to end- users.

Donor transparency. Although donors are pushing institutional reforms that increase transparency for developing countries, they themselves resist openness when it comes to particular aspects of TC, especially those relating to the cost of advisors. This hinders rational decisions and evaluations about efficient use of resources, and contributes to waste of valuable development resources.

Institutional weaknesses hinder capacity development, the effectiveness of TC and the possibility of TC reform.

Priority of institutions and governance. Public sector frameworks often fail to provide adequate continuity or incentives, and may harbour high levels of corruption. Strengthening institutional frameworks and making them more conducive to developing and sustaining capacity should be a priority of governments and donors alike. This includes both working to improve the quality of governance generally, and establishing incentives for performance and for individual and organizational capacity development.

Issues around expertise and TC personnel are difficult, yet central to transforming TC.

Local vs. expatriate personnel. Donors should exercise great restraint in utilizing or encouraging the use of expatriate personnel. They should be open about their relative cost. When expertise outside the implementing institution is needed, local expertise should be used whenever and as fully as possible.

Building capacity of local research and consulting sectors. The extent to which local expertise can take over the role of providing knowledge services will depend substantially on the strength of the local universities, research institutes and consulting sectors. Donors and partner governments should therefore invest in building the capacity of these sectors as well as demanding their services.

Personnel and jobs data bank. If donors and governments are to gain access to local expertise, there needs to be a better base of information about available expertise. Establishing and maintaining a system that collects information on both the supply and demand — experts and job opportunities

— would be valuable. Donors, partner governments and research institutions could work together to develop and maintain such a system.

TC needs to be "mainstreamed" into existing capacity development institutions.

Integration of TC into local institutions. Technical cooperation and its capacity development efforts should be integrated as fully as possible with implementing institutions. To the extent that project management units remain necessary, keeping them within the purview of the relevant ministry or organization is more likely to have positive results for capacity development.

Strengthening human capital-building institutions. Technical cooperation should aim to build capacity not only in government, but should invest in higher education and other relevant knowledge institutions and NGOs. This will support the development of human capital more broadly, and will strengthen the country's ability to nurture, sustain, update and regenerate capacity over time.

References

Balihuta, Arsene, et al. 2002. *Technical Cooperation and Capacity Development in Uganda,* paper prepared for Reforming Technical Cooperation for Capacity Development, United Nations Development Programme.

Baris, Pierre, and Zaslavsky, Jean. 2001. *Reforming Technical Cooperation for Capacity Development: A Review of Statistical Evidence 1969-1999.* Summary. Based on a paper prepared for Reforming Technical Cooperation for Capacity Development, United Nations Development Programme.

Berg, Elliot and United Nations Development Programme (UNDP). 1993. *Rethinking Technical Cooperation,* New York: UNDP.

Cukrowski, Jacek, et al. 2002. *Technical Cooperation and Capacity Development: The Kyrgyz Republic,* paper prepared for Reforming Technical Cooperation for Capacity Development, United Nations Development Programme.

El-Refaie, Faika, et al. 2002. *Technical Cooperation and Capacity Building: The Case of Egypt,* paper prepared for Reforming Technical Cooperation for Capacity Development, United Nations Development Programme.

Gray Molina, George, and Chávez, Gonzalo. 2002. *Technical Cooperation and Capacity Development: Bolivian Case Study,* paper prepared for Reforming Technical Cooperation for Capacity Development, United Nations Development Programme.

Illo, Jeanne Frances I., et al. 2002. *Reforming Technical Cooperation: Philippines,* paper prepared for Reforming Technical Cooperation for Capacity Development, United Nations Development Programme.

Sobhan, Rehman, et al. 2002. *Technical Cooperation for Capacity Development: Bangladesh Experience,* paper prepared for Reforming Technical Cooperation for Capacity Development, United Nations Development Programme.

OECD/DAC, *International Development Statistics.*

3 *Bangladesh*[1]

APPLYING TECHNICAL COOPERATION TO HEALTH AND FINANCIAL REFORM

Introduction

Bangladesh is one of the largest recipients of official development assistance (ODA). Average ODA was around $1.5 billion for the period 1994-1999, although total ODA receipts, as a share of GDP, have declined in recent years and in 1999 were about four percent of GDP. Technical cooperation (TC), sometimes referred to as technical assistance (TA), constitutes about one-sixth of ODA, again making Bangladesh a major recipient. This chapter evaluates the performance of TC during the 1990s in order to identify the factors behind success and failure. Technical cooperation here refers to assistance intended to enhance the capacity of institutions and individuals, so that they are better able to undertake tasks and improve performance. Technical cooperation covers a wide range of activities, including consultancy services, workshops, training and the supply of equipment. Significant amounts are also provided under the umbrella of so-called project aid.

Following a brief economic background section, this chapter provides an overall picture of ODA and TC in Bangladesh. Thereafter, it focuses on two case studies – one

[1] This paper was co-written by Rehman Sobhan, Executive Chairman, and Debapriya Bhattacharya, Executive Director, at the Centre for Policy Dialogue in Dhaka. The larger research team included Fouzul Kabir Khan, Chief Executive Officer, Infrastructure Development Company Ltd.; Sayed Alamgir Farrouk Chowdhury, Former Secretary, Ministry of Health and Family Welfare, Bangladesh; and Riffat Zaman, Assistant Professor, Department of Economics, University of Dhaka.

in the health sector and the other in the area of economic reform, where a considerable amount of TC was provided during the 1990s.

Technical cooperation to the health sector was initially provided through projects. Since 1997, TC has been provided within the framework of a sector-wide strategy through the Health and Population Sector Programme (HPSP). This approach has permitted a greater level of coordination among donors and the Government in a sector that is critical to the welfare of the country. A significant component of this TC is investment-related.

The second case study on economic reform deals with free-standing TC provided to the Ministry of Finance. The programmes implemented in the Ministry are directly linked to the wider process of economic reform that is being undertaken in Bangladesh, in cooperation with the country's development partners and within the framework of the Consultative Group process.

Economic Background

Bangladesh is a Least Developed Country. With a population of 123 million, its average GDP for the years 1997-1999 was about $36 billion, which converts into a per capita GDP of around $300. This same period witnessed a GDP growth rate of around five percent. There has been considerable progress in macroeconomic stability, and the rate of inflation has been low – below 10% – for most of the last decade. An important achievement is a sustained increase in exports, rising from $1.7 billion in 1990/91 to $5.8 billion in 1999/00. Meanwhile, ODA as a share of exports declined from 104% in 1990/91 to 28% in 1999/00. This is an appropriate illustration of the respective roles of aid and trade.

Despite improvements in performance on the Human Development Index – Bangladesh's HDI value improved from 0.335 in 1975 to 0.478 in 2000 – the country remains in the low human development category, at 145th place out of 173 countries ranked on the HDI. In 2000, life expectancy for the average Bangladeshi was 59.4 years, just below the South Asian regional average of 62.9 years. According to data from 1999, the country performs well below the regional average in adult literacy (41.3% against 55.6%) and combined enrolment ratios (37% to 53%). Average income per head in 2000, at $1,602 (PPP US$) is also well below the regional average of $2,404.

Trends in ODA and TC

Official development assistance has played an important role in Bangladesh's development scenario in four principal forms: food, commodity, and project aid (which includes investment-related technical assistance), and free-standing TC. Commitments totalling nearly $44 billion in ODA were made between 1971/72 and 1999/00, of which $36 billion was disbursed. In the 1990s, the amount of ODA disbursed was $16 billion.

Table 3.1 shows declining ODA disbursements for the period 1990/91-1999/00. Disbursements dropped from $1,733 million in 1990/91 to $1,251 million in 1997/98, but registered a modest rise in subsequent years, to $1,588 million in 1999/00 (in connection with post-flood relief and rehabilitation support).

Official development assistance disbursements, as a percentage of GDP, revenue, expenditure and exports, experienced a declining trend over the last decade. From 1990/91 to 1999/00, the share of ODA in GDP declined from 7.4% to 4.3%; government revenue as a percentage of GDP increased from 9.56% to 11.42%; government expenditure (as a percentage of GDP) increased from 16.1% to 20.3%; and the share of exports (again as a percentage of GDP) increased from 7.14% to 15.5%. These trends indicate that the domestic capacity to finance expenditure through greater domestic resource mobilization has risen over the last 10 years.

Disbursements exceeded commitments in 1990/91, 1994/95, 1995/96 and 1999/00; in other years, more aid was committed than used. This provides a crude measure of the deterioration in the absorptive capacity for foreign aid, and explains the large volume of unutilized aid. More than $5 billion, mostly in the form of project aid, remains untapped in the pipeline.

Commitment and disbursement figures of ODA and its components show a fall in aid commitments, with the exception of fiscal years 1993/94 and 1997/98. The increase in 1998/99 is most likely a reflection of additional aid commitments for post-flood rehabilitation projects. The volume of food aid was $160 million in 1990/91, but dropped to $50 million in 1999/00. Commodity aid declined from $431 million to $174 million over the same period.

The same trend did not apply to project aid. Many development activities in Bangladesh are undertaken within the context of projects, and project aid is an influential factor in national development. In 2000, the amount of project aid committed was $1,250.74 million, which makes up 84.79% of ODA. Project aid contains an important TC component, generally ranging from five to 10%.

Technical cooperation is integrated into the Annual Development Programme (ADP) through the budget for publicly funded projects, including those underwritten by foreign assistance. Table 3.2 shows that from 1990-91 to 1999-00, the total ADP allocation was $24,739 million, $11,308 million (45.7%) of which was for PA. Some $894 million was allocated to TC.

The share of TC in the ADP has seen a declining trend. It was slightly more than three percent between 1990/91 and 1995/96, rising to 4.2% and 5.1% in the following two years, before falling back to 2.7% in 1999/00. The total amount of TC declined from a high of $126 million in 1997-98 to a low of $81 million in 1998-99. It rose again to $89 million in 1999-2000, which is still below allocations in every year from 1993 to 1998. The share of TC in project aid grew until 1997/98 to a peak of 11.16%, and has since fallen back quite sharply.

Free-standing TC has two components. One is the government component (consisting of matching funds, overhead facilities or some personnel cost), and the other

TABLE 3.1: KEY ECONOMIC DATA, 1990-2000

Year	(US$ millions)		As share of GDP (%)			
	GDP	ODA	ODA	Govt Revenue	Govt Expenditure	Exports
1990-91	23,372.32	1,732.58	7.41	9.56	16.10	7.14
1991-92	23,767.75	1,611.47	6.78	10.50	16.60	8.01
1992-93	24,218.00	1,675.01	6.92	11.67	18.27	9.84
1993-94	25,759.13	1,558.64	6.05	12.12	16.37	9.84
1994-95	29,110.61	1,739.09	5.97	12.11	17.82	11.93
1995-96	31,855.75	1,443.75	4.53	11.49	16.66	12.19
1996-97	32,857.00	1,481.23	4.51	12.22	16.80	13.47
1997-98	34,062.03	1,251.37	3.67	12.38	17.46	15.18
1998-99	36,394.01	1,536.06	4.22	11.26	16.74	14.63
1999-00	37,153.58	1,587.95	4.27	11.42	20.30	15.51
Trend growth rate (%)	5.87	-1.77	-1.77	7.30	7.03	14.55

Source: Economic Relations Division (ERD), Ministry of Finance.

TABLE 3.2: ANNUAL DEVELOPMENT PROGRAMME (ADP) ALLOCATIONS AND DISBURSEMENTS (US$ MILLIONS)

	Allocations			Disbursements		Shares of TC (%) in allocation	
Fiscal year	ADP	Project Aid	TC	ADP	Project Aid	TC in ADP	TC in Project Aid
1990-91	1,714.57	1,029.85	63.65	1,476.16	832.63	3.71	6.18
1991-92	1,874.67	1,061.88	71.37	1,579.44	889.38	3.81	6.72
1992-93	2,074.86	1,080.60	68.44	1,673.56	865.51	3.30	6.33
1993-94	2,400.00	1,090.00	90.68	2,245.88	1,024.50	3.78	8.32
1994-95	2,773.63	1,154.23	95.12	2,562.93	1,072.18	3.43	8.24
1995-96	2,556.78	1,091.53	94.56	2,451.22	968.19	3.70	8.66
1996-97	2,740.05	1,153.10	113.64	2,585.71	991.33	4.15	9.86
1997-98	2,463.70	1,124.95	125.56	2,427.85	926.97	5.10	11.16
1998-99	2,860.65	1,179.81	81.73	2,555.99	953.21	2.86	6.93
1999-00	3,279.67	1,341.68	89.11	2,827.55	1,127.27	2.72	6.64
Total	24,738.58	11,307.63	893.86	22,386.29	9,651.17	3.61	7.90

Source: Implementation, Monitoring and Evaluation Division (IMED), Planning Commission.

TABLE 3.3: TECHNICAL COOPERATION BY SECTOR, 1990/91-99/00

Sectors	Allocation			Utilization		
	GOB-TA	PA-TA	Total	TA	As % of total allocation	As % of total utilization
Agriculture	9.36	83.77	93.13	30.69	32.95	13.39
Industry	3.01	65.21	68.22	11.18	16.39	4.88
Health, Pop. & Family Welfare	22.5	64.99	87.49	23.69	27.08	10.34
Family Welfare	1.76	50.05	51.81	6.65	12.84	2.90
Social Welfare, Women's Affairs & Youth Development	0.79	10.98	11.77	3.86	32.80	1.68
Labour, Manpower	0.72	4.11	4.83	0	0.00	0.00
Power	3.18	22.07	25.25	9	35.64	3.39
Oil, Gas, Natural Resources	2.49	26.09	28.58	9.05	31.67	3.95
Water	42.44	199.04	241.48	50.39	20.87	21.99
Phys. Plan, Water Supply & Housing	4.41	35.87	40.28	5.12	12.71	2.23
Rural Development & Institutions	1.27	38	39.27	10.61	27.02	4.63
Transport	8.59	66.03	74.62	22.22	29.78	9.70
Communication	0.32	3.52	3.84	0.58	15.10	0.25
Mass Media	0.62	1.99	2.61	1.36	52.11	0.59
Public Administration	15.13	90.28	105.41	25.35	24.05	11.06
Education & Religious Affairs	3.23	28.83	32.06	19.4	60.51	8.46
Science & Technology Research	0.32	5.39	5.71	0	0.00	0.00
Sports & Culture	0.09	0.46	0.55	0.03	5.45	0.01
TOTAL (1990/91-1999/00)	120.23	796.68	916.91	229.18	24.99	100.00

Source: Economic Relations Division (ERD), Ministry of Finance; and Implementation Monitoring and Evaluation Division (IMED), Planning Commission.

is the foreign aid component under project aid. Table 3.3 shows TC disbursed directly through the budget and as a component of PA for the period 1990/91-1999/00, categorized under 18 ministries.

Total TC allocation over the decade was $916.9 million. The largest portion went to the Ministry of Water Resources ($241.5 million), followed by the Ministry of Public Administration ($105.4 million), Agriculture ($93.1 million), Health, Population and Family Planning ($87.5 million) and Transport ($74.6 million).

The level of TC disbursements, however, was much lower than the allocated amounts. TC utilization was only $229 million, or about 25% of the total. Technical cooperation use by the respective ministries was highest for Water Resources (22.0%), followed by Agriculture (13.4%), Public Administration (11.1%), and Health, Population and Family Welfare (10.3%).

The major TC donors are the World Bank (International Development Association), the United Kingdom, the Netherlands, Germany, UNDP and the Asian Development Bank. Table 3.4 shows commitment data by donor, and their preferred sectors.

In sum, TC trends in Bangladesh depict an overall declining trend that is expressive of both the restrictive supply-side situation, as well as improved demand conditions. Flows of TC slowed with falling ODA disbursements. Improvements in human and institutional development indicators, along with mixed results from past TC, also contributed to low "off-take".

Process Analysis of TC

Technical cooperation projects in Bangladesh theoretically evolve through long, multi-layered consultation. Donors talk to implementing agencies first to identify needs and priorities. They then consult the administrative ministries to ascertain whether the needs and priorities named by the implementing agencies are consistent with government policies. In the formal sense, the Planning Commission comes in at a much later stage for approval. Donors, implementation agencies and the ministries consult the Planning Commission earlier, however – even if informally – to avoid rejection or protraction of the process at the approval stage. Once donors and implementation agencies reach agreements on priorities and preliminary design – and the concurrence of the Planning Commission has a high probability – formal steps to "process" the project commence.

The donors and the Government then hold programming meetings wherein they formally agree to the types of assistance to be provided, and the time frames, which are generally longer than 12 months, and usually for three years. If the changes called for under the proposed programmes are major, i.e. fundamentally changing sectors and institutions, a review of previous programmes is generally undertaken. Donors also produce feasibility studies and other pre-project analysis before they can commit resources.

Once agreements have been reached, government agencies prepare Technical Assistance Project Proforma (TAPP). The Planning Commission examines the proforma and submits it to the Executive Committee of the National Economic Council (ECNEC), headed by the Prime Minister, for approval. It is rare for the Planning Commission or the ECNEC to reject a TC project, though they may raise objections that need to be addressed by the ministries and the implementation agencies.

The donors also prepare their own documentation, which generally resembles the proforma with respect to objectives, technical specifications, implementation arrangements and budget, but differs in terms of format and structure. Differences between the Government and donors, and within the Government itself, lie in details and procedures, and hardly ever on issues of substance. Once agreement on fundamental issues is established, TC project articulation and documentation formalizes the commitment.

TABLE 3.4: TA BY DONOR ALLOCATION (US$ MILLIONS)

Donor/source	Main Sectors	Allocated Amount in 1991-00
ADB	Agriculture, Water, Transport	27.21
BELGIUM	Power	0.23
CANADA	Water	9.59
DENMARK	Water	2.88
E.E.C.	Water	2.63
F.A.O.	Agriculture	2.154
F.R.G	Agriculture, Communication	13.54
FRANCE	Natural Resources	4.06
GERMANY	Finance, Education, Water	21.31
IDA	Transport, Physical Infrastructure	141.10
INDIA	Education	1.72
JAPAN	Education	1.19
NETHERLANDS	Water, Health, Physical Infrastructure	90.85
NORWAY	Finance	1.60
RUSSIA	Power	4.88
SAUDI ARABIA	Health	2.03
SWEDEN	Health, Population	1.42
UK	Health, Oil, Gas & Natural Resources	155.70
UNDP	Public Administration, Education, Family Welfare, Water	56.36
USA	Public Administration, Finance	15.00
TOTAL		555.45

Source: Economic Relations Division (ERD), Ministry of Finance.

TABLE 3.5: TC AND TA TO HEALTH AND FAMILY PLANNING, 1991-2003 (US$ MILLIONS)

Period	Total Dev. Exp	TC	TC as % of Total Dev. Exp	TA under loan
1991-98	1,241.1	415.5	33.5	40
1998-03	1,875.2	432.1	23.0	120

The External Resources Division (ERD) of the Ministry of Finance plays a moderating role between implementation agencies, ministries, the Planning Commission and donors. Its concern lies in mobilizing external resources for sectors and ministries. In cases where there are disagreements between implementation agencies and ministries or donors, ERD tries to narrow down or remove the difference. In the event that the Planning Commission raises objections, ERD sides with the ministry's judgment, and points to the need for external resources for the sectoral programme (and particularly the direct and indirect need for foreign exchange). For judgments on substantive contents and merits, ERD relies more on the relevant ministry and the implementation agency, which have a better grasp of the technical/ engineering contents of projects.

Aid is now being directed increasingly to institutional capacity building and reform – the so-called "software" of development. Analysis and design have become much more important and more complex in these areas. Judgments and value perceptions of donor and government functionaries play a crucial role in the "software" of aid and development.

Donors often expect more fundamental changes than the institutional capacity can deliver. On the other hand, accelerating development entails many of these changes – at least according to donors who base their recommendations on neo-classical economic theory and their own experiences in institutional and economic development. As long as the basic approaches to development are conditioned by this cognitive structure and the country is dependent on aid, the role of TC will remain important.

TC in Health and Family Planning Sector

This section examines TC support to the health sector, mainly with reference to the Fourth Population and Health Project (FPHP, 1990-97) and the Health and Population Sector Programme (HPSP, 1998-03). These were the largest aid programmes over the last decade, supported mainly by Australia, Canada, Germany, the Netherlands, Norway, Sweden, the United Kingdom, USAID, UNICEF, WHO and UNFPA.

The overall FPHP goals included reducing fertility, lowering morbidity and mortality in children under 5, reducing maternal mortality, reducing mortality from common poverty-related diseases and enhancing the nutritional status of women and children. The HPSP objective is to achieve improved health and family welfare among the most vulnerable women, children and the poor. It is intended to put in place a comprehensive system that ensures client-centred provision of primary health care and related services.

The figures in Table 3.5 show a comparison of TC disbursements between the 4th and 5th Government Plan periods (projected in the case of the latter period), which show sustained high levels of TC. The data on TC for the first period includes support to 64 FPHP projects. The Government adopted sector-wide approaches (SWAps) in 1998, and the HPSP and the National Nutrition Project account for a larger share of total aid and TC to the sector. Technical cooperation associated with loans was also significant in both periods.

Ideally, all foreign support is pooled under a SWAps arrangement that serves as the basis for identifying priority clusters of activities. There is, however, some resistance from both donors and the Government to aggregating all aid programmes in the health sector under one head – on the part of donors because of a desire to establish their authority over the HPSP, and on the part of recipients because of concern that subjecting all expenditures to World Bank oversight norms might slacken the pace of implementation.

The nature and extent of government involvement in TC is a commonly debated issue. Officials complain about non-involvement in the formulation and implementation of programme activities associated with the HPSP, mainly where TC is not pooled.

More importantly, there is a sense that HPSP funds are spent on activities that do not reflect government priorities, leaving critical areas untouched. For example, despite substantial disbursements during the last decade, the Ministry of Health still does not have a serviceable personnel data base, a computerized MIS system, or a training programme focused on increasing clinical knowledge and skills. Important programmes such as English-language training for medical students have been dropped on grounds that cannot be linked to shortage of funds. Procurement is stalled because of a lack of skilled manpower, which is a deficiency that could be met through consultancy services financed by grants. Important research activities, such as epidemiological studies on a number of non-communicable diseases, remain uninitiated for lack of funds.

A significant amount of total aid to the sector – around one-fifth – is allocated to NGOs, largely at the discretion of donors. The involvement of NGOs in the sector is wholly appropriate, but there is no collective oversight of their activities, either by donors or the Government.

Expenditures for most activities financed under grant aid through the HPSP are controlled by bilateral donors, including direct disbursements for NGOs, consultancies, workshops and research. In contrast, when loan funds are used, programme details are legally required to be finalized in consultation with the stakeholder. Here also, recipients sometimes have to acquiesce to the will of the donor.

It is important to note that official opposition to donor-proposed consultancies, for example, does not necessarily mean such services are not needed. The Government may be averse to TC programmes that are likely to precipitate politically or strategically unpalatable change. Inhibitions towards integrating the Family Planning and Health departments and the introduction of user fees for public health services are examples of official resistance to donor-initiated reforms under the HPSP.

With respect to modalities of TC, available data suggests that expenditure on consultancies has tended to fall, while spending on training activities has increased. Again the trend appears appropriate, given the emphasis being given to primary health care and family planning, mainly for rural and disadvantaged populations.

There is also a general feeling that a significant part of TC is being channeled into "soft" management-related issues, where achievements are difficult to quantify and evaluate. Expenditure details and interviews with officials reveal that sector-wide management, decentralization and planning are some of the areas that receive excessive attention and funds.

There is also concern about foreign tours and study visits by officials in the Health and Population sectors, much of which is redundant because of the rapid turnover in personnel. Support from concerned officials, however, ensures prioritization of such programming. Although it is difficult to estimate the extent of this 'padding', it is the opinion of the research team that rationalization would lead to significant economies, particularly under the HPSP.

As a management device, the sector-wide approach introduced by the HPSP has improved coordination. Related activities are clustered into line programmes. However, bilateral aid to the health sector that falls outside the pooled funds of the HPSP still continues to support activities under different line directors, who exert their own autonomy vis-à-vis the HPSP. Planning, management, human resource and MIS issues are thus dealt with by more than one line director, each unaware of the programmes implemented in other areas. This undermines the integrity of the HPSP.

HPSP discipline can be undermined for other reasons. Implementing agencies remain reluctant to become involved with the process of procurement and hiring out of fear of getting embroiled in complaints and accusations that could end with investigations by the Anti-Corruption Bureau. There is also the concern that expenditures will bring them within the purview of the national audit system, which scrutinizes all accounts according to national rules, even when the spending is done by the donors, in conformity with their own procedures.

The TC experience in the health sector raises a number of related issues.

Use of local consultants. Bangladesh has qualified local consultants in most sectors. More use could be made of them under the HPSP, since local experts are more familiar with national procedures and social conditions. In practice, while more local consultants are being used under TC than before, there are still marked differences in remuneration when compared with expatriate experts. Current competitive bidding systems tend to drive down compensation rates for local consultants, even though they are as qualified as expatriates.

It is proposed by the study team that the outcomes of consultancies, research, workshops and other TC activities be more widely disseminated to policy makers and civil society so that the professional competency of these services, and particularly those of more costly expatriate consultants, can be put under greater public scrutiny. Initial reviews of TC programmes indicate that this is rarely done, and that the lack of scrutiny probably helps to conceal substandard consultancy work within donor-funded TC.

Aid effectiveness and sustainability. Although it is clearly desirable for the Government to establish greater control over TC programmes, there are evident problems in realizing this goal, given prevailing governance practices. Effectiveness of TC can be compromised by the protracted nature of the consultant selection process when the Government is responsible for recruitment, and when loan funds are used. Government regulations on co-financing can also be a hindrance. Training and workshop programmes, for example, require counterpart funds. Government rules, however, limit the amounts of funds that may be drawn, or the volume of 'imprest' funds made available to support such activities.

The sustainability issue of TC-related activities is of concern, particularly as foreign assistance begins to decline. There are both funding and capacity dimensions to sustainability. It is clear that the Government cannot continue funding programmes at the level realized under the HPSP from its own resources. Given the somewhat superfluous nature of some activities funded under TC, equivalent levels of funding may not be necessary if the reduced allocations are used more effectively. The Government will need to apply stricter priorities to its expenditures.

The permanent creation and retention of capacity is the other challenge arising out of the TC process. If recipient organizations are able to capture or retain capacity built up through TC, then dependence on such assistance is likely to decrease. In practice, however, a significant part of TC training and research is not directly targeted at enhancing the health sector's organizational capacity in designing and implementing its own programmes. Personnel retention is also a key problem. Frequent turnovers of civil servants trained under TC programmes and limited career prospects within the public service sector drain away knowledge and skills.

Accountability and cost-effectiveness. Any assessment of development expenditure, to be meaningful, requires that outcomes or benefits be evaluated against costs. Research studies and surveys indicate that there have been improvements in health indicators: a fall in infant and maternal mortality and total fertility rates, as well as progress in life expectancy and nutritional conditions. It is less clear how these improved health indicators are causally related to the HPSP. More studies relating component-specific expenditures to health outcomes are required. Here again, precise estimates of the HPSP's cost-effectiveness are not easily discernible, because data on expenditure broken down by activity are not readily available. The general conclusion is that the HPSP has been positive, but that the extent to which society has extracted value for money from the HPSP varies according to different components of the programme.

While the achievements in the health sector are encouraging, the sector continues to be a source of major developmental concern. In a country where even primary health care services are still fragmented and there is ample scope for improvement both in terms of coverage and quality of service, there is at the same time a parallel demand for providing specialist services for treatment of complicated diseases. As in the past, emphasis on primary health care has to be measured against the demand for tertiary care provided by better-trained medical personnel.

Enhancing TC Effectiveness in Health, Family Planning Sectors

Technical cooperation will continue to play an important catalytic role as Bangladesh strives for a better and more equitable health care system. Such support is financed through both grants and concessional loans from multilateral finance institutions, although the Government has a clear preference for grant assistance. If necessary, it should be feasible to shift some of the TC obtained as loans – especially when tied to investment projects – to sources that will provide TC in grant form. However, as discussed in the next section, grants are not necessarily a less costly source of aid.

It is also unclear whether grant preference works in the interests of capacity development. Since TC is largely provided in grants and is not considered a cost incurred by the Government, there is no financial incentive for closer scrutiny and control. Consultants are thus retained to undertake tasks that should normally be carried out by local officials. The Government also appears to accept TC for activities of low priority in the health sector, for fear of compromising opportunities for larger volumes of project aid.

A more purposeful Government with a greater understanding of expenditure priorities – which requires more than a fundamental change in attitude – would help to ensure a better use of aid resources. A more effective role for the Government can emerge from the sector-wide approach, but will call for major changes in institutions and procedures.

TC and Financial Reform

In the early 1990s, Bangladesh embarked on a large number of reform initiatives covering a wide range of public sector activities. The efforts of the Government were complemented by various donor-supported TC projects. Donors include the United Kingdom's Department for International Development (DFID), the World Bank (IDA) and the Asian Development Bank. This section focuses on macro-economic reforms carried out through TC and capacity development programmes in the Ministry of Finance during the period 1992-2001. The TC projects analyzed here addressed a broad range of issues in the areas of budgeting and expenditure control, revenue administration and macroeconomic policy analysis. The three TC programmes are summarized below.

Reforms in Budgeting and Expenditure Control (RIBEC) was implemented in three phases (RIBEC1, RIBEC2 – subsequently restructured as RIBEC 2A and 2B – and RIBEC2000), with a new phase in the offing. These three DFID grant-funded projects covered budgeting and expenditure control issues. In RIBEC1, two private consultancy firms – one from the UK and other from Bangladesh – carried out a diagnostic study. The report identified the weaknesses in budgetary and expenditure controls, with recommendations for reforms. RIBEC2 followed up on the report. Subsequent to a review, the activities of RIBEC2 were reduced to focus on a smaller number of issues. Phase 3 (RIBEC 2000) continues with various key tasks, especially focusing on strengthening the training functions of the Financial Management Academy and reforming government audit processes and financial management capacities. The RIBEC programmes are indicated under Table 3.6.

Excise Taxes and Customs Data Computerization (ETAC) and its successor, the *Customs Administration Project* (CAM1), focused on computerizing the National Board of Revenue (NBR) and modernizing customs procedures. Both were funded through an IDA credit, and targeted improvements in revenue administration. ETAC was implemented through individual consultants, while a private consulting consortium is handling CAM1. Expenditures under these programmes are presented in Table 3.7.

Institutional Support to the Ministry of Finance (ISMOF) and its follow-up project, *Efficiency Enhancement of Fiscal Management* (EEFM), were funded by grants from the Asian Development Bank. The primary aim of these projects is to improve the Ministry's research and analytical capacities in fiscal, monetary and external economy policy. The programme has developed a computerized general equilibrium model to enable the Government to address key monetary and fiscal policy issues. These programmes are presented in Table 3.8.

The three TC projects identified above represent three different donors and two different types of financing (grants and credit). Out of the seven projects, RIBEC, ISMOF and EEFM are stand-alone TC projects, ETAC is a sub-project under an umbrella group of TC projects, and CAM1 is one of the TC components of the broader Export Diversification Project. All the projects under review are ongoing in the sense that although one or more phases of the project have been completed, a successor project is in place or is being contemplated.

The projects exemplify a process by which TC projects originate, and the way donors are involved. RIBEC was created within the finance division of the Ministry of Finance, and DFID worked alongside national officials in developing the programme to improve budgetary processes and public expenditure management. The ISMOF/EEFM programme was driven by a Government push to improve capacities within the Ministry of Finance, with ADB support. There was a shared mutual interest between donors and the Government in designing and implementing these projects.

Key Issues in Design and Implementation

The three programmes in the Ministry of Finance – RIBEC, ETAC/CAM1 and ISMOF/EEFM – would appear to have been successful in terms of capacity development. The RIBEC programme has brought about improvements in the quality of accounting, and enhanced capacities in financial management, particularly at the sectoral level. The ETAC/CAM programme has speeded up data transfer and reporting through computerization. Customs procedures and documentation are faster and more transparent. Finally, ISMOF/EEFM has improved research and analytical capabilities in the Finance Ministry – manifested by several series of regular reports – and has begun to strengthen capacities in domestic debt management and monitoring of state-owned enterprises.

TABLE 3.6: TC UNDER REFORM IN BUDGETING AND EXPENDITURE CONTROL (RIBEC) PROJECTS

| Project | Duration | Amount (in £millions) | | | |
		Local Consultants	Foreign Consultants	Other Costs	Total
RIBEC1	October 1992 - April 1993	NA	NA	NA	£2.14
RIBEC2	1 Year				
RIBEC2A and 2B	September 1994 - March 1998	£0.83	£3.46	£5.52	£9.81
RIBEC 2000	January 1999 - September 2001	£0.61	£1.58	£1.29	£3.48

TABLE 3.7: EXPENDITURES UNDER REFORMS IN BUDGETING AND EXPENDITURE CONTROL (RIBEC) PROJECTS

| Project | Duration | Method of Implementa-tion | Amount (in £millions) | | | |
			Local Consultants	Foreign Consultants	Other Costs	Total
ETAC	June 1992 - June 1999	Consultants	NA	NA	NA	$3.44
CAM1	June 1999 - July 2002	Consulting Firm	$1.32	$2.83	$5.46	$9.61

TABLE 3.8: TC UNDER ISMOF AND EEFM PROJECTS

| Project | Duration | Method of Implementa-tion | Amount (in £millions) | | | |
			Local Consultants	Foreign Consultants	Other Costs	Total
ISMOF	August 1995- September 1998	Consultants	$0.08	$0.17	$0.40	$0.65
EEFM	October 1998- March 2002	Consulting Firm	$0.20	$0.27	$0.31	$0.78

In all groups, challenges remain in order to ensure that the capacity gains are consolidated and made sustainable. The TC projects have highlighted a number of issues that have more general application.

Ownership. The Government can claim ownership of the economic reform projects, as they address its priority concerns. The donors themselves have attached priority to these issues and have supported the Government. There was strong commitment at the level of senior policy makers and administrators, as well as from the political leadership. Ownership can be claimed only when there is this degree of commitment. The projects were also designed after an extensive process of consultation between the Government and TC donors, which involved the participation of a wide range of stakeholders.

Institutional capacity building. Tensions can arise from integrating a TC project into the administrative practices of a ministry or organization. The existing organization has its mission, culture, and pattern of formal and informal relationships and work methods. If the project builds on what already exists and is largely compatible with the existing organization, integration does not pose a problem. However, if the project aims at changing existing structures more fundamentally, then it poses a challenge to managers and administrators. In the public sector, the tension can be more pronounced. Government is a large and complex set of organizations, and its parts interact with each other and with the whole in varied and complex ways. The introduction of new methods and values will always be resisted. Capacity development programmes, therefore, need to select strategic units that affect and influence other parts. The reform of financial management is strategic from that point of view.

One interesting innovation has been the creation of project implementing units (PIUs) within projects. Currently serving government officials with the requisite background have been recruited as consultants to these PIUs, and they are paid a higher remuneration than their normal government salaries through the project budget. The employment of these officials in this capacity has enabled projects to collaborate with related government offices during implementation.

Some of the potential impediments to successful integration and change occur when:

- new and higher levels of professional and managerial skills are required, but incumbents are unwilling to learn new skills and resist change;

- there are no incentives to help motivate employees (remuneration and prospects of career advancement do not improve with new skills);

- there is no innovation in decision making methods, and therefore no demand, reward or recognition for new skills; and

- the structure of administration and the civil service system, organized as generalist cadres, do not attach value to professional or higher levels of skills. (The functional cadres are also generalists in that they do not need pre-entry professional qualifications. The cadres with technical qualifications have a limited or little role in policy making, and when they attain senior positions in ministries, they rotate in the same way as generalist officers).

These problems cannot be solved within one project or a single organization in the public sector. To ensure productive and sustainable processes of capacity development, these systemic problems need to be addressed at a government-wide level.

Nonetheless, the RIBEC group of projects appears to have addressed, largely successfully, the problems of assimilating a project into the main structure of an administration, potentially ensuring its sustainability (though this is yet to be fully tested). The ingredients of success would seem to have been the following: the project originated from the Government; expatriate and local consultants, and retired and serving government servants worked together in designing the programme; government officials working as consultants provided a channel for transfer of knowledge; and there was sustained political commitment at top levels. The RIBEC experience may be treated as an example of a "good practice" and examined carefully to ascertain whether and to what extent it can be applied to other projects.

Grants vs. loans. As mentioned in the previous section, the Government depends on aid for TC for capacity building programmes, and has a strong preference for grants. This preference could reflect a perception that such programmes have low priority and should be implemented at no or lowest possible cost to the Government. This rationale does not seem justified by facts. Soft loans also contain a high grant element – in the range of 80% - 90%. Where the alternative is tied grant assistance, the procurement of goods and services with such grants is reportedly 20% - 30% higher. Allowing for the higher cost of tied grants and the expected efficiency of more competitive procurement, TC grants are not necessarily more cost-effective than soft loans. The Government should consider allocating adequate resources of its own for capacity development and for efficiency-enhancement interventions, and should not discriminate against soft loans.

Sustainability. Here there are more worries. Technical cooperation projects seem to lack a clear exit policy, implying that extensions have become inevitable. This absence of a phase-out is obviously beneficial to all parties involved, other than the real development stakeholders, i.e., the public. Expatriate consultants and firms get paid, irrespective of project performance, the donor portfolio is enlarged by the project extension, and local officials and consultants continue to benefit from training, travel and fees. This experience makes the case for more developmental, rather than merely intrinsic project accountability.

Information technology. The TC projects above have important components of technology, particularly IT. But the benefits that should accrue from implementing these components have not been full realized for several reasons. Local staff are inadequately trained, and there is an aversion to IT among some public officials. There is also the problem of out-sourcing: IT activities are often contracted out to consultancy firms, which means capacities are not built up within government institutions. When the TC project is over, the Goverment cannot afford to continue paying for the consultancy services.

By whatever means it was done, the introduction of IT and computers should have led to more efficient management of government tasks. Even within the same ministry, however, there was no project interface: the ISMOF project, for example, failed to utilize the expenditure data developed under the RIBEC project. Also, RIBEC introduced a common classification for revenue and development budgets, but the integration of the two budgets was not attempted in order to prevent inter-ministerial conflict. (The revenue budget and overall resource programming rests with the Finance Division of the Ministry of Finance, while the Planning Commission is responsible for programming development expenditure.

Consultancy firms. In these projects, extensive use was made of consultancy firms, which reduce the administrative burden of project management for both the Government and donors. Several aspects of these arrangements need to be considered. Both multilateral and bilateral donors make only limited provision for local consultancy services. As noted in the previous section, there is plenty of opportunity for more extensive use of national consultants who possess internationally recognized qualifications. If this practice is widely adopted, it will make an important contribution to capacity building.

Enhancing Effectiveness of TC in Financial Reform

In sum, the TC programmes within the Ministry of Finance appear to have been at least partially successful, and have led to enhanced capacity in three areas of strategic management concern. The following are among the principal reasons for success:

- The Finance Ministry felt the need for capacity building in these areas, and programmes were designed with close involvement of officials who knew the problems and stood to benefit from the process.

- The recognition of this need for capacity building was not idiosyncratic in the sense that it was not confined to an individual civil servant or minister. This need was widely perceived and shared, and when individual civil servants changed, their successors continued to support the programmes. The programmes were thus embedded in the institutions.

- The projects lent support to the ongoing activities of the Ministry, which helped its integration into mainstream activities. This added to overall understanding of the benefits associated with programmes, and thus their acceptance.

- The projects employed local consultants, including individuals who had previously worked, or were currently working in government, and could thus tap local knowledge and informal channels of contacts. Many of the civil servants who worked on the project later occupied important positions in the Ministry. The projects thus became opportunities for learning new skills, and resulted in mechanisms for transmitting that knowledge to the mainstream organization.

The factors responsible for change have been identified above. If these factors are present, TC projects are more likely to be successful in capacity building. And for capacities to be sustained, it is crucial to have the following conditions: institutional recognition of need, incorporation of experiential knowledge in design, concurrent help to the mainstream activities of the institution, removal of the artificial barrier between projects and mainstream administrative systems, and integration of personnel from the earliest period.

Concluding Remarks

The TC assessment exercise and the two case studies provide some general observations about TC and its utilization in Bangladesh. These are summarized below.

Foreign aid to Bangladesh has undergone significant changes. During the 1990s, donors generally shifted from a project to a programme approach, but continued to exercise control over their respective TC programmes. This is evident in the case of TC to the health sector. Programmes often became management-intensive, with much of the TC going to "soft" areas. There was "overuse" of TC, substitution of local capacity, and a lack of interface between TC programmes despite the sector-wide approach.

From the recipient's perspective, there is now a better understanding and demand for client-oriented TC, and there have been institutional changes in line with SWAps. There remains, however, evidence of an ambivalent operational approach: complaints about lack of transparency and ownership are expressed, even as TC-related perks and the absence of auditing systems pass muster.

A number of other changes have become apparent in recent years, including more involvement by local consulting firms and academics in bidding for TC projects, and more extensive use of local subcontractors for substantive work (at much lower cost). Foreign experts hired for projects are also increasingly being replaced by less expensive personnel.

In the health sector, the new programme structure and requisite managerial changes were initiated mostly from the donor's side, while the Government's response was divided with respect to the new changes. The agencies and relevant sections of the Planning Commission required to undergo change were against it, as it meant an erosion of their influence. The health sector programme did not achieve its objectives primarily because too many changes were proposed in too short a time, and because of bureaucratic resistance to diminished authority.

The Finance Ministry was more effective in using TC to meet its goals primarily because the motivation for change originated from Government. The project was split into phases, and designed or re-designed on the basis of the organization's capacity for absorbing change. The distinction between project and mainstream personnel was eliminated by hiring permanent civil servants with higher remunerations. Finally, the activities of TC personnel were integrated into the work of the Ministry from the very beginning, and could thus be easily retained and utilized.

References

Centre for Policy Dialogue. 2001. *Principles for New Orientations in Technical Co-operation.* Dhaka: Centre for Policy Dialogue.

Cleland, David I., and King, William R. *Systems Analysis and Project Management.* New York: McGraw-Hill.

Garida, S. and Hauge, A. 2001. "Easy to evoke, hard to measure." Framing paper for the Reforming Technical Cooperation for Capacity Development initiative at the United Nations Development Programme. New York.

Grindle, Merillee S. and Hilderbrand, Mary E. 1995. "Building sustainable capacity in the public sector - what can be done?" *Public Administration and Development,* Vol 15. pgs. 441-463.

Khan, Zakir A., Thornton, N. and Frazer, M. "Experience of a Financial Reform Project in Bangladesh."

Michael, Stephen R., et.al. 1981. *Techniques of Organizational Change.* New York: McGraw-Hill.

Organ, Dennis W. and Hamner, W. Clay. 1982. *Organizational Behavior.* Business Publications.

Government of Bangladesh and Asian Development Bank. 1991. "Technical Assistance for Institutional Support to Ministry of Finance." Dhaka.

————. 1991. "Technical Assistance to Bangladesh for the Efficiency Enhancement of Fiscal Management." Dhaka.

Government of Bangladesh and the Department for International Development (UK). 1998. "Reforms in Budgeting and Expenditure Control - RIBEC Phase 2B." Dhaka.

————. 2001. "Reforms in Budgeting and Expenditure Control. Final Report." Dhaka.

International Management Consultants Limited and S. F. Ahmed and Co. 1993. "Reforms in Budgeting and Expenditure Control." Dhaka.

Robey, Daniel. 1982. *Designing Organizations: A Macro Perspective.* Richard D. Irwin.

Sobhan, Rehman. 1996. *Rethinking Technical Assistance.* Dhaka: Centre for Policy Dialogue.

World Bank. 1999. "Project Appraisal Document for an Export Diversification Project: Custom Modernization - Phase 1." Washington, DC.

————. 2000. "Implementation Completion Report for A Sixth Technical Assistance Project." Washington, DC.

4 *Bolivia* [1]

THE POLITICAL CONTEXT OF CAPACITY DEVELOPMENT

This study considers four aspects of technical cooperation and capacity development in Bolivia over the past decade. The first part presents a profile of technical cooperation (TC), describing changes in TC over the past decade with preliminary hypotheses concerning key problems. The second presents two case studies of TC (civil service and education reform) through process and stakeholder analysis of TC and capacity development in both sectors. The third documents innovations in TC and capacity development over the past decade, and suggests a preliminary assessment of successes and failures across sectors. The fourth part of the study concludes with recommendations on how to reform TC in view of the case study evidence.

Background

This chapter describes Bolivia's economic performance from 1990 to 1999 and the scope of first- and second-generation reform programmes. Bolivia is regarded as a case study in economic orthodoxy in the 1980s, and in institutional heterodoxy in the 1990s. Much of the increase and decline in official development assistance (ODA) and TC can be linked to these two waves of reform. Both the level and characteristics of TC suggest changes in the way the Government, donors and non-governmental actors interacted between the two periods.

---

[1] This paper was prepared by George Gray Molina, Director, Masters of Public Policy and Management, and Gonzalo Chávez, Professor of Economics, both at Maestrias para el Desarrollo, at the Universidad Catolica Boliviana.

Economic Performance

Bolivia is one of the poorest countries in the Latin America and Caribbean region. Its GDP per capita is around $1,000 and social indicators are similar to Sub-Saharan African countries. Nearly two-thirds of Bolivians live below the poverty line, with low levels of education, health and nutrition. The average years of schooling for 20-year-olds and up is less than eight; infant mortality stands at 92 per 1,000 live births (0 to 5 years), and 10% of the children under five are malnourished.

Bolivia is landlocked, and its undeveloped road infrastructure constrains access to export markets. After significant macroeconomic stabilization and structural adjustment policies (1980s - 1990s), international reserves and foreign direct investment have increased substantially. And while the burdensome external debt remains high, it has eased, thanks to the Heavily Indebted Poor Country (HIPC) initiative, which Bolivia joined in 1998.

Bolivia is a segmented society, with insufficient investment, weak institutional capacity and entrenched vested interests hampering the private sector. According to the World Bank, Bolivia is also a good example of a country that has achieved successful stabilization and implemented innovative market reforms, yet made only limited progress in the fight against poverty.

Overall, Bolivia experienced moderate but sustained economic growth throughout the 1990s, averaging 4.1% over the decade (0.6% more than the Latin American regional average, see Table 4.2). GDP growth per capita suggests an important demographic constraint slowing economic development and poverty reduction. Despite a decrease in the relative urban poverty rate from 54% in 1989 to 47% in 1999, the absolute number of people living in urban poverty increased by close to 30,000 per year (EBRP 2001). High population growth, averaging 2.4% throughout the decade, also slowed the rate of effective economic growth.

Inflation rates were moderate and dipped into the single digits by 1993. Investment levels increased from 12.6% of GDP in 1990 to 18.9% in 1999. The composition of investment also changed. In 1990, public investment accounted for almost two-thirds of total investment. By 1999, private investment accounted for two-thirds of total investment, led by a significant increase in foreign direct investment (FDI). The total savings rate increased from approximately 15% of GDP in 1990 to 19% in 1999. Private domestic savings accounted for more than half of this rate. The other half is equally split between domestic public savings and foreign savings. By the late 1990s, foreign savings were averaging over seven percent of GDP.

Reform Chronology

Over the past decade, Bolivia was also among the most reform-oriented countries in the region. A comprehensive set of first-generation (structural adjustment) and second-generation (institutional) reforms left few state organizations and institutions unchanged. Structural adjustment, stabilization and liberalization were followed by constitutional

TABLE 4.1: MAIN HUMAN DEVELOPMENT INDICATORS

DESCRIPTION	TOTAL	EXPRESSED BY PERIOD	REFERENCE	SOURCE
Population	8,274,325	Inhabitants	Sep. 05, 2001	INE/2001 census
Child mortality rate (0-5 years)	92	Per 1,000 live births	1994 - 1998	INE/ENDSA-98
Illiteracy rate	13.83	Percentage	2000	INE/MECOVI
Men	7.41	Percentage	2000	INE/MECOVI
Women	19.63	Percentage	2000	INE/MECOVI
Average rate of schooling for 20-year-olds and up	7.46	Years	2000	INE/MECOVI
Equivalent unemployment rate	11.49	Percentage	Nov. 2000	INE/MECOVI
Underemployment net rate	18.89	Percentage	Nov. 2000	INE/MECOVI
Human Development Index rank	104		1999	UNDP
Poverty incidence				
Total	61.25	Percentage	2000	INE/MECOVI
Urban	49.54	Percentage	2000	INE/MECOVI
Rural	81.79	Percentage	2000	INE/MECOVI
Poverty gap				
Total	30.94	Percentage	2000	INE/MECOVI
Urban	21.71	Percentage	2000	INE/MECOVI
Rural	47.13	Percentage	2000	INE/MECOVI

Source: Instituto Nacional de Estadistica, Encuesta de Mejoramiento de Condiciones de Vida, Encuesta Nacional de Demografia y Salud

reform, then capitalization, decentralization, and education, judicial, civil service and land tenure reform, among others. Both waves of reform were sustained by a fragile system of coalition politics led by the three largest political parties. To the extent that political stability provided room to design and implement ambitious policy reforms, the Bolivian reform programme owes as much to politicians and political parties as to technocrats and economic policy makers.

A political economy approach to the reform programme also draws attention to a key structural feature of the Bolivian policy system: the coexistence of formal and informal institutions that facilitate room to design ambitious policy reforms, but hinder attempts to build sustainable organizational and institutional capacity that is beyond "particularistic" or "clientelistic" political reach. The timeline of reforms can be described in terms of windows for reform, followed by waves of counter-reform.

1985-1989: Victor Paz Estenssoro and first-generation reforms: August 1985 is a milestone in Bolivian reform efforts. The then recently-elected Government of former

TABLE 4.2: ECONOMIC INDICATORS 1990-1999 (%)

	1990	1991	1992	1993	1994	1995	1996	1997	1998	1999
MACRO										
GDP growth	4.6	5.3	1.6	4.3	4.7	4.7	4.4	5.0	5.5	0.6
GDP growth per capita	2.2	2.8	(0.9)	1.8	2.2	2.3	1.9	2.5	3.1	(1.7)
Inflation	18.0	14.5	10.5	9.3	8.5	12.6	7.9	6.7	4.4	3.1
INVESTMENT										
Public	8.3	8.7	10.0	9.2	9.0	8.2	7.3	7.2	6.3	6.7
Private	4.3	6.9	6.7	7.4	5.4	7.0	9.0	12.4	16.8	12.2
SAVINGS										
Public	3.9	4.4	5.6	3.1	6.0	6.4	5.3	4.2	2.3	2.9
Private	10.7	7.1	3.9	6.3	7.2	4.4	5.9	9.0	12.9	9.3
Foreign	-2.0	4.1	7.3	7.1	1.2	4.5	5.1	6.5	8.0	6.7

Source: Estrategia Boliviana de Reducción de la Pobreza (2001).

President Victor Paz Estenssoro, leader of the Bolivian national revolution, enacted a stiff package of liberal reforms called the *Nueva Política Económica* that was designed to counter hyperinflation and set the basis for structural adjustment. Paz secured legislative support for his Presidency through an alliance with Acción Democrática Nacionalista (ADN). Although the *Pacto por la Democracia* alliance provided Paz with much-needed room to govern, the alliance also set a precedent for patronage-led negotiations between coalition partners throughout the decade. Paz Estenssoro's reform included steep devaluation, liberalization of trade and exchange rate regimes, tax reform and a social emergency programme.

1989-1993: Jaime Paz Zamora and problems with coalition politics: The post-crisis administration led by former President Jaime Paz Zamora sustained moderate growth rates and initiated electoral and constitutional reforms that would set the stage for further institutional change. Many of the fiscal and monetary constraints developed during the previous administration provided a backdrop for policy reform during the Paz Zamora administration. Unlike the previous political coalition agreement, the Movimiento de Izquirda Revolucionario (MIR) / ADN *Pacto por la Democracia* agreement signed in 1989 included explicit political quotas for ministries and vice ministries. Rather than entrust ministries along party colors, the agreement distributed ministry-level posts to one party and vice ministry posts to the other, thus consolidating a skewed set of political incentives for public officials throughout the public administration. Much of the Paz Zamora administration was marked by inter-party conflict and ministerial instability.

1993-1997: Gonzalo Sánchez de Lozada and second-generation reforms: In 1993, the Movimiento Nacionalista Revolucionario (MNR) won the national elections with a

36% plurality of the vote. A new political agreement between the MNR, Unión Cívica Solidaridad (UCS) and Movimiento Bolivia Libre (MBL) provided ample legislative support for an activist President. Unlike the two previous administrations, the Sanchez de Lozada Presidency followed its electoral plan to completion. The *Plan de Todos*, an electoral pamphlet circulated in the latter part of the electoral campaign, provided a policy blueprint for an ambitious set of reforms. Education, decentralization, popular participation, capitalization, pension, land tenure and judicial reforms paved the way for four years of intense political and institutional change. As with previous administrations, the MNR/UCS/MBL coalition was glued together by patronage. Unlike others, the privatization of public enterprises and the decentralization of public investment initiated by Sanchez de Lozada dismantled the coalition monopoly over patronage. By 1997, with new elections, the central administration could no longer mobilize resources and employment to ensure stability within the coalition, and social stability outside of it.

1997-2002: Hugo Banzer/Jorge Quiroga and the unraveling of coalition politics: The Banzer administration secured a large coalition of small parties dubbed the *Megacoalición*. The politics of keeping an eight-party coalition together with diminishing state resources proved difficult and ushered in a new era of political and social instability that threatened to topple the Banzer Presidency in April and September 2000. In August 2001, Banzer resigned due to ill health, leaving the Presidency to Jorge Quioroga Ramírez. Two policy themes ran through the Banzer/Quiroga administration: coca-leaf eradication and natural gas discoveries. By 2002, Bolivia became the smallest producer of coca-leaf and illicit drugs within the Andean region. The discovery of natural gas in the southern department of Tarija ushered in a new era of natural resource extraction. Proven reserves, estimated at 47 trillion cubic feet, make Bolivia the second-largest producer in the region. The Banzer/Quiroga administration also faced a sustained wave of social discontent and violence.

Technical Cooperation Profile

Data Over 10 Years

Bolivia is the second-largest recipient of official development assistance (ODA) in the LAC region. It averaged close to $80 per capita over the past decade, ranging from $498 million or 11% of GDP in 1989 to $569 million, or 6.8 percent of GDP in 1999. Official development assistance peaked in the mid-1990s and dropped gradually to levels seen earlier in the decade.

Technical cooperation, defined to include "activities whose primary purpose is to augment the level of knowledge, skills, technical know-how, or productive aptitudes of the population of developing countries", increased from $93 million in 1989 to $192 million in 1999. Capacity development is understood as the process by which "individuals, organizations, institutions and societies develop abilities (individually and collectively) to perform functions, solve problems and set and achieve objectives." Technical cooperation flows across the past decade can be broken down into three distinct periods: first-generation reforms (1985-1992), second-generation reforms (1993-1997)

TABLE 4.3: OFFICIAL DEVELOPMENT ASSISTANCE AND TC FROM 1989-1999 (US$ MILLIONS)

	1989	1990	1991	1992	1993	1994	1995	1996	1997	1998	1999
ODA Grants	270.7	310.5	717.8	438.9	365	471.4	544.9	587.1	498.7	418	398.7
ODA Loans	227.6	236.8	-211.9	232.0	199.4	97.4	173.9	244.6	201.6	210.7	170.4
ODA Total	498.3	547.3	505.9	670.9	564.4	568.8	718.8	831.7	700.3	628.7	569.1
TC	93.1	108.3	156.0	174.3	189.7	189.8	217.3	195.1	199.2	185.4	192.6
ODA (G) p/c	41.2	47.2	106.6	63.7	51.7	65.2	73.5	77.4	64.3	52.6	49.0
ODA (L) p/c	34.6	36.0	-31.3	33.7	28.2	13.5	23.4	32.3	25.9	26.5	21.0
ODA (T) p/c	75.8	83.2	75.3	97.4	79.9	78.5	96.9	109.7	90.2	79.1	70.0
TC p/c	14.1	16.5	23.2	25.3	26.8	26.2	29.3	25.7	25.7	23.3	23.7

Source: OECD Development Assistance Cooperation (DAC) dataset.

TABLE 4.4: HUMAN RESOURCES FOR TECHNICAL COOPERATION (1989-1999)

	1989	1990	1991	1992	1993	1994	1995	1996	1997	1998	1999
Students (#)	213	148	225	388	260	205	91	333	411	216	237
Trainees (#)	175	286	303	251	614	321	236	583	782	82	276
TC personnel (#)	249	553	640	395	694	663	671	705	763	511	686
TC experts (#)	249	369	425	302	484	399	535	407	545	317	498
TC exp p/m	1,081	1,857	2,366	1,967	2,370	1,709	900	2,312	3,344	1,852	2,249

Source: OECD Development Assistance Cooperation (DAC) dataset.

and HIPC-II reform assistance (1997-present). Each period suggests a distinct portrait of ODA flows, TC and capacity development.

The first period is characterized by a significant inflow of balance of payments assistance for structural adjustment and macroeconomic stabilization. Most ODA was geared toward non-capacity development activities. The second period, however, inaugurates a process of intensive institutional reform, backed by high levels of TC. In particular, education, decentralization, popular participation and judicial reform included a significant capacity development component. A preliminary review of the impact of TC during this period, however, suggests a heightened divorce between institutionalized and non-institutionalized capacity development efforts. The mid-1990s are characterized by a sharp increase in the number and influence of non-governmental, international and parastatal consultancies leading reform. The third period was inaugurated by Bolivia's entry into the HIPC-II agreements, which set out a new framework for donor assistance, and within it, a shift from project-centred TC to policy-level dialogue and long-term planning.

Technical cooperation increased significantly during the Sanchez de Lozada reform period. Approximately 1,300 students received scholarships for short- and long-term academic training, and approximately 2,000 trainees received financing for on-the-job training. Technical cooperation peaked during this period, involving 1,800 TC experts totaling over 8,000 person / months in economic, social and institutional reform-oriented consultancies. Technical cooperation largely followed a decentralized pattern of assistance. Line ministries hosted hundreds of TC experts via multilateral and bilateral donor assistance programmes, often prodded by donor agencies themselves. The largest recipients of TC aid were the capitalization and education reforms, which were intensive in expatriate expertise, and linked to a region-wide wave of institutional reforms developing over the decade.

In terms of research and technology, Bolivia has not achieved much success. According to the National Secretary of Investigation, Science and Technology (NSIST), chronic low budgets and human resource scarcity have restricted opportunities for Bolivian researchers, academics and professionals to successfully conduct scientific and technological research. In 2001, NSIST estimated that there was an approximate rate of 100 researchers per million Bolivians, which is far lower than other Latin American countries, and miniscule compared with 8,401 per million in Japan and 5,959 per million in the United States.[2]

In spite of such unpromising figures, a number of interesting projects have been accomplished through international TC over the past decade. In 1990 for instance, the Institute of Hydraulics and Hydrology (IHH) granted doctoral degrees to four professors with the cooperation of the Berlin Technical University. At the moment, IHH enjoys three financial cooperation agreements that deal mainly with river, lake and glacial research studies. Among the most important donor agencies supplying TC to IHH are the International Hydrology Programme of UNESCO, the Institute of Research for Development (IRD) of France, and the Asdi-SAREC of Sweden.[3]

By the same token, many Bolivian universities, especially the state-financed Universidad Mayor de San Andrés (UMSA), have been able to procure a number of TC projects from countries like Cuba, France, Germany and Spain. Health services have been dramatically improved by a continuous flow of Cuban professors and doctors who have come to the country to conduct training sessions, seminars and know-how transfer, all free of charge.

With respect to TC projects that enhance upper-level education performance, it is essential to recognize the graduate-level programmes at the Bolivian Catholic University as one of the country's top academic achievements. Framed as a "Human Resources for Development Project", it was initiated in 1994 with the assistance of USAID-Bolivia and the Harvard Institute for International Development. The project was established to strengthen democracy by enhancing managerial skills and increasing accountability and transparency in both public and private spheres. The present outcome and impact of the project is self-evident. There are more than 480 masters graduates working as development leaders in both private and public organizations.

---

[2] Secretaria Nacional de Investigacion Ciencia y Tecnologia, Memorias VII Renacit, Potosi – Bolivia, 2001
[3] Instituto de Hidraulica e Hidrologia, http://www.megalink.com/ihh/

The programme has also consistently executive programmes, reaching some 2,000 students to date. At the moment, the alumni network includes professionals working in Congress, government ministries, municipalities, superintendencies, embassies, financial institutions, banks, consulting firms, and oil & gas, mining, electricity, and communications companies, among others.

Environment for Capacity Development: Institutional Dualism

An assessment of capacity development can be analyzed at two levels. The first considers capacity development at the programme level itself – capacity development for capitalization, decentralization, civil service and education reform, and so on. A second level, however, involves a more general assessment of statewide opportunities and constraints for capacity development. At this more general level, Bolivia faces a singular challenge in developing institutions that attract, train and promote well-qualified professional and technical staff. Efforts at constructing formal institutional incentives for capacity development are continuously being undermined by powerful informal practices based on patronage and clientelistic networks within public administration.

This brand of "institutional dualism" provides a skewed set of incentives for TC and sustained capacity development. Well-designed programmes from a meritocratic and performance-oriented perspective are often split between formal compliance and informal pressure to "get things done" – including bending the hiring, training and promotion rules along the way. From an institutional perspective, informality acts as a pervasive constraint on capacity development. Informality itself is perhaps best explained as a result of a coalition politics that create space for innovative reform, but lessen the possibility of sustaining reform through non-clientelistic or patronage means.

Since 1985, every administration has faced a similar political predicament: a highly fragmented political system delivers a weak mandate at the electoral polls. Congress is then tasked to form fragile coalitions with multiple political partners. The glue that keeps coalitions together, above and beyond ideological or programmatic affinity, often involves patronage in the form of employment or access to the spoils of public office. The political space created by coalition politics has been a significant determinant of the success of ambitious policy reform. Paradoxically, to the extent that second-generation reforms have succeeded, thus reducing access to patronage through privatization, decentralization or civil service reform, coalition politics have unraveled. The most recent period of political fragmentation observed between 1999 and 2000 suggests an end to a 15-year formula of governance. The executive power is less and less able to mobilize the political resources needed to drive reform.

A key indicator of dual institutionalism in the public sector is the number of non-staff employees working in the central and decentralized government offices. Consultants make up close to 25% of central administration personnel, according to a Ministry of Sustainable Development study (4,200 of 16,500 total staff). In addition, close to 75% of staff were hired for a single administration. High rotation and levels of informality hinder efforts to promote institutional development and sustained capacity development at the national level. Central government practices are amplified at the departmental and municipal levels, where local political clienteles, NGOs and other key players substitute for a non-existent administrative career path.

General Assessment: Success and Failure

The key TC problems confronted by policy makers and the donor community are summarized below:

(i) As ODA dropped as a proportion of GDP, absolute levels of TC increased significantly throughout the decade. Increased TC, in turn, has led to a perception of donor over-involvement. The largest multilateral donor (the World Bank) today accounts for more investment than the entire domestic private sector. Donor presence inadvertently conspires against "driver's seat/ownership" mandates.

(ii) Increased TC has sharpened a dual institutional structure that cuts across party, clientelistic and regional lines. The formal bureaucracy is undercut by an equally institutionalized informal network of part-time consultants, political appointees, technocrats and NGO staff linked to TC projects. This network is particularly important during agenda formation and policy design. The standing bureaucracy plays a more prominent role during policy implementation. A dual structure skews incentives, generating donor interest in TC early in the policy cycle, and less during implementation.

(iii) Increased TC has also shifted donor priorities away from short-term project lending toward longer-term programme or policy support. Sustainability and ownership have replaced earlier donor concerns for efficiency and effectiveness. Recent interest in "policy dialogue", "civil society consultations" and "participatory decision making" has increased donor influence over policy making. Not all TC experiences have been negative. Capacity development in decentralization/ popular participation has proven relatively effective, and has incited further interest in long-term knowledge, human resource and capacity development.

(iv) At times, donor efforts to promote "country ownership" have themselves undermined bureaucratic and political ownership. Multi-donor tables that pool donor efforts under the Bolivian Poverty Reduction Strategy (PRSP) and HIPC II, have adverse effects. They constitute the single most influential lobby over domestic policy makers – each "next big idea" discussed by donors tends to eclipse other initiatives presented by domestic pressure groups, political parties or regional organizations. Donor tables tend to focus attention on issues that are paramount to donor effectiveness: budgeting, reporting and accounting mechanisms, for example. These are not necessarily seen as important for government effectiveness as are decision making, participation and inclusion mechanisms.

Brief History of TC in Bolivia

Before and during the early 1990s, there was essentially no coordination between the Bolivian Government and international TC donors. There was no official or reliable donor record. Large disbursement providers like the World Bank Group, the Inter-American Development Bank, the Corporación Andina de Fomento and the kind, were the only ones with whom the Government used to keep some sort of interaction. The absence of coordination and agenda alignment was absolute. The donor-driven environment stifled TC.

There was also no NGO or bilateral donor record whatsoever. The Government had a heavily centralized political structure, which deprived economic improvement to more remote regions. On top of that, the national decision makers were unfamiliar with regional needs and priorities that may have benefited from TC. Rampant economic crises, political turmoil and social distress made TC a waste of opportunities at best, and corruption at worst. Today both the Government and donors are moving forward to reverse negative past experiences, and to redesign TC in Bolivia.

In the past, many public servants, academics and even international donors perceived the lack of coordination as not being dramatically harmful to the Bolivian economy and its development. The Bolivian situation was considered so critical that any source of cooperation – either technical or financial – was welcome regardless of basic considerations such as priorities, adequacy, methodology, impact and sustainability.

Accordingly, much TC and cash flowed in through many cooperation sources. Unfortunately, the unregulated and uncoordinated system undermined assistance intentions, mainly as a result of unfinished projects, inflated costs, derailed funds, and a lack of follow-up programmes and real means of accountability.

A strong characteristic of TC in the past was the overwhelming participation of foreign consultants. Bolivia received numerous consultants from abroad who usually enjoyed huge compensations for their services. In many cases, these compensations mirrored an irrational distribution of funds both in relation to the status of the Bolivian economy, and to the overall project budget. The budget lines in a 1996 FAO-funded Post Harvesting TC Programme in Santa Cruz illustrates this imbalance (see table 4.5).

Moreover, there were an unknown number of private organizations, NGOs, and foundations running a wide variety of TC projects. Most of the time, there was no record of fund disbursement, performance accountability or follow-up evaluation. International and domestic counterparts held disparate agendas. Considering this TC environment, positive outcomes were understandably rarely seen.

Around the mid-1990s, both the Bolivian Government and donors fully understood the urgent necessity for coordination, and for defining objectives, priorities and agendas. Under these circumstances, the Bolivian Government instituted a new administrative structure of public offices to manage and coordinate TC and financial cooperation more adequately.

TABLE 4.5: FAO POST HARVESTING TC PROGRAMME

Project Number	TCP/BOL/6611
Domestic institutions in charge of programme	Secretaria Nacional de Agricultura y Ganadería (SNAG) Centro de Investigación Agrícola Tropical (CIAT)
Time framework From To Total	May 1, 1996 Dec. 31, 1996 8 months
FAO contribution	$197,000
Budget breakdown Int'l consultant National expert National consultants Administrative support Official trips Capacitating Equipment and supplies Maintenance/Others Total	96,000 19,000 5 consultants x $400 x 8 months 16,000 8,000 10,000 26,000 7,000 15,000 197,000

Source: http://www.fao.org/Gender/static/tcp/bol66112.htm

In addition to this new administrative organizational structure, the Bolivian Government convoked National Dialogues *(Dialogo Nacional)* in 1997 and 2000 to debate the country's economic situation and prospects. The Government was experiencing difficulties in restoring confidence in its economy, particularly after the hyperinflation and shortfalls during structural reforms. The country's fundamentally weak institutional capacity and constrained private sector contributed to an average yearly growth rate of 4.2% between 1990-97, which was well below potential.

In response to this alarming situation and after the 1997 National Dialogue, the Government endorsed a National Action Plan *(Plan Operativo de Accion)* based on four pillars:

- Opportunity (growth generation and better distribution)
- Institutional strengthening
- Equity (an improvement in the living standards of the poor)
- Dignity (removal of the country from the drug circuit by the year 2002)

The 2000 National Dialogue

The 2000 National Dialogue (ND) from June through August 2000 was focused mainly on fighting poverty. It contributed boosting mechanisms for enhancing participative democracy by strengthening the relationship between civil society and the Bolivian national and local governments.

During the ND, a variety of different viewpoints addressed the country's general situation. The ND debated three big topics: society, politics and the economy. Many actors played an active role during the discussion meetings: representatives from national and local government, academia, think tanks, labour unions, indigenous organizations, political parties, NGOs, the private sector and the Catholic Church, among others. Many workshops concluded with solid recommendations on a wide scope of topics.[4]

Community representatives addressed TC as a powerful mechanism for the poverty-fighting crusade. Municipalities concluded that rural development was undoubtedly linked to the quality and quantity of opportunities rendered to the poor. Accordingly, 56% of the municipalities highlighted the need for training and TC. This demand may be related to two issues: the necessity of technical education in order to access the labour markets, and the need for agricultural technology transfers in order to increase productivity. In terms of capacity development in education, municipalities noted the urgent need for better faculty training.

One feature that made ND so special and illustrative was that municipalities determined their own necessities and priorities through their own perspectives, rather than that of the national Government. With rural poverty incidence at an outrageous 81.79% (INE/MECOVI, 2000), it is interesting to note that the majority of municipalities ranked capacity development and TC at second place in terms of priorities, and before other basic, unsatisfied needs. Figure 4.1 shows ND data on rural development priorities according to municipalities.

Teams working on the economy highlighted a number of strategic areas that needed special attention. Workshops were comprised of representatives from the production, services and exports sectors, and from the food and manufacturing industries. Most important discussion topics included infrastructure, research, financing, trade, exports, information, investments, tariffs and taxes, nationwide institutional reforms and public policies.

During the workshops, there was a clear recognition of the importance of research, development, innovation and technological assistance. A clear majority of the production, export, and industry representatives called for designing and making TC programmes available at the municipal level.

Participants agreed that next in importance was the strengthening of existing TC, research and technology transfer institutions, and highlighted the need for creating new institutions in accordance with regional necessities. There was also a firm stand on the need for establishing a legal product frameworks for addressing concerns with quality, classification and standardization.

---

4 Public Expenditure Review Workshop Recommendations: (i) Education: Improve teacher quality by modifying the compensation scheme and reducing public resources allocated to higher education; (ii) Health: A need to: (a) analyze salary levels, regional distribution of personnel, service demands, expenditure allocation, and impact evaluation; (b) establish a sustainable financing source consistent with decentralization; and (c) coordinate donor participation; (iii) Water/sanitation: Need to ensure that regulations to water/sanitation law consolidate the regulatory framework. Project sustainability must be improved; (iv) Roads: Need for a master plan estimating maintenance costs/expansion plans; (v) Decentralization: Need to hold a workshop to prioritize donor assistance; and (vi) Resource Mobilization: the PER tax reform recommendations to be implemented as a package.

FIGURE 4.1: RURAL DEVELOPMENT PRIORITIES ACCORDING TO MUNICIPALITIES

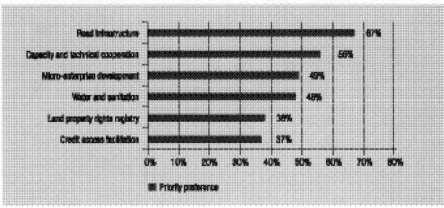

Source: Municipal polls, National Dialogue 2000.

Municipalities expressed their desire for more decentralized management of resources, and as the direct executing entities, demanded administration over the HIPC Initiative. Allocations of such resources were defined under poverty-level criteria, but also under criterion of population, number of municipalities and departments.

Figure 4.2 shows how principal representatives of the Bolivian economy prioritized their needs for innovation, technology and TC. It is important to note that an overwhelming majority agreed on having unmet capacity development and TC demands.

During the ND, the Vice Ministry of Public Investments and External Financing (VIPFE) performed an active role in chairing meetings and defining means of coordination with donors. It was then that many objectives were defined in order to channel TC in the future. Even after many structural and conceptual improvements, there is still a long way to go towards outstanding TC management in Bolivia.

What Has Changed?

The three periods of policy reform (structural adjustment, institutional reform and HIPC-II) described above suggest alternative scenarios for evaluating TC and capacity development efforts. What has changed? Three aspects of the donor/government/NGO partnership are reviewed here.

(i) The nature of donor involvement has changed. Structural adjustment ODA was based primarily on balance of payment support during stabilization, liberalization and devaluation. Technical cooperation revolved around fiscal and monetary reform as well as incipient institutional reform. After 1993, a period of intense institutional reform moved the TC focus to expatriate expertise for policy

FIGURE 4.2: INNOVATION AND TECHNICAL COOPERATION DEMANDS

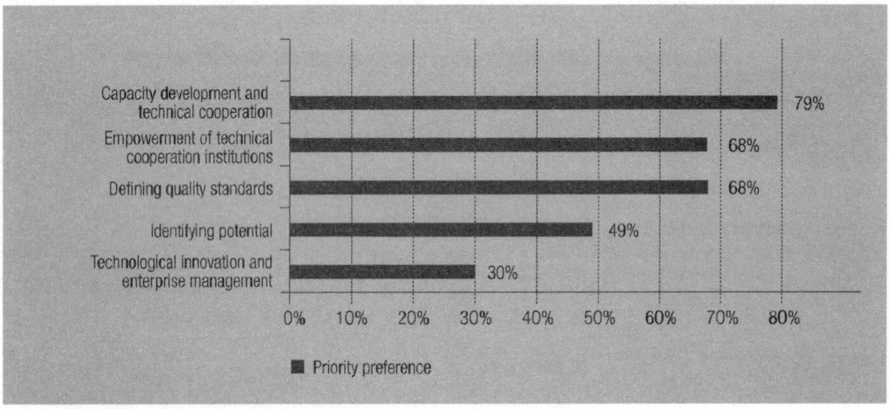

Source: Economy polls, National Diaologue 2000.

design and implementation. The mid-1990s witnessed a significant increase in both ODA and TC. A third period began with the signing of HIPC-II agreements. The focus of ODA and TC then shifted toward poverty alleviation. The Comprehensive Development Framework adopted by HIPC countries resulted in a new set of rules for government and donor relations. The National Dialogues and Jubilee meetings held in 2000 resulted in a new framework for government/civil society relations. The new frameworks are incipient and suggest closer alignment over policy focus, but introduce a new source of conditionality that more closely resembles the structural adjustment period than the late 1990s.

(ii) The focus on human resources, organizations and institutions has changed. While most of the last decade's reform initiatives revolved around policy design, this decade's emphasis is on implementation, with a particular focus on strategic management, policy ownership and social dialogue. The Bolivian Government has adopted much of the language of public sector reform, i.e., "institutional development", "ownership" and "sustainability". Renewed talk of hiring practices, personnel management and career ladders follows a decade of administrative re-design. Much of this occurs under the broad umbrella of anti-corruption and transparency campaigns, rather than management concerns. While it is clearly too early to assess whether the "organizational turn" sticks, public sector reform, human resource management and capacity development are clearly on the agenda.

(iii) The political economy of reform has changed. For over 15 years, coalition politics provided space for reform. A key lubricant was state patronage, employment and access to state-owned enterprises. Since 1999, coalition politics has lost its shine.

A strong wave of anti-party sentiment, coupled with a shrinking pool of patron-age possibilities has fractured the ruling coalition and pushed the majority coalition into a minority in congress. From a political economy of "coalition-led" policy reform, Bolivia has crossed to "social movement-led" policy response.

Government TC Management, Coordination Efforts

In 1998, the Government initiated dynamic coordination efforts with donors. That year, a positive alignment of ideas between Bolivia and the World Bank originated the new relationship framework, *Nuevo Marco de Relacionamiento Gobierno – Cooperacion Internacional hacia el Siglo XXI,* which settled the basis for the dialogue and coordi-nation means used today.

This new framework sets the basis for improving the efficiency and efficacy of the relationship between the Government and international donors. It identifies common problems, fixes core relationship principles and defines actions to carry out the required improvements.

(i) Common problems
- Scarcity of highly-qualified human resources
- Low availability of domestic counterpart funds
- Donor-driven persistence
- Centralized decision making process
- Lack of information
- Lack of coordination between NGOs and the private sector
- Different programming cycles
- Non-systematic application of legal frameworks regarding goods and services acquisition
- Weak institutional structures at national and local levels

(ii) Core principles
- Compatibility with government development goals
- Bolivian definition of objectives and programme "ownership"
- Efficacy
- Accountability
- Sustainability
- Institutional strengthening
- Cooperative policy
- Transparency

(iii) Actions
- Definition of the strategic framework
- Definition of priorities
- Definition of programmes
- Outcome-based programming
- Supervision, monitoring and evaluation

- Promotion of enhanced decentralization
- Reprogramming and reassignment of funds
- Elaboration of multi-year budgets
- Joint financing fundraising
- Goods and services acquisition

In accordance with this new approach on TC management, the Bolivian Government has initiated a gradual but steady process to improve TC administration. To begin with, the Government has reassigned TC management within the Executive Power. Under this new structure, the Ministry of Economy, through the VIPFE, replaces the Ministry of Planning with regard to all TC and financial aid matters.

In order to improve the benefits from TC, the Bolivian Government has taken a number of actions. Among others, it has recognized the need for programme and donor coordination, in-house organization, and definition of priorities and objectives by municipalities.

- Programme and donor coordination

  The Ministry of Finance has shaped a new way of TC coordination. First, it eliminated endless, year-round meetings with the entire cast of donors. The education reform programme, for example, convened eight to 10 mission meetings a year, overwhelming ministry staff with logistical work. At a certain point, the ministry was much busier attending to administrative matters than working on education reform.

  Now, government policy consists in opening information channels and trans- mitting national and regional priorities to all donors. In spite of this well-intentioned management policy, many donors dislike the lack of person- alized attention. For many TC providers, the "ownership" component and the imprint of their personal stamp are essential. Claiming sponsorship and gain- ing visibility for TC projects seem to be quite valuable politically among the vast majority of international donors.

  In terms of the existing relationship among donors, the VIPFE has acknowledged that bilateral donors have historically felt resentful towards multilateral donors. Bilateral donors reportedly have the impression that the Government pays greater attention to the World Bank and the Inter-American Development Bank, for example. To minimize this tension, the Government now focuses on working with all donors, no matter the size of their contributions, on jointly defining programmes and projects based on the real necessities in the country.

  A heavily-funded World Bank and Inter-American Development Bank TC pro- gramme on decentralization now underway illustrates this policy change. Every elaboration and follow-up process has been carried out by committees comprised of both large and small donors. By the same token, small and large donors join workshops within the Consulting Group in order to align agendas and reach common conclusions.

One of the most important goals is simply to share the same information with all donors, to let them know of the necessities and priorities that are being identified, agreed to, and framed as grounds for policy and strategy making. Information flow is thus being noticeably improved. The purpose is to promote proactive definition of national and local needs rather than reactive accommodation to donor agendas. This effort is strongly intended to enhance decision making abilities within the national Government and municipalities.

Today, one-to-one negotiations with donors are still held, but only for specific matters of fund amount definition. New room for dialogue has been promoted in order to attempt comprehensive coordination between donor and Bolivian agendas. Unlike past practices, there are now joint project evaluation missions. For instance, in education and health reform, follow-up evaluation missions bring together representatives from the Inter-American Development Bank, the World Bank, the Netherlands, Denmark, Sweden and Bolivia. Meetings are held twice a year, and important joint decisions are made from conclusions and recommendations.

- In-house organization

Technical cooperation comes to Bolivia in many forms, according to the programmes, projects, objectives and even particular development perspectives of donors. This usually makes it difficult to completely separate TC from financial assistance. Moreover, there are unusual cases where both definitions seem to be reversed by daily practice. For instance, a current Inter-American Development Bank credit line to the Ministry of Sustainable Development is provided as reimbursable TC.

A clear-cut distinction between financial aid and TC has proven to be unrealistic. Countries like Bolivia that receive these two cooperation components benefit most if they functionally link them. Best practices generally come from implementing TC in a way that supports the completion of programmes and projects funded by financial aid.

Because both TC and financial aid are usually designated to a single project or programme, the Ministry of Finance has come to realize that having a separate office for each was a waste of resources. The staffs from the financial aid and TC offices have now been merged into one national office within the VIPFE. For many, the key element in this changing process is the different magnitude of funds between the two. Although financial assistance is by far greater than TC, the Government is jointly managing them under an assimilated system for operational and administrative reasons.

It appears that the very concept of TC has significantly changed throughout the last decade. Ten years ago TC was conceived more as a sort of "ideas laboratory" that contributed to structural reform as a whole. Now that the Government, through the VIPFE, has changed that TC macro vision into a more project-focused concept, the general TC scheme is directed towards regional needs. In other words, the call for TC development is at the municipal level.

- Definition of priorities and objectives

The National Dialogue defined itself as a clear turning point in recognizing the need to give municipalities the role of defining and executing TC projects and programmes. Municipalities are now considered the responsible executing agents for defining objectives and priorities, and for managing their own TC projects. The need for strengthening municipalities to accomplish such goals is also clear.

In spite of the Government's efforts, TC does not yet fully respond to objectives set by national or local representatives. Donors still play an important role in setting TC objectives and priorities while the Government struggles to match different agendas by establishing countrywide programmes. At the moment, the most important government policy pillar is poverty reduction. Technical cooperation programmes are intended to accommodate that vision. Unfortunately, fighting poverty remains an "over-inclusive" idea when decision makers need to define actions.

Zoomed-in programmes are still difficult to frame. There are too many contradictory demands from local governments and community representatives. At the same time, it is not uncommon to field offers for TC that support low priority objectives. Coordination discussions with donors may sometimes be difficult. Japan is among the few examples where coordination efforts have paid back satisfactorily. For the last three to four years, a number of assistance areas have been clearly set, and TC programmes have worked accordingly.

However, the real problem in channeling and executing TC is not simply a matter of coordination with donors. The problem goes much further, and deals with a lack of a clear definition of objectives and priorities by the potential local beneficiaries. Few sectors have well-planned and comprehensive programmes. The education reform is one of them, and its "definition" process has taken a number of years to prepare. Other sectors remain weak in terms of programme organization and defining objectives, and many sectors simply accept what donors are willing to provide in terms of TC projects. Local governments, both rural and urban, need to learn how to structure their objectives, priorities and policy actions.

For the last few years, TC has focused on institutional strengthening at both national and local levels. Technical cooperation objectives are much more strongly elaborated and defined at the national level than the municipal, and the Vice Ministry of Popular Participation is working hard to identify the best mechanisms for strengthening institutions in municipalities. The absence of defined policy actions has pushed many donors to work with a variety of different municipalities.

Many projects were only partially concluded, and problems in distributing TC benefits equitably among municipalities have also been evident. At the municipal level, multilateral and bilateral donors manage various schemes for institutional strengthening while the municipalities themselves – especially small ones in rural areas – seem to be struggling with the long-term process of developing basic institutional structures.

At present, the Ministry of Finance, through the VIPFE, is concentrating on legitimately defining the TC objectives of municipalities. One important goal is to diminish donor discretion in defining and executing TC projects and programmes. The VIPFE thus centralizes all TC, collecting demands form departmental and municipal governments, evaluating requests, filing petitions and negotiating with donors. The ultimate target is to complete institutional strengthening and make the decentralization process more viable.

In sum, many achievements have been accomplished from 1998 up to this moment, but there is a long way to go in terms of strengthening municipalities. The Bolivian Government is betting on TC as the best choice for that endeavor. The problem now is to allocate resources and explore the most efficient way to reach each of the 314 municipalities. These municipalities have special characteristics that make them remarkably different from one another. Differences in poverty and education levels, tradition, idiom and social structure are just a few examples of the characteristics that make them so distinct.

Technical Cooperation Cases

The civil service and education reform initiatives below illustrate different experiences with TC and capacity development over the past decade. The study team conducted process and stakeholder analyses for each sector, and discuss hypotheses to explain successes and failures. The team found that both reform initiatives are hampered by micro (institutional) and macro (political) constraints that skew incentives for capacity development toward patronage, clientelism and dual arenas of political and bureaucratic development. We identify a number of first-order institutional constraints for each sector and trace the roots of most institutional problems to second-order, and longer-term, political determinants of dual institutional development.

Civil Service

i. Process analysis

Civil service reform in Bolivia developed along four distinct phases. The first phase, toward the end of the structural adjustment and stabilization period (1989-1992), followed a "key posts" approach, aimed at building a civil service programme for 700 senior posts across the state administration. This limited attempt, led by joint government and donor efforts, was launched under the expectation that structural adjustment required the "professionalization" of key macroeconomic and technocratic positions held by consultants linked to political appointees in the ministries of finance and planning, and at the Central Bank. The key posts approach floundered both because of an unsustainable institutional design financed almost exclusively by multilateral donors, as well as because of deeper constraints in converting political technocrats into civil service employees.

A second phase began in 1992 under the Administrative Reform Programme (ARP), which unlike the key posts programme, aimed at expanding the civil service throughout the entire central government administration system. The objectives of the programme were to (i) reduce the size of the public workforce, (ii) install a hierarchical and competitive scale, (iii) design and adopt a meritocratic system of human resource management to eliminate political influence over hiring, paying, promoting and dismissing public employees, and (iv) instill a public culture of transparency and accountability for results. Despite these objectives, the Government by 1993 had begun to question the viability of extending the civil service programme to the entire central government administration.

A third phase started in 1993 with the Civil Service and Administrative Reform (CSAR) project. It was considerably less ambitious than the previous approach, but included a projected expansion to 2,566 posts. The CSAR project promoted a "critical mass" approach to civil service reform. Offices and line ministries would institutionalize critical masses of civil servants at different hierarchical levels to provide continuity and provide a career ladder for trained bureaucrats. The objectives of the programme included creating a critical mass in 11 ministries and 3 decentralized agencies, strengthening political support for the implementation of the civil service, and developing selected agencies' institutional capacity. The results of the CSAR were disappointing. The targets for reaching "critical masses" were not achieved in any agency except the Ministry of Justice. By 1997, only 248 posts out of a projected 729 had been filled.

A fourth period was launched during the Banzer administration (1998-2001) under the National Integrity Plan (PNI), focusing on a new legal framework for the civil service (Ley de Organización del Poder Ejecutivo, Estatuto del Funcionario Público), the creation of the position of Superintendent for Civil Service, and an ambitious institutional re-engineering programme (Programa de Reforma Institucional). The Government's key objectives were to initiate a re-engineering of public agencies, reduce the size of the public sector and improve salaries to attract and retain a new cadre of public managers.

The most recent effort at civil service reform incorporates approximately 2,500 recruits in mid-level central government administration. Table 4.6 shows the current structure of personnel at central and departmental offices. Approximately 12,000 mid-level positions make up the heart of public administration today. Directive positions occupy 14% of central administration, mid-level technical staff make up 42%, and support staff 44%. This structure is largely replicated at the departmental level. Payroll currently accounts for close to 1.3 percent of GDP. The Civil Service Programme is largely funded by donor credit. Table 4.7 shows a 10-year projection of cost and staff replacement. The projection aims to substitute existing long-term staff and consultants for civil service personnel. By 2008, 2,566 civil service posts will replace 631 consultants and 2,379 current long-term staff.

Table 4.8 shows the financing strategy pursued by the Bolivian Government for its fourth attempt at civil service reform. A sliding scale of donor commitments phases out credit by years eight, nine and 10, to be substituted by Treasury support averaging close to half a percentage of GDP by year 10. Political and fiscal support is deemed critical by donors for civil service reform, but is consistently downplayed by government officials as a key constraint. Political will, organizational complexity and labour instability are cited as more pressing constraints to effective implementation. The future of civil service reform is likely to depend on both sets of constraints, particularly on the recognition of first-order and second-order causes of informality and dual institutionalism.

The World Bank is undoubtedly one of the most important donors promoting civil service reform in Bolivia. In 1998, it promoted a 10-year public sector modernization programme that was initiated with a Bank-funded institutional reform project in March 1999.[5] In this regard, the World Bank's intention is to support the Government's programme to improve the effectiveness, efficiency and transparency of the public sector, with the ultimate aim of strengthening the country's ability to implement its economic and social development programmes.

The World Bank project is being carried out under the new Adaptable Programme Loan (APL) instrument, whose benefits include longer-term project financing and flexibility in project design and implementation. Under the APL, subsequent projects expanding the reform programme to other national or local public offices are triggered by the achievement of benchmark indicators set by the first project. In these success cases, no additional approval by the Bank's Board of Directors is needed.

In order to achieve the Government's goals, the World Bank provides TC in training, goods and equipment, and incremental recurrent costs. The project aims at improving government-wide management systems, implemented in different public offices in a phased manner. The components of the project include both "horizontal" systemic and "vertical" organizational reforms as illustrated in tables 4.9 and 4.10.

These horizontal reforms are scheduled for implementation in six pilot agencies selected by the Bolivian Government (tentatively the Ministry of Finance, the Internal Revenue Service, the Customs Service, the Ministry of Health, the Ministry of Justice and the National Statistics Institute) during phase 1 of the programme (2002).

The overall cost of the project is estimated at $50 million (including contingencies), and the financing plan includes an International Development Association credit of $40 million. It is interesting to note that after receiving initial help focused on organizational restructuring from the World Bank, the Government has taken strong ownership of this particular project.

---

5 The World Bank Group, Project: Bolivia - Institutional Reform, ID Number BOPE62790, Board date March, 1999

TABLE 4.6: GOVERNMENT PERSONNEL: PRE-REFORM (US$ THOUSANDS)

	No Posts	Percent	Average Salary	Annual Cost
Central Administration	**9,365**	**100%**		**47,585**
-Directive	1,320	14%	10.08	13,310
-Technical	3,943	42%	5.56	21,917
-Support	4,102	44%	3.01	12,359
Prefects	**3,594**	**100%**		**17,859**
-Directive	246	7%	13.55	3,326
-Technical	1,663	46%	6.08	10,113
-Support	1,685	47%	2.62	4,419
Total	**12,959**			**65,444**
Other Personnel Expenses				**11,847**
Total Treasury Expenses				**77,291**
% GDP				**1.27%**

Source: National Budget 1998.

TABLE 4.7: CIVIL SERVICE COSTS (US$ THOUSANDS)

Years	Future CS Posts	CS Costs	Current System Posts	Current System Costs	Consultants	Consultant Costs	Total Annual Costs
1	187	3,610	2,379	6,902	631	12,400	22,912
2	457	6,609	2,089	5,856	550	10,711	23,176
3	729	11,395	1,799	5,460	423	8,221	25,076
4	1,003	16,274	1,509	4,816	297	5,754	26,844
5	1,279	20,643	1,225	4,199	169	3,247	28,089
6	1,556	25,076	945	3,578	46	887	29,541
7	1,830	29,133	670	2,731	0	0	31,864
8	2,078	32,782	405	1,810	0	0	34,592
9	2,322	36,252	140	906	0	0	37,158
10	2,566	39,698	0	0	0	0	39,698

Source: Civil Service Programme, 1998; SNAP.

The World Bank noted two issues that urgently need to be addressed in order to avoid another failure of public service reform. First, the practice of financing of political parties by deducting a percentage of public officials' salaries should be abolished. Without addressing strong, underlying political forces, it doesn't seem feasible to implement any merit system of promotion, hiring and firing. Second, even though

TABLE 4.8: FINANCING STRATEGY (US$ THOUSANDS)

Years	Annual Costs	Donor Financing	%	Government Financing	%	% GDP
1	22,912	10,469	46%	12,443	54%	0.214
2	23,176	10,197	44%	12,979	56%	0.214
3	25,076	9,780	39%	15,296	61%	0.241
4	26,844	9,127	34%	17,717	66%	0.267
5	28,089	8,146	29%	19,943	71%	0.288
6	29,541	7,090	24%	22,451	76%	0.310
7	31,864	6,054	19%	25,810	81%	0.342
8	34,592	4,843	14%	29,749	86%	0.376
9	37,158	3,344	9%	33,814	91%	0.409
10	39,698	1,985	5%	37,713	95%	0.436
Increase	73%	-81%		203%		0.315
Cumulative	298,950	71,035		227,915		

Source: Civil Service Programme, 1998; SNAP.

Bolivian public officials are generally poorly paid, there is also evidence of a serious overstaffing problem, which in turn is a consequence of a strong patronage culture among public servants.

ii. Stakeholder analysis

We identify four micro (institutional) and macro (political) constraints to TC/capacity development within the civil service reform programme.

(i) A lack of political and fiscal backing from the executive power has induced an exclusive dependence on donor funds and a vicious cycle of donor involvement/government disengagement/reform. Four attempts at civil service reform in 10 years have not broken this cycle. Until early this year, the organization in charge of implementing the CSAR programme had not received any budget allocation from the Treasury.

(ii) A second institutional factor blocking effective TC within civil service concerns the administrative scope of the project. By centering attention exclusively on the central government administration, civil service reform initiatives have overlooked the fact that most public investment and service delivery is today done at the prefectural and municipal levels. A large group of latent stakeholders are systematically excluded from the reform process. Future reform success is likely to depend on the mobilization of these stakeholders.

TABLE 4.9: HORIZONTAL SYSTEMIC REFORM

Component	Goals and Cooperation	TC Outputs
Civil service reform	Creation of a new merit-based, performance-oriented civil service system. Technical cooperation, consisting primarily of assistance in drafting legislation, regulations, and civil service procedure manuals, as well as institution building activities.	• a new Civil Service Law and regulatory framework • establishment of a civil service directorate to serve as the principal institution for modern, government-wide human resource management. Its responsibilities would focus on establishing and adapting the regulations relating to the Civil Service Law, supporting the human resource units in line ministries, and overseeing the integrity of the government-wide human resources system • creating up-to-date terms of references and job classification capabilities, establishment registers, and personnel data files • establishing adequate salary schedules and pay adjust-ment schemes • improving training programmes, career development and personnel evaluation processes
National integrity	Establishment of a broad-based anti-corruption programme in collaboration with civil society. Technical cooperation through training, some goods, and institution building activities.	• new legal framework for government ethics • design of an asset declaration programme for public officials • strengthening of institutions involved in the investigation of corruption, including the Office of the Public Defender, the Public Ministry and the Office of the Comptroller General • simplification of bureaucratic procedures • reform of public procurement processes • public education campaign
Performance evaluation	Creation of legal and institutional framework for a national evaluation system with the aim of facilitating creation of results-oriented agen-cies, including: the design of a national evaluation system including budgeting by results (procedures, responsibilities, incentive structure, etc.) aimed at establishing, monitor-ing, and facilitating the improvement in performance by public organizations and personnel	

Source: http://www-wds.worldbank.org/

(iii) Third, behind institutional factors lie deeper political constraints that shape the way institutional reforms play out. First, civil service reform is particularly vulnerable to political pressures that are derived from a tradition of patronage and clientelism within the executive power. The stability and governability often attributed to the Bolivian reform period is directly linked to this politi-cal reality. Governing coalitions are glued together by redistributive pacts over public employment and public contracts. Privatization, capitalization, decentralization and popular participation have exacerbated this problem by reducing the availability of patronage to a minimum.

TABLE 4.10: VERTICAL ORGANIZATIONAL REFORM

Component	Goals and Cooperation	TC Outputs
Organizational restructuring	Integrated restructuring and reform of six pilot agencies. Technical cooperation, including training, some goods, and institution strengthening activities	• structure and functional diagnostics of pilot agencies • Organizational Restructuring Agreements (ORA), designed with the full participation of the agency, to be reviewed and approved by the policy level National Integrity Commission (CNI), chaired by the Vice President of the Republic • implementation of the ORAs with the aim of adjusting the agency's structure and function to permit it to execute a well-defined, service-oriented mission. Particular emphasis will be placed on implanting new human resources systems in line with the Civil Service component, implanting new decentralized financial management systems in line with Bolivia's ongoing integrated financial management programme, budget reform to support medium-term budget planning and budgeting by results, reengineering core business processes, and creating personnel and programme evaluation processes within the agency in line with the performance evaluation component. Under separate contracts, private firm(s) are expected to assist the government in selecting professional and managerial staff for the pilot agencies. Existing staff who choose to reapply to the agency and external candidates would be hired on a competitive basis using competency tests, background checks, and personal interviews. A major element in the programme is that the Bank, in parallel with the civil service programme financed by bilateral donors, plans to fund (on a declining basis over four years) the salaries of professional and managerial-level civil servants hired into the restructuring agencies. The government wishes to expand the pilot civil service programme to cover all professional and managerial staff in the central government, and to implement the new system on a phased basis in organizations undergoing an integrated restructuring process. This would direct new staff to reforming agencies to better ensure creation of results-oriented organizations that would be sustainable and replicable. The government is simultaneously seeking to maintain bilateral donor funding for key civil service positions outside of the pilot ministries during the interim period before these agencies are restructured and higher salaries are assured.

Source: http://www-wds.worldbank.org/

(iv) Fourth, donors are also influenced by the political rules that lie behind policy reform in Bolivia. Elite pacts between donors and the Government tend to reinforce the political pacts made between coalition partners by excluding political opposition, thus stifling reform and making benign neglect more likely. In the case of civil service reform, opposition parties constitute a natural countervailing power to patronage-led distribution of public employment. These latent stakeholders, however, are rarely included in policy discussions over the future of the civil service programme. Paradoxically, donor interest in remaining "apolitical" plays into the hands of entrenched political interests.

Education Reform

i. Process analysis

The Bolivian Education Reform, launched in 1996, is one of the most politically and institutionally complex among the package of reforms launched in the 1980s and 1990s. The reform has followed three phases of gradual implementation. The first phase (1992-1996) focused on policy design and consensus building. The second and current phase focuses on the implementation of curricular, organizational and teacher training programmes at the primary school level (1996-2002). The third phase aims to extend these efforts to secondary school (2002-2010).

Expenditures on primary and secondary schooling account for an average 3.9 percent of GDP and approximately 16% of the total national budget since 1996. As of this year, 2,200,000 students attend primary and secondary schools in the country and approximately 1,200,000 are under the education reform programme. Over 90,000 teachers and 9,000 administrative staff are covered under the reform. Since 1995, the education reform has accounted for $142 million in capital and recurrent expenditures, $100 million of which is financed by multilateral and bilateral donors.

The TC component of the education reform is significant and is the largest of all reform programmes. Since 1995, approximately $32 million was allocated to teacher training and $1.7 million to administrative training linked to the reform. In addition, $12 million was allocated to institutional strengthening and $4.7 million to curricular development programmes for primary education. The logistics of TC under the education reform are highly decentralized and managed by departmental and municipal educational authorities. Over 10,000 schools, organized into 2,000 "nucleos escolares" in 314 municipalities and 9 departments, provide a decentralized architecture for TC and capacity development.

The education reform includes a wide variety of TC throughout the whole programme. It comprises approximately 150 activities / consultancies, including:[6]

- training and orientation for community organizations and parents
- establishment of an education management information system
- incorporation of community participation in administration
- development of a core curriculum for grades 1 through 8
- development, production and distribution of textbooks, materials, computers and teachers' guides
- development of an education assessment programme
- programme support and monitoring

The education reform sets out four objectives: to transform public management of educational services; to improve teacher training in accordance with the basic tenets of bilingual and intercultural curricula; to transform the curriculum and structure of primary and secondary education; and to promote community participation in educational

---

[6] Inter-American Development Bank, Education Reform Programme (931/SF-BO; ATN/SF-4718-BO), Approved November 16, 1994

decision making, control and evaluation. While the initial adoption of reform was met with widespread teacher resistance, gradual implementation has created arenas for government/union negotiation over the content and pace of reform. Teachers' unions are today full – though partially unwilling – stakeholders in the reform process.

Table 4.11 shows the education reform budget for 1995-2001. Three aspects are worth highlighting. First, the education reform is the most important state reform in terms of both donor and government outlays. Over $142 million was disbursed between 1995 and 2001. Second, donor outlays equal approximately $95 million, or 67% of the total. The largest donors are the World Bank and the Inter-American Development Bank. Third, government commitments have been growing over the last three years. During the first three years, the reform was overwhelmingly financed by multilateral and bilateral donors.

Table 4.12 shows figures for the education reform's teacher training programme. The programme accounts for almost $33 million, or almost a quarter of the total reform budget. As with the general budget, multilateral donors account for most of the financing. The Bolivian Government has steadily increased its participation since 1998. The teacher training programme reaches over half of current teachers and almost 80% of all primary level teachers. It includes training on learning-centred education strategies and bilingual and intercultural education.

ii. Stakeholder analysis

We identify micro (institutional) and macro (political) factors to help explain the impact of TC and capacity development within the education reform programme.

(i) First, from a micro (institutional) perspective, we find that education reform TC and capacity development (teacher and administrative training) is a highly complex institutional operation involving over 20,000 teachers across the country. This is magnified by the high turnover rates and inter-regional mobility observed among urban and rural teachers. Capacity development involves a continuous process of learning and classroom adaptation of new curricula, teaching methods and bilingual learning content.

(ii) Second, despite the scope of teacher training and capacity development, the implementation of TC is highly decentralized in the Bolivian experience. This provides more room for local appropriation and modification of TC to suit local needs and experiences. Dozens of regional universities, NGOs and training institutes are involved in capacity development under central government monitoring and quality control.

(iii) Third, from a macro (political) perspective, education reform has encountered visible political opposition from teacher unions across the country. Political concessions made by the Government on payroll issues have attenuated opposition, but yearly negotiations between the Government and unions continue to be marked by stand-offs, strikes and prolonged negotiations. The

TABLE 4.11: EDUCATION REFORM BUDGET 1995-2001 (US$)

Year	GOV	GOV COUNTER	OTHER GOV	DONORS	TOTAL
1995	0	0	0	14,858,244.37	14,858,244.37
1996	0	3,548,343.05	3,120,835.49	11,736,802.23	18,405,980.77
1997	0	5,071,673.00	1,874,669.42	7,523,927.95	14,470,270.37
1998	0	543,084.72	0	12,717,415.33	13,260,500.05
1999	3,631,036.34	779,607.04	0	18,995,540.97	23,406,184.35
2000	10,278,460.36	285,194.15	0	23,058,532.89	33,622,187.40
Oct 2001	13,113,023.67	141.12	0	11,542,926.03	24,656,090.15
TOTAL	32,483,239.54	10,228,043.08	4,995,504.91	94,972,671.93	142,679,459.46

Source: Contaduría General de la República

TABLE 4.12: TEACHER TRAINING BUDGET (US$)

YEAR	GOV-Treas	GOV-EdRef	GOV COUNTER	OTHER GOV	DONORS	TOTAL
1995	0	0	0	0	220,238	220,238
1996	0	0	199,500	62,610	3,753,387	4,015,497
1997	0	0	161,597	244,516	506,987	913,100
1998	0	0	18,829	0	3,486,126	3,504,955
1999	463,890	0	139,150	0	1,359,694	1,962,734
2000	12,477,344	160,514	481,541	0	8,980,131	22,099,530
Total	12,941,234	160,514	1,000,617	307,127	18,306,563	32,716,055

Source: Contaduría General de la República

politics of teacher participation plays a key constraint over continued capacity development in the education sector. Union politics are not monolithic either, as both Government and opposition parties are represented at the central teachers' union.

(iv) Fourth, donor involvement in teacher training provides an effective means of balancing the political tug-of-war between unions and Government. The threat of losing donor funds has been repeatedly used to force a compromise during salary and working condition negotiations. At times, the presence of donor commitments such as those by the World Bank and IDB has also worked against capacity development, as unions denounced external conditionality over the scope and course of reform efforts. Teachers' unions continue to be among the best-organized and most radical union groups in Bolivia.

Technical Cooperation Agreements in Progress

Technical cooperation projects currently being executed are so diverse that they range from health and education reform to indigenous and census projects. Even though TC levels have dropped markedly during the past decade, there is no doubt about its impact at both national and local levels. At the moment, 22 donors are supporting TC agreements in a wide variety of projects and programmes.

For the most part, the Government applies "size-based" project management. For instance, there are many small TC projects that may simply involve one highly qualified person working at a Bolivian institution for one or two years. Likewise, every now and then there are more integrated TC projects comprising a whole working team. It is also not uncommon to find small infrastructure components supporting large TC projects. The Japanese have many of the kind, and promote that sort of knowledge transfer in many fields.

Many donors provide a variety of workshops, seminars, training programmes, and scholarships. The Organization of American States, the United Kingdom, Spain, Japan, Belgium, Germany, other European countries, and the United States provide the most important scholarships and training programmes. In the past, the Ministry of Planning administered most scholarships channeled through the Government. Unfortunately, the Ministry was known to divert well-intentioned TC projects by means of patronage and clientelism. Today, such responsibility is granted to the National Personnel Administration Service, which has proven to provide better and more systematic management.

Other recent, positive changes deal with a better allocation of consultants. A large majority of donors are increasingly hiring Bolivian rather than foreign consultants. The United Nations agencies and UNDP in particular were the first ones to initiate such practices. It is needless to state the importance of promoting Bolivian professionals not only in terms of fund allocation, but also in terms of creating job opportunities that may fit more accurately the particular needs of the country.

Innovations in TC

During the 1980s and the first part of the 1990s, Bolivia was perceived as a "model reformer". Ambitious policy reforms aimed at setting the framework for sustained growth and increased democratic development attracted the attention of donors and academics alike. By the end of the decade, however, policy analysts agreed that the Bolivian experience had led to disenchantment both with the processes and benefits of reform. Donors and the Government turned to implementation and management issues linked to institutional change. An increased awareness of the political and institutional fragility of many reform initiatives led to an explicit focus on issues of sustainability, ownership and accountability. The new scenario also suggests innovations in the way donors, the Government and the development industry confront the challenge of making reforms, particularly TC, "stick".

From Short- to Long-Term Planning (Sustainability)

The relatively fragmented and piecemeal approach to institutional reform adopted in Bolivia – particularly with respect to the education, popular participation / decentralization, and judicial reforms — tended to induce a multiplication of similarly fragmented and piecemeal TC and capacity development initiatives for each reform. A fixation on the short-term accomplishment of reform-specific targets betrayed a bias against longer-term, comprehensive and systemic TC planning. The Bolivian entry into the HIPC agreement in 1998 marked a turning point in donor and government relations. A key requirement of HIPC funding hinged around long-term (15-year) policy planning and continuous consensus building. The Bolivian National Dialogues of 1998 and 2000 provided a kick-off point for the World Bank's own Comprehensive Development Framework, and set the groundwork for a significant shift from short- to long-term policy planning.

Among the positive consequences of this shift are increased discussion of the need for comprehensive and long-term TC and capacity development plans. This means the inclusion of long-term policy issues (including Bolivia's strategic gas interests, international trade competitiveness, and the aftermath of coca-leaf eradication) on the government agenda, and an increased acknowledgement of the critical role of good public management, particularly a stable, meritocratic and well-qualified civil service.

From Conditionality to HIPC-II (Ownership)

The move from structural adjustment and stabilization policies to institutional and poverty reduction reforms was also accompanied by a shift from strict conditionality measures to relatively flexible conditionality between the Government and donors. "Ownership" refers, in this context, to a milder form of accountability, as donors attach dialogue, participation and social control clauses to PRSP and HIPC-II approval. The overall effect of this shift is mixed. On the one hand, governments are asked to take control of the content and pace of reforms. On the other hand, they are also expected to comply with an expanded set of poverty reduction targets, participation quotas and macroeconomic stability conditions.

How much has Bolivia advanced on the road to ownership? The civil service case reviewed in this document would suggest not much. Four donor-led attempts at reform have failed over the past decade, and have illustrated TC and capacity development initiatives at their worst. The education reform case, however, would suggest a different picture. Technical cooperation for teacher training worked through a highly decentralized system of capacity development that was well-attuned to local needs and demands of teachers and unions. As with popular participation and decentralization reform, the politicization of key actors was not necessarily a significant deterrent for effective TC. What mattered most was the effective appropriation and tailoring of capacity development programmes at the local or school level.

BOX 4.1: The Japanese experience

Since the beginning of diplomatic relations, the Japanese Government has contributed to Bolivian development in many ways. Loan and grant aid and TC have been channeled to a wide variety of projects, and coordination between both Governments has been smooth and cooperative. A longstanding policy of flexibility has encouraged a vibrant relationship. In this spirit, many loan agreements are constantly rescheduled.

Another active aid provider is the Japan International Cooperation Agency, which manages government-based TC. JICA conducts training programmes in Japan, an expert dispatch programme and provides equipment and material. It also runs Japanese Overseas Cooperation Volunteer programmes, immigration (assistance for immigrants of Japanese descent) and emergency disaster-relief programmes.

Yet TC has been subject to a gradual reduction over the past 10 years. The following table shows Japan's ODA disbursements from 1994 to 1998, and the amounts programmed as of April 2002.[7]

Japanese TC disbursements to Bolivia (US$ millions):

Year	1994	1995	1996	1997	1998	2002
Amount	28.56	31.21	22.00	20.76	18.99	16.51

Source: *Reforming Technical Cooperation for Capacity Development/UNDP (2002),*
http://www.mofa.go.jp/policy/oda

Changing Roles of Donors, Recipients and Development Industry (Accountability)

The Bolivian reforms would not have been possible without the active participation of donors and a vibrant development industry. In recent years, the design issues tackled in the early 1990s have been overshadowed by a new concern for implementation, sustainability and long-term development. The focus of donor efforts has also shifted from project to policy concerns, and from short-lived development fads to longer-term development objectives. This does not mean that donors have relinquished control over development policy making, nor that Bolivia has succeeded at institutionalizing a functioning technocracy / bureaucracy. In fact, the dual state structure described in the first chapter of this study shows every sign of having hardened in recent years. The institutional determinants of poor public sector performance are complemented by political determinants of entrenched public sector informality.

Lessons and Recommendations

The preliminary evidence gathered in the case studies and buttressed by figures on ODA, TC and capacity development trends would suggest that TC is going through significant changes in Bolivia. Among key lessons emerging from the Bolivian experience:

(i) First, increased TC has helped to promote capacity development for second-generation reforms in Bolivia. The cases suggest the importance of considering TC as part of a larger problem linked to developing capacities within the formal and informal public sectors. A dual bureaucratic structure, as described in this study, provides a perverse set of institutional incentives for sustainable TC efforts.

---

[7] Japan's Official Development Assistance (ODA), http://www.mofa.go.jp/policy/oda/

(ii) Second, micro (institutional) and macro (political) determinants of public sector performance help to identify significant constraints to effective capacity
development in the Bolivian public sector. An entrenched system of patronage
and clientelism driven by coalition politics (the backbone of political stability
in the Bolivian context) provides the backdrop for any attempt at institutional
re-engineering. Technocratic isolation, political quota-sharing and other political
devices have been used with varying degrees of success, but all point to the
importance of managing political conflict for effective capacity development.

(iii) Third, the objectives of TC have also changed throughout the decade. An
early focus on TC and capacity development for policy design and agenda setting has been replaced by a new focus on TC for policy implementation. There
is an increasing demand, furthermore, for decentralized capacity development at prefectural and municipal levels of government.

Among preliminary recommendations:

(i) First, TC for capacity development must be tailored to overcome significant
political and institutional constraints that skew incentives toward patronage,
clientelism or other forms of political particularism. The neglect of politics is
perhaps the most effective way of sustaining vicious cycles of reform / iner-
tia/counter-reform.

(ii) Second, at the micro-level, the case studies suggest a significant role for
individual leadership/entrepreneurship in pushing for, and overseeing successful capacity development. Learning, knowledge accumulation and diffusion
are heightened by highly-motivated and well-qualified public sector leaders.

(iii) Third, TC needs to be promoted within a larger framework of human capital
development in order for political leaders and opinion makers to lobby for
capacity development. The perception that TC is "merely bureaucratic" poses a
significant constraint to effective political action and public support for this effort.

(iv) Fourth, TC needs to move from an exclusively central government focus to
more decentralized forms of sustained capacity development. As municipalities gain more fiscal and administrative power, the needs of decentralized
training and capacity development will undoubtedly grow. Local and regional
government already account for over two-thirds of public investment and a significant proportion of social expenditure.

5 *Egypt* [1]

BUILDING PRIVATE SECTOR CAPACITY THROUGH TECHNICAL COOPERATION

Introduction

Egypt is a middle-income country, with a total GDP of around $84 billion (1999/00), or $1,404 per capita. The private sector plays a prominent role in the economy. In recent years, inflation has been brought under control and macroeconomic performance has improved, with the economic growth rate averaging over five percent in the years 1995-2000. The budget deficit in 1999/00, however, was nearly five percent of GDP. Egypt's external debt is manageable, amounting to $28.5 billion (2001), or about 32% of GDP. In 1990/91, Egypt embarked on a reform programme, with structural adjustment supported by the World Bank and the International Monetary Fund (IMF). In 1997/98, the process of relatively successful reform led to major cancellations of debt through the Paris Club. The economic programme included major financial sector reforms, including budgetary and fiscal policy, and other trade and economic reforms. It also focused on giving a greater role to the private sector.

With 67.9 million people, Egypt is the 18th most populated country in the world. Population growth rate averaged about 2.3% in the 1990s, compared with 2.6% during

[1] This paper was prepared by Faika El-Refaie, Member of Parliament and the National Council for Women; Ihab Ibrahim El Dissouki, Lecturer, Economics Department, Sadat Academy for Management Sciences; Omneia Amin Helmy, Associate Professor of Economics, Cairo University and Senior Economist at the Egyptian Centre for Economic Studies; Maha El Essawy, Undersecretary for US Grants at the Ministry of International Cooperation; and Rawia Atef Mokhtar, Economist and Business Development Manager, Allied Corporation Egypt.

the 1980s. Gauged by its performance on the 2002 Human Development Index (0.642 in 2000), Egypt is in the middle category of countries, ranking 115 out of 173 countries in the global table. Egypt still has far to go in developing its human resources and capacities, but there are elements in its human development profile that reflect the country's potential for an accelerated process of capacity development. The adult literacy rate (2000) is 55.3%, compared with the regional aggregate of 62%. Egypt's combined gross enrolment ratio, however, is 76% against the region's 62% (1999). Life expectancy at birth is 67.3 years, a shade above the regional average. It has 202 doctors per 100,000 people, compared with 162 for China and 48 for India. Public spending on education is about 5% of GDP (1995-1997), nearly one-third of which goes to higher education. Egypt has a substantial cohort of highly educated people when compared with many other developing countries.

This chapter is in two parts. It begins with an overview of official development assistance (ODA) and technical cooperation (TC). The second part focuses on a study of the private sector, since Egypt is a unique example of a country where the bulk of TC resources has been focused on this area.

Patterns of ODA and TC

The ODA figures for Egypt presented here, based on the OECD definition, cover the whole range of assistance, including grants, TC and soft loans. Egypt ranks among the largest recipients of ODA worldwide. Donor assistance has been an important part of the country's development strategy, with average flows of $2 billion per year from approximately 35 donors. It received a total of $25 billion between 1990 and 1999. Official development assistance to Egypt has begun to decline, and is expected to continue to do so. The government and its major donor, the United States, have agreed on a reduction by five percent annually from 1998 to 2007.

Official development assistance flows reached a peak of $5,439 million in 1990, but dropped by a substantial margin to $1,579 million in 1999. With population growth from 52.6 million in 1990 to 63.3 million in 1999, ODA per capita has dropped from $103 in 1990 to a low of $25 in 1999 (see Table 5.1).

The major donors are the United States Agency for International Development (USAID), the European Commission (EC) and European Union member states, Japan, the World Bank, the International Monetary Fund, UNDP, and regional development organizations such as the African Development Bank and the Arab Fund for Economic and Social Development.

The United States is the dominant donor, on average accounting for almost half of total development assistance flows to Egypt in the 1990s. Because of its location, large and growing market, history, culture and role as a moderating influence in the Middle East, Egypt has long been the United States' strategic partner. Since 1979, Egypt has used its political leadership to foster peace in the region. Both the United States and Egypt have recognized that Egypt must be prosperous and stable for wider regional stability. Technical cooperation to support economic development in Egypt therefore became vitally important. Project assistance alone amounted to over $400 million yearly during the 1990s, of which 50% was TC up to 1998, and 80% since then. The agriculture sector received an average of $50 million annually for policy reform, including training, advisory services and new technologies.

The EC and the EU member states contributed 28% of ODA flows to Egypt during the 1990s. Most of the EU assistance has been directed to small and micro enterprises, industrial modernization, poverty alleviation, employment generation, gender issues and capacity development.

Japan comes next. Its cumulative flows during the last decade reached about $1 billion, of which the most significant component financed the first bridge spanning the Suez Canal. After a decade-long moratorium on lending, Japan reopened its soft loan window in 2000 to focus on the environment, technology, human development and small and medium enterprises.

Arab countries constituted most of the balance of total ODA flows to Egypt during the 1990s. The volume has become quite modest, declining from $2.2 billion in 1990 to less than $50 million in 1999.

Official development assistance flows to Egypt through international or regional institutions represented on average about three percent of the total during the 1990s. United Nations agencies contributed 1.3% of total ODA flows to Egypt during this period. Although international and regional institution contributions to ODA flows were not large, their contribution to capacity development was significant because of their influence on both the volume of aid and the focus on TC by major donors.

Total TC flows to Egypt have been very substantial, amounting to $7 billion during the 1990s. Annual inflows of TC were much better sustained than ODA, ending the decade at about the same level as they began. As a proportion of total ODA, TC climbed from less than one-sixth to almost half. In terms of GDP and budget revenue, TC declined steadily until 1998, and then increased (see Table 5.2).

The United States provided the bulk of TC, while EU members and the European Commission ranked second, followed by Japan. The USA and EU together offered 89% of the total, while Japan's share was about three percent during the same period (see Table 5.3).

Available statistics on sectoral distribution of TC indicate that during the 1990s as a whole, the agriculture sector was the largest beneficiary, but that the private sector received increasing amounts during the second half of the decade. The private sector received over $300 million during the 1990s from USAID alone.

TC Practices and Policies

The government established the Ministry of International Cooperation (MIC) in the mid-1970s to manage foreign assistance. In December 2001, the MIC became the

TABLE 5.1: ODA FLOWS, 1990-99

	1990	1991	1992	1993	1994	1995	1996	1997	1998	1999
ODA (US$ millions)	5,439	5,025	3,603	2,401	2,695	2,014	2,199	1,981	1,951	1,579
ODA per capita	103.4	93.6	65.7	43.0	47.2	34.6	37.0	32.6	31.5	24.9
ODA/GDP (%)	11.3	15.0	8.7	5.1	5.2	3.3	3.3	2.6	2.4	1.8
ODA/Gov. budget (%)	46.3	58.6	29.1	17.3	17.4	12.3	12.2	10.4	9.7	7.3
ODA/Exports of G&S (%)	39.8	34.7	21.3	12.4	17.9	11.3	12.2	10.2	10.2	8.4

Sources: World Bank Global Finance Development 1999 and 2000; IFS Yearbook 2000; Joint Arab Economic Report, 1999; www.cbe.org.eg/annual time series, and www.OECD.org.

TABLE 5.2: TC FLOWS, 1990-99

	1990	1991	1992	1993	1994	1995	1996	1997	1998	1999
TC (US$ millions)	812	757	827	975	594	744	635	570	472	768
TC/ODA (%)	14.9	15.1	23.0	40.6	22.0	36.9	28.9	28.8	24.2	48.6
TC/GDP (%)	1.7	2.3	2.0	2.1	1.2	1.2	0.9	0.8	0.6	0.9
TC/budget revenue (%)	6.9	8.8	6.7	7.0	3.8	4.5	3.5	3.0	2.4	3.6

Sources: World Bank Global Finance Development 1999 and 2000; IFS Yearbook 2000; Joint Arab Economic Report, 1999; www.cbe.org.eg/annual time series, and www.OECD.org.

TABLE 5.3: DONORS' SHARE OF TC IN THE 1990S

	Total	USA	EU & EC	Japan	UN Agencies	Other
US$ billions	7.16	5.44	0.91	0.24	0.16	0.41
% of total	100.0	76.4	12.6	3.3	2.2	5.7

Source: OECD 2001

Department of International Cooperation (DIC) within the Ministry of Foreign Affairs, headed by a State Minister.

Practices regarding the appropriation of TC vary according to different donors. In some cases, donors take the initiative in proposing grants and loans for specific pro-grammes and sectors. The DIC then consults the concerned ministry regarding its priorities. After reviewing and agreeing on priorities, terms and conditions, DIC and representatives from the concerned ministry discuss the TC agreement with the donor. The donor then prepares the final agreement for a TC project/programme, and may submit a draft Memorandum of Understanding (MOU) to allocate the local currency

TABLE 5.4: TC FLOWS FROM SELECTED DONORS BY SECTOR, 1990-99 (US$ MILLIONS)

	USAID	EU	AFSED	Total
Private Sector	326.4	265.5	0.3	592.2
Banking Reform	-	3.3	-	3.3
Social Fund	-	16.6	-	16.6
Agriculture	1,184.8	106.8	-	1,291.6
Health	346.9	139.5	1.8	488.2
Education	263.3	90.0	-	353.3
Tourism	15.0	-	7.3	22.3
Environment	5.4	18.3	23.7	47.3
Power	200.0	-	0.5	200.5
Telecommunication	200.0	-	-	200.0
Sector Policy Reform	66.3	38.7	-	105.0
Promoting Democracy	34.3	-	-	34.3
NGOs & PVOs	29.5	-	-	29.5
Total	2,672.0	678.7	33.5	3,384.0

Sources: USAID, EC, Arab Fund for Social & Economic Development (AFSED)

counterpart funds associated with some programmes. Agreement is reached, often after long consultations.

Aid and TC have been hitherto managed in a somewhat *ad hoc* fashion. Since there was no overall national strategy setting out clear priorities, the government did not attempt to match requirements with specific offers. There was no mechanism for systematically reviewing, monitoring and assessing implementation, and review sessions between government and donors relied heavily on donor documents, reporting and statistics. Some projects received TC from a number of different donors, but for the same purposes. Training provided to individuals was not always based on a coordinated assessment of priority needs among government agencies. Despite this, there was no evident movement of individuals from the public to the private sector, because of relatively secure working conditions in government.

Management is also complicated by the fact that TC procedures and processes differ from one donor to another. Donor systems and policies affect the modalities and priorities of TC. During the 1990s, however, there has been a tendency for donors to favour programme over project-based TC. In part, this shift reflects changes in the direction of development as a whole. In the 1980s, TC heavily supported infrastructure projects. Under the economic reform programme, policy formulation, social development and poverty alleviation received higher priority, with TC shifting to support these objectives. The programme approach has given more flexibility in the use of funds and enabled quicker disbursement, and cuts administrative burdens for both the donors and the Government. More importantly, it is more conducive to capacity development than the project approach. A mix of project/programme approaches continues to operate, although the programme approach is expected to predominate in the future.

Among bilaterals donors, the programme approach has been adopted increasingly by the United States and the European Commission, while Japan has retained its preference for project-based TC. Technical cooperation from UNDP has also been programme-oriented and designed to address the main priorities of the National Development Plan: agriculture, industry, human resource development, information systems, public services and advanced technology. The programme approach has been an important change and has helped to concentrate TC more on the priority objectives of Egypt's development.

Several recent changes can be noted in the TC practices of donors and the Government. Apart from the greater focus on programmes, with TC increasingly linked to policy reform and sector-wide approaches (SWAps), donor-side changes include more emphasis on social development (i.e. the Social Development Fund) and poverty reduction issues. Technical cooperation has also helped to bring the human development dimension into the mainstream of policy making and public discussion.

Donors are also more actively engaged with the private sector, enabling them to play a lead role in economic development, particularly through business expansion and export promotion. Finally, donors have improved coordination among themselves through a number of informal arrangements, and are tapping more into the local expertise.

On the government side, changes have included a greater focus on institutional capacity building. There is also a greater awareness of the potential role of TC, which has led to increased demand.

Conjointly, there is a better mutual understanding as a result of more extensive donor-government consultations in defining sector priorities and policy implications. This has led to more participation and ownership by national authorities in the implementation of TC.

Donor Coordination

Donor coordination takes place at three levels. The Consultative Group (CG) meeting, chaired by the World Bank, is held every three years. There is good coordination between donors and the Government in such meetings. In the mid-1990s, bilateral and multilateral donors also formed the Donor Assistance Group (DAG), consisting of 40 members excluding Arab countries. The DAG meets monthly in Cairo, and it has eight sectoral subgroups that convene as needed. The CG and the DAG deal with issues of both capital and technical cooperation.

The DAG has recently succeeded in inducing Egypt to focus more on its social development agenda and to pay more attention to democratic and institutional reforms. National institutions are invited to DAG meetings from time to time. The National Council for Women, for example, is a member of a DAG subgroup. The formation of DAG is a major improvement in harmonizing donor and government efforts. Instead of repetitive discussions with individual donors, the government can hold collective meetings. This arrangement, however, needs to be strengthened. "Coordination" among donors mainly consists of an exchange of views and information. There has been no systematic attempt to concert common positions, for example, regarding the effectiveness of TC with respect to capacity development. Mutual efforts by both donors and government in this regard are essential. A DAG Position Paper on Social Development in Egypt addressing issues related to poverty and the main challenges for the future was recently prepared for a Consultative Group meeting.

The Impact of TC on Capacity Development

The general perception that TC has had a generally positive impact on capacity development in the country is largely based on impressionistic evidence. Most institutions that have received TC, viewed it positively, not surprisingly. What follows is a brief assessment of selected projects by different donors, from which the nature and extent of capacity development can be discerned.

 Economic Policy Initiative Consortia (EPIC): The project began in 1996 and ran for a four-year period. The US-based International Center for Economic Growth provided technical and research support towards building a community of Egyptian scholars and institutions committed to research. It also provided advice on economic policy reform to Egyptian policy makers, and engaged business, academia, media and research communities in its programmes. The project included a component to train young Egyptian economists through doctoral and post-doctoral studies in the United States. The project developed a strong sense of local ownership and participation and contributed to developing capacities in economic policy analysis. The quality of these analytical skills (as seen from resulting documents) has improved significantly as a result.

 Education Sector Assistance Strategy: The education system in Egypt faces enormous challenges if it is to contribute to the country's development agenda. In recognition of this, the government has worked with the World Bank and the European Commission since 1996 on a framework for education reform at all levels. In 1997, the Ministry of Education articulated a long-term vision with input from both partners that recognized the need to improve the quality, efficiency, equality and quantity of education. The paper called for a national dialogue and increased community participation, focusing on enhancing quality as a priority. The Bank produced an informal sector note consistent with this vision.

 The assistance included informal policy advice to the four ministerial committees in charge of formulating the national strategy for educational reform by 2000. The World Bank (IDA) financed interventions that supported the strategies being developed. This work in the education sector exemplifies the principles of the Comprehensive

Development Framework. It focused on a long-term vision for the economy and recognized the need for structural changes within the sector. It involved strong ownership at the Government level, and Ministry staff gained useful knowledge from the experience.

UNDP Programme at the Institute of National Planning (INP): The programme's objective is to produce and publish an annual report on human development in Egypt. The institute undertook the preparation of the report with support from UNDP, and since 1997, with additional contributions from UNICEF, UNFPA, WFP and the Social Fund for Development. The reports issued by INP since 1994 have been guided by the conceptual framework and methods developed by UNDP in its 1990 Human Development Report. The concepts and indices used then have been modified in light of the valuable contributions of a large number of experts and specialists in development. In the adaptation process, Egyptian intellectuals have provided an added value that has helped refine the global report in a mutually reinforcing manner. Such an endeavour reflects a good example of putting TC partnership and participation principles into practice, while helping to shape and influence social policy.

External Debt Management Unit at the Central Bank: The EDM Unit publishes Egypt's external debt statistics in a quarterly series, with monthly and daily issues produced for internal use. The Unit has been transformed into a full-fledged separate department at the Central Bank. It uses the United Nations Conference on Trade and Development database software package, which is regularly updated. The Unit became technically independent three years after it started operations, and now provides its expertise and systems to other countries in the region and in Africa. This service has been acknowledged by recipient entities. The EDM documents the impact of TC on capacity development of individuals and institutions domestically, and also on institutional capacities in other countries.

The Banking Institute: The Banking Institute was established in 1991 with financing by a consortium of donors (USAID, EC, the United Kingdom, the Bundesbank of Germany, the Canadian International Development Agency and the Banque de France). The Institute's objective was to enhance the capacity development and expertise of Egyptian bankers, and to strengthen the banking leadership. Its impact has been felt in the upgrading of individual bankers' performances as well as improvements in the institutional capacities of the banking sector. The Institute has since expanded its activities to Central and Eastern Europe, the Arab region and Africa. The number of participants in different programmes undertaken by the Institute increased from 714 in 1991/92 to 15,382 in 2000/01.

Other projects in the Central Bank: In the context of the World Bank's financial sector reform programme, the EC offered $20 million to undertake six TC projects in the areas of organization, automation, payments systems, bank supervision, reserve management and monetary policy. The projects essentially consisted of a series of studies recommending measures to be implemented. The organizational study has been completed, but was not implemented because decision makers did not accept its recommendations. The automation study was completed and its implementation is proceeding slowly. The payments system study has been completed and implementation is now under way. The Bank Supervision Department did not apply the recommendations of the study in their entirety, due to lack of expertise. The other projects were confronted with bureaucratic obstacles, lack of competence among local staff, and an equivalent lack of interest form the foreign-staffed Project Management Unit. In terms of capacity development, the projects mostly fell short of their objectives. The PMU did not have a strategy to enable local staff to participate effectively in these projects and owner-ship/partnership was clearly lacking. The programme was extended twice, ultimately utilizing only $4 million out of the original $20 million commitment. The programme has now been terminated.

Technical Cooperation to the Private Sector

The two leading donors – the United States and the European Commission – have pro-vided a considerable amount of TC for private sector development. The Economic Reform Programme called on the country's private sector to build capacities for a process of dynamic engagement with the world economy. The projects that are described below can be viewed as TC activities that have enabled Egypt to address immediate and practical concerns arising from globalization. The objective of these projects was to improve the business practices of enterprises and to enable them to upgrade their technology and skills. Eight of the nine projects listed below with their starting dates were funded by the United States, one by the European Commission.

- Small and Micro Enterprise Development - 1988

- Credit Guarantee Corporation - 1989

- Privatization Support - 1990

- Small Enterprise Credit - 1991

- Egyptian Centre for Economic Studies - 1992

- Growth Through Globalization - 1996

- EEA/Expo-link - 1997

- Centre for Business Support - 2000

- The Private Sector Development Programme - 1996 (EC-funded)

Small and Micro Enterprise Development (SMED): Business associations were selected by USAID as implementing agencies to create viable credit delivery systems for small and micro enterprises. The associations that administer the funds in coordination with local banks are: Alexandria Business Association, Egyptian Small Enterprise Development Association, Assiut Businessmen Association, Small Enterprise Development Sharkeya Association and Dakahleya Businessmen Association for Investment and

Community Development. Their specialized loan officers have reached out to targeted poor areas. Each designs its strategy in collaboration with USAID, with approval by MIC/DIC.

The $44 million programme is aimed at enabling small and micro enterprises to invest, expand, buy raw materials, upgrade equipment and hire staff. In addition, TC includes training for clients to develop administrative and financial skills, and to solve technical problems. Training was provided by technical experts, advisors and trainers hired locally or from the United States, and USAID selected the auditing and accounting firm. The programme has provided loans valued at approximately $600 million to more than 220,000 borrowers, resulting in the creation of over 180,000 jobs. From profits generated, another association was established in Kafr Aldawar. The very positive results of this programme led USAID to extend its duration to 2005. In October 1999, the Alexandria Business Association launched a poverty-lending programme targeting female-headed households in poor areas. To date, more than 3,700 women have benefited from this programme, with a 100% repayment rate.

Credit Guarantee Company for Small and Medium Scale Enterprises (CGC): As part of a policy to liberalize the Egyptian economy, alleviate unemployment and encourage the private sector, the government commissioned a local consulting firm to undertake a feasibility study on establishing a private sector credit guarantee scheme. The CGC was then set up with funding in Egyptian Pounds from USAID special counterpart funds. The major partners in this project are the MIC/DIC, USAID and Italy. The United States provided assistance and training support to the staff of CGC (individualized capacity building) and supported a management framework for expanding and diversifying SMEs lending agents (institutional capacity building). The CGC opened in Cairo and now has branches in five more cities.

The Privatization Programme: The USAID provided $35 million to help government implement its privatization programme through two projects. Four foreign consulting agencies were entrusted with the implementation of the first project, partnering with the technical office of the Minister of Public Sector Enterprises, MIC/DIC and USAID.

Two implementing agencies (foreign but located in Cairo) were selected on the basis of international bidding for the second project, and the main partners were senior officials from the ministries of economy, foreign trade, electricity, transport, communication, housing and construction, public enterprises and MIC/DIC. One of the implementing agencies was tasked with evaluating and preparing companies for privatization, and researching particular industries in order to identify new markets. The second agency was responsible for quarterly follow-up reports on the privatization programme.

The project contributed to capacity development through a total of 80 training courses and seminars for public service personnel. Through continuous consultation and close contact with their Egyptian partners, foreign experts have contributed to capacity development. Implementing agencies have also been hiring Egyptian staff. Auditing by USAID and follow-up by MIC ensure accountability.

Small Enterprise Credit (SEC): The objectives of the SEC were to provide financial, technical and other services to support traditional crafts, familiarize small borrowers with banking rules and procedures, and provide advice on how to regulate their accounts. A national network of lending organizations, NGOs and community development associations was utilized to undertake this work. The major partners in this project are the senior officials of the MIC/DIC, the Ministry of Social Affairs and the National Development Bank (NDB). The NDB has become full owner of the project, relying on its own resources and staff. The bank has been able to organize seminars and symposiums for training banking cadres from Arab countries on this type of financing. It also sends its staff to attend seminars organized by the World Association of Small and Medium Enterprise. This is in addition to creating nearly 50,000 job opportunities and familiarizing the informal sector with banking rules and procedures.

The Egyptian Centre for Economic Studies (ECES): The ECES is an independent, non-profit research institution founded in 1992 by prominent private entrepreneurs. Its objective is to promote economic development by assisting policy makers and the business community in identifying the need for reform, and then implementing change. To expand its activities, the Centre requested USAID support.

The Centre is becoming a key player in providing independent analytical advice to policy makers, and in engaging communities in productive dialogues on economic issues. As a research institution dedicated to serving the government's public policy, the ECES draws heavily on foreign expertise to maintain high standards of service. The Centre is contributing to capacity development for researchers not only within government, but also for the benefit of universities, research institutes and journalists. The Centre is playing an active role in enhancing the economic knowledge of other players in the economy, including NGOs, to widen constituencies supporting the reform process. The Centre has recently received an endowment to ensure its sustainability.

Growth Through Globalization (GTG): This project was initiated with a $149 million from USAID. Its aim is to promote the adoption of improved technologies and management practices, increase access to market information, promote financial services and build strong private sector associations that can advocate reforms favourable to private sector-led growth. An important priority of the project is export development.

The Egyptian Exporters Association (EEA/Expo-Link): The business sector in coordination with the Government established the Egyptian Exporters Association as a private sector-led organization to assist firms in expanding export activities. The EEA's "action arm" was Expo-Link, a non-profit organization founded under USAID Exporter Service Programmes to increase non-traditional exports. Under the agreement, Expo-Link was to provide assistance to approximately 150 firms and increase Egyptian exports by $150 million over the life of the project (1997-2001). Expo-Link provided assistance to firms already exporting, or with potential to export, by identifying markets and requirements, and developing marketing strategies. All 47 staff members were Egyptian. Short-term experts, local or foreign, were recruited to respond to specific client needs and after consultation between the Egyptian client and Expo-Link.

There were an average of 30 foreign experts a year; Egyptian consultants were mainly recruited for start-up firms. Expo-Link staff and consultants were available throughout the process for a range of activities, from diagnosing business needs and developing service packages, to ensuring that new techniques and technologies were adapted appropriately.

This process contributed to capacity development at the individual and institutional levels. Exports increased by $206 million, easily exceeding the target. This achievement is attributed to a large extent to Expo-Link's success in solving the technical and marketing problems of client firms. Egyptian firms traditionally lack strong export departments equipped with trained staff, and this project helped to stimulate a needed export culture.

The Centre for Business Support (CBS): The Centre is a $12.5 million export-business development programme funded by USAID. The USAID agreement requires CBS to increase Egyptian exports by $36 million over the life of the project (2000-2003) by supporting the efforts of client firms to compete in the global market. This includes improving business operations, staff development and establishing viable business alliances abroad. The Centre is managed by the US International Executive Service Corps, which has operated in Egypt since 1976 and has completed over 1,900 projects for 1,200 companies. It delivers specialized expertise to small and medium-sized companies and NGOs. Experts, whether local or foreign, are selected after identification of clients' specific needs through consultation between the Egyptian firm and CBS. On average, there are some 200 foreign experts a year, the majority of whom are American. Local counterparts are recruited for short-term assignments and for Egyptian start-up firms.

Private Sector Development Programme: The Private Sector Development Programme (PSDP) for business upgrading, set up with 25 million Egyptian Pounds from the European Commission, provides customized technical and professional expertise to private sector companies and business associations. Services are provided in response to demand and most activities apply the principle of cost-sharing. Because of its success, the PSDP has begun to receive refunds for its services. The components of the programme include:

- **Business training:** More than 125 courses are offered at the European Management Centre, which has trained some 4,000 Egyptian executives.

- **Marketing and export:** Advice has been provided to more than 180 companies producing a wide range of consumer goods.

- **Business cooperation:** More than 100 companies have received assistance in forming strategic alliances with European companies.

- **Information services:** Commercial data and market information is provided to the PSDP and other donor programmes.

- **Institutional development:** The Centre's institutional development division has provided direct assistance to nine business associations.

In conclusion, these examples reveal that Egypt's private sector has benefited from a considerable amount of technical cooperation, including a large proportion of foreign expertise. This support has resulted in readily measurable and tangible bene-fits in many cases, and sustainability can be gauged by the continuing solvency of the enterprises assisted.

References

Berg, E. and the United Nations Development Programme (UNDP). 1993. *Rethinking Technical Cooperation: Reforms for Capacity Building in Africa.* New York.

Berger L.& Checchi, (YEAR) "Donor Assistance to Egypt Past/Present/Future." Washington, DC.

Central Bank of Egypt (CBE). "Annual Report." Various issues. Cairo: Central Bank of Egypt.

————. "Quarterly Economic Review." Various issues. Cairo: Central Bank of Egypt.

Consultative Group Meeting. 1999. "Survey of Donor Support for Social Development in the Arab Republic of Egypt." A survey compiled by UNDP. Paris.

El-Refaie, F. 2000. "Coordination of Monetary and Fiscal Policy in Egypt." Cairo: Egyptian Center for Economic Studies.

El-Mikawy, Noha. 2001. "Institutional Reform to Improve Economic Performance: Challenges and Sequences in the Case of Egypt." In El-Mikawy, Noha, and Handousa, Heba (eds.), *Institutional Reform and Economic Development in Egypt.* Cairo.

European Union. 2000 "Annual Report." Delegation of The European Commission in Egypt.

European Commission. 2001. "Report on the Implementation of the European Commission External Assistance Situation at 01/01/2001." Europe Aid Cooperation Office, Staff Working Document. (http://europa.eu.int/comm/europeaid/reports/status_report_2001_en.pdf)

European Union and Member States. 2001. "Analysis of a Survey Conducted Among EC Delegation and Member States- Annual Stocktaking." Cairo.

Egyptian Center for Economic Studies (ECES). 2001. "Business Barometer." Cairo.

Handy, H. 2000. "Monetary Policy and Financial Sector Reform in Egypt: The Record and the Challenges Ahead." Cairo: Egyptian Center for Economic Studies.

International Monetary Fund. *International Financial Statistics Yearbook.* Various issues. Washington, DC.

————. 1998. "Egypt Beyond Stabilization, Toward a Dynamic Market Economy." Occasional Paper/98/163. Washington, DC.

Ministry of Economy and Foreign Trade. *Monthly Economic Digest.* Various issues. Cairo.

Ministry of International Cooperation. 2000. "Implementation Status of USAID In Egypt." Cairo.

Namazi, Banquer. 1998. "Assessment of Human Development Advocacy Initiatives." Paper prepared for the United Nations Development Programme.

Organisation for Economic Co-operation and Development/Development Assistance Committee (OECD/DAC). 2000. *Development Co-operation 2000*. Paris.

————. 1996. "DAC Seminar on Technical Co-operation And Capacity Development: Synthesis Report." Paris.

————. 1991. "Geographical Distribution of Financial Flows to Developing Countries." Paris.

Ragui, Assaad. 2000. "The Transformation of the Egyptian Labor Market: 1988-1998." Cairo: Egypt Labor Market Project, Economic Research Forum (ERF) for the Arab Countries Iran, and Turkey.

Siddiqui, Farid. 2000. "Conducting a Joint Country Review of the Agencies in Egypt: Issues and Recommendation." Final Report. Cairo.

Subramanian, Arvind. 1997. "The Egyptian Stabilization Experience." Cairo: Egyptian Centre for Economic Studies.

United Nations Development Programme. 1997. "Capacity Development." New York.

————. 2001. "Fifth Country Programme for Egypt." DP/CP/EGP/5. Cairo.

————. 2002. *Human Development Report 2002*. New York: Oxford University Press.

United States Agency for International Development (USAID). 2000. "USAID/Egypt Strategic Plan FY2000-2009, Advancing the Partnership." Cairo.

————. 2000. "Egypt Country Assistance Evaluation." Operations Evaluation Department. Cairo

————. 2000. "Egypt Social and Structural Review." Report No. 22397- EGT. Washington, DC.

————. 1999/2000. "Egypt: Action Plan for Improving the Business Environment, Civil Service, and Business Linkages." Cairo.

World Bank. 2001. *Global Development Finance 2001*. Washington, DC.

————. 2001. *World Development Indicators 2001*. Washington, DC.

————. 2001. "Memorandum of the President of the IBRD and the IFC to the Executive Directors on a Country Assistance Strategy for the Arab Republic of Egypt." Report No. 22163-EGT. Washington, DC.

————. 2002. *Building Institutions for Markets*. New York: Oxford University Press.

6 The Kyrgyz Republic[1]

DEVELOPING NEW CAPACITIES IN A POST-TRANSITION COUNTRY

Introduction

Capacity development is characterized by three main activities: skills upgrading (both general and job-specific), organizational strengthening and procedural improvements. The skills enhancement component includes general education, on-the-job training and professional improvements in crosscutting skills such as accounting, policy analysis and information technology. Organizational strengthening covers what some have defined as institutional development – reinforcing the capacity of an organization to use available funds and staff more effectively. The procedural improvement refers to functional changes or systemic reforms. In the volume preceding this work, UNDP has referred to a facet of capacity development as the "societal" dimension, involving capacities of society as a whole (Fukuda-Parr et al, 2002).

Over the last decade, several factors have increased the significance of technical cooperation (TC), including globalization, the information revolution, the growth in international markets, and an acceleration of the democratization and decentralization of national authority. Technical cooperation itself, however, has undergone little change. The purpose of this chapter is to analyze TC and the role it can play in developing

[1] This paper was prepared by Jacek Cukrowski, Senior Expert, Center for Social and Economic Research (CASE) and Professor, University of Finance and Management, Poland. Contributing authors include Roman Mogilevsky, Executive Director and Senior Economist, CASE-Kyrgyzstan; Radislawa Gortat, Collaborator, CASE-Warsaw and Senior Lecturer, Warsaw University; Marek Dabrowski, Chairman of the Council, CASE-Warsaw, and Member of Poland's Monetary Board.

lasting capacities in Kyrgyzstan. The main focus is an analysis and assessment of the following five issues: (i) the overall record, dynamics and profile of the TC relationship; (ii) TC's contribution to capacity development, (iii) donor and government TC policies and practices; (iv) promising alternatives and options; and (v) factors and conditions that enable or constrain TC's contribution to capacity development.

Background

The Central Asian Republic of Kyrgyzstan attained independence just 10 years ago. It has a population of nearly five million and is land-locked. Its presidential system of government and two-chamber Parliament are elected by universal franchise. More than 65% of the population is Kyrgyz, and there are two minority ethnic groups, Russian (Slav) and Uzbek. A majority of the population is Muslim, but other religions are practiced. As part of the former Soviet Union (FSU), its economy was organized through a central planning system.

One of the poorest FSU republics, Kyrgyzstan was historically dependent on trans-fers from the centre. In 1990, prior to independence, transfers from the central Soviet budget were equivalent to almost 11% of GDP. With the collapse of the Soviet Union and independence in 1991, the subsidies ceased. The triple transition to nationhood, democracy and the market economy has prompted an urgent need to build national capacity in all dimensions. In the first years of independence, with scarce financial resources, disintegrating economic links and hyperinflation, the country was forced to borrow from external sources in order to achieve macroeconomic stability and eco-nomic growth. After 10 years of independence, the situation has not changed much. External assistance still has a vital role to play in supporting the process of economic, social and political reforms by strengthening institutions, developing management systems and promoting the development of human capital.

The post-independence period can be divided into the phase of transformation (1992-1995), in which output declined rapidly, and the period of stabilization and growth (1996 onwards), in which there was a renewal of economic expansion. In the first phase, GDP declined by 45% and standards of living fell sharply, a trend exacer-bated by high inflation. The change from a controlled to a market economy took a heavy toll on the population. Since 1996, growth in GDP has resumed, and there is greater macroeconomic stability. Kyrgyzstan is a low-income country and its GDP per capita in the year 2000 was about $270, ($2,521 in purchasing power parity terms). The country's economy is relatively open, with exports accounting for about 44% of GDP, and imports around 55%.

Kyrgyzstan placed 102nd out of 173 countries on UNDP's 2002 Human Development Index, compared with neighboring Kazakhstan's 79th place ranking. With less than half of Kazakhstan's income per head, however, Kyrgyzstan's life expectancy, at 67.8 years, is a shade higher than its wealthier neighbor. Kyrgyzstan also performs comparatively well on the two other components of the index: adult literacy and gross enrolment ratios (97% against 99%, and 68% to 77%, respectively). Government expenditure on education has remained above 20% of the total since 1985.

TC – Overall Features

Technical cooperation for capacity development is of special importance to countries such as Kyrgyzstan, which are not rich in natural resources, and where opportunities for economic development are related mainly to effective economic management and use of available human potential. It is consequently scarcely surprising that Kyrgyzstan is vitally interested in all forms of TC.

Kyrgyzstan has come under increasing pressure to reform TC since the early 1980s, well before the start of the transition process in former communist countries. In spite of these pressures, TC has not lived up to its potential, and is still being criticized for being inefficient, donor-driven, and even undermining indigenous capacities. There are weaknesses on all sides: in recipient countries, among donors and in the development industry.

Recipient countries often suffer from weak leadership and thus lack strategic vision and ownership of reform processes. They are criticized for having inadequate systems of accountability and public participation, misguided policies and priorities, a lack of transparency, corruption, "demotivated officials", bureaucratic red tape, inflexibility and disinterest in development. In some cases, local governments, NGOs and civil society organizations serve their own interests with donor resources. Domestic pressures often result in competition rather than cooperation with other partners. Bilateral and multilateral partners drive and maintain existing attitudes and approaches.

Donors, particularly through the OECD/DAC, have in principle agreed to new partnership approaches that place national ownership at the centre of development efforts. There is a common consensus, however, that donors still tend to dominate the identification, design and implementation of projects. As a result, provision of TC is largely supply-driven. Key criticisms directed towards donors practices include: inappropriate development concepts and incentives; lack of downward accountability and transparency in processes and reporting; hidden strategic agendas; inhibitory procedures and rules; inappropriate capacities; and for undermining local capacities, institutions and organizations. High levels of funding also create serious distortions in the recipient country labour market, with local experts increasingly seeking levels of remuneration that only international organizations can provide.

The development industry is driven, to a great degree, by a genuine motivation to help the poor and enable governments and civil society actors to better perform their tasks. In reality, however, the staff and procedures of many development agencies seem poorly equipped to make the necessary reforms. The development industry has a vested interest in "staying on the job" and attracting sources of funding. It has also been recognized that international aid has worked primarily with an established pool of service providers at arguably high costs. In many cases, the pricing of TC services remains largely insulated from the principles of comparative advantage and immune to the forces of market competition.

Main Sources of TC

Kyrgyzstan has been the recipient of quite significant amounts of official development assistance (ODA) since independence, reaching over 9% of its GDP in 1999 (see Table 6.1).

Technical cooperation began to flow into Kyrgyzstan in 1992, and in some years constituted more than half of the total value of ODA. According to the database created at UNDP's Kyrgyzstan country office, the amount of TC increased steadily until 1998, when it topped out at $35 million, before falling back in 1999 and 2000 (see Table 6.2 and Figure 6.1). Total TC during the nine-year period 1992-2000 amounted to $204.6 million or $45 per capita, which is quite a high level by international standards.

The major donors among international organizations are the United Nations (UNDP in particular), the Asian Development Bank (ADB), the World Bank and the European Union (through its grant-financed TACIS programme). Among bilaterals, Germany, Turkey, Switzerland and Japan contribute a significant share. Among non-governmental organizations, the Soros Foundation made the biggest contribution. Major donors, which provided more than $20 million each, are Germany (21% of total TC amount), the Soros Foundation (12%), Turkey (11%) and the UN system (10%).

At various periods, different donors played the leading role in the provision of TC. After independence in 1992-1994, Turkey was the largest foreign partner, but its contribution subsequently fell back as Germany and the Soros Foundation became the country's major donors. The UN contribution has also greatly increased since 1997 (see Table 6.3).

In terms of TC allocation by sector, the pattern has been very diverse, covering 20 sectors. Nine received more than $1 million per year on average, reflecting the fact that after independence, many spheres of public activity and social life had to be developed almost from nothing.

The most heavily supported sectors were human resource development ($37.9 million or 18.5% of total TC), economic management ($29.4 million or 14.4%), health ($25.5 million or 12.4%), agriculture ($23.4 million or 11.5%) and public administration ($19.3 million or 9.4%).

The main components of TC (in terms of money spent) in these sectors included the following: consulting services; assistance in developing sectoral policy, legislation, planning and management; building information systems; and institutional and organizational support to local authorities. The basic characteristics of TC projects in these five major sectors are presented briefly below.

Human resource development – Within this sector, education and cultural cooperation programmes have dominated. Projects have included assistance in founding

TABLE 6.1: TRENDS IN OFFICIAL DEVELOPMENT ASSISTANCE (ODA), 1992-99

Year	1992	1993	1994	1995	1996	1997	1998	1999
Total, US$ millions	3.43	69.4	86.96	96.83	99.37	50.42	79.81	115.56
% of GDP	0.15	1.61	2.72	2.91	5.44	2.84	4.85	9.18
% of Gov. Revenue	0.93	10.38	17.43	17.44	36.74	18.55	27.55	70.58
% of Budget (revenue+deficit)	0.50	7.12	11.67	10.33	26.92	13.98	23.54	59.19
% of Exports	1.21	19.93	23.33	21.61	17.66	7.46	13.47	21.85
Per capita	0.76	15.48	19.44	21.45	21.72	10.88	17.12	24.04

Sources: OECD, World Bank

TABLE 6.2: TRENDS IN TECHNICAL COOPERATION, 1992-99

Year	1992	1993	1994	1995	1996	1997	1998	1999	2000
Total, US$ millions	3.03	3.93	14.17	25.53	30.49	33.67	35.04	30.04	28.65
% of GDP	0.13	0.09	0.44	0.77	1.67	1.89	2.13	2.39	2.20
% of ODA	88.34	5.66	16.29	26.37	30.68	66.78	43.90	26.00	13.34
% of Gov. Revenue	0.82	0.59	2.84	4.60	11.27	12.38	12.10	18.35	14.65
% of Budget	0.44	0.40	1.90	2.72	8.26	9.33	10.33	15.39	12.93
% of Exports	1.06	1.13	3.80	5.70	5.42	4.98	5.91	5.68	5.11
Per capita, USD	0.67	0.88	3.17	5.66	6.66	7.26	7.52	6.25	5.83

Sources: UNDP, World Bank

FIGURE 6.1: TRENDS IN TECHNICAL COOPERATION VOLUME, 1992-2000

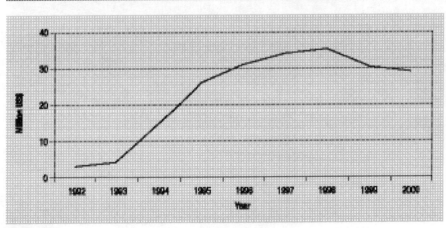

Source: UNDP

TABLE 6.3: TECHNICAL COOPERATION BY DONOR, 1992-2000 (US$ THOUSANDS)

Year	1992	1993	1994	1995	1996	1997	1998	1999	2000	Total
GRAND TOTAL	3,031	3,925	14,171	25,532	30,491	33,671	35,041	30,048	28,649	204,559
Germany	0	915	2,435	4,590	4,428	5,600	6,771	5,582	12,278	42,599
Soros Foundation	0	0	0	3,364	3,541	4,162	4,551	4,722	3,854	24,194
Turkey	3,031	1,818	4,681	3,567	2,645	2,822	4,323	0	0	22,887
UN Organizations	0	350	809	1,048	1,147	2,774	4,838	5,735	4,554	21,255
Asian Development Bank	0	0	30	1,190	5,342	3,585	2,970	4,577	2,058	19,752
Switzerland	0	365	1,343	2,690	3,607	2,481	2,006	2,366	2,115	16,973
World Bank	0	0	400	1,981	1,524	2,349	2,483	2,599	1,586	12,922
Japan	0	230	1,980	3,210	2,850	2,860	1,310	373	40	12,853
European Commission	0	0	0	0	1,841	1,844	1,789	2,577	990	9,041
EBRD	0	45	1,019	1,787	1,321	787	930	700	0	6,589
Netherlands	0	202	759	1,287	1,363	458	360	159	10	4,598
Denmark	0	0	707	568	342	2673	0	0	217	4,507
Finland	0	0	0	0	0	600	1,900	1	5	2,506
Islamic Development Bank	0	0	0	250	200	98	340	90	0	978
DFID	0	0	8	0	340	410	58	0	0	816
Sweden	0	0	0	0	0	0	0	112	484	596
USA	0	0	0	0	0	98	151	230	0	479
IOM	0	0	0	0	0	70	78	130	0	278
IMF	0	0	0	0	0	0	0	0	200	200
China	0	0	0	0	0	0	183	0	0	183
Bill & Melinda Gates Foundation	0	0	0	0	0	0	0	0	138	138
OSCE	0	0	0	0	0	0	0	23	109	132
Centre For Diseases Control	0	0	0	0	0	0	0	37	0	37
Canada	0	0	0	0	0	0	0	35	0	35
Ireland	0	0	0	0	0	0	0	0	6	6
Norway	0	0	0	0	0	0	0	0	5	5

Source: UNDP

TABLE 6.4: TECHNICAL COOPERATION BY MAJOR DONOR, 1992-2000 (% OF TOTAL)

Year	1992	1995	1998	2000
Finland	0.00	17.98	19.32	42.86
Sweden	100.00	13.97	12.34	0.00
USA	0.00	10.54	5.72	7.38
Canada	0.00	12.57	3.74	0.14
Other bilateral	0.00	7.26	7.40	2.51
UN Organisations	0.00	4.10	13.81	15.90
Asian Development Bank	0.00	4.66	8.48	7.18
World Bank	0.00	7.76	7.09	5.54
European Commission	0.00	0.00	5.11	3.46
EBRD	0.00	7.00	2.65	0.00
Other multilateral	0.00	7.98	4.01	1.56
Soros Foundation	0.00	13.18	12.99	13.45
Total bilateral	100.00	62.32	48.53	52.92
Total multilateral	0.00	24.50	38.49	33.63

Source:UNDP

new colleges such as the American University in Kyrgyzstan and the Kyrgyz-Turkish University; assistance in vocational and foreign languages training systems; publishing and purchasing textbooks and other training literature; grants for local researchers to participate in international conferences; programmes for improving professional skills; and assistance to libraries and other cultural institutions.

Economic management – Technical cooperation to this sector has focused on training programmes and strengthening training centres for civil servants employed in the major economic agencies (including the Ministry of Finance and the National Bank). A considerable portion was composed of investment-related TC projects aimed at preparing capital projects in different sectors of the economy (such as energy and agriculture) that were later funded by international organizations.

Health Care – Technical cooperation to this sector has consisted in the provision of medicines, equipment, training for medical personnel, and advocacy programmes for various health protection issues such as AIDS and reproductive health.

Agriculture – In this area, TC has targeted land reform efforts and new forms of farm management. This includes restructuring large state and collective farms into private ones, creating water-user associations and developing agricultural infrastructure. Considerable attention has been paid to the creation of a system for financing agricultural enterprises – in particular, strengthening the Kyrgyz Agricultural Financial Corporation. Numerous projects providing microfinance for agricultural (and non-agricultural) activities in rural areas have been implemented and considerable resources have been directed to forestry support.

Public administration – Technical cooperation programmes within this sector have been quite diversified, but mainly oriented towards supporting selected government agencies (such as the Presidential Administration, the Prime Minister's Office, ministries) and local authorities. Technical cooperation included numerous civil service training programmes, support to the country's participation in international organizations, and efforts at creating elements of an e-governance system, including "Shailoo", an automated information system for electoral processes.

The main recipients were the following ministries: Health (8.4% of the total), Agriculture and Water Resources (6.9%), Finance (6.9%) and Education and Culture (5.1%). The top 10 major recipients are all central government bodies, reflecting priority sectors of assistance. Another notable characteristic, however, was the large number of smaller organizations receiving TC – those that fall under the "Other" category. All together, this group's allocation comprises more than 40% of total TC.

Detailed analysis of information about TC reveals its prevailing forms.

Institution building – Many TC projects were directed towards the development of government organizations, because of the need to establish them from scratch. These projects included support in developing the public administration system, clarifying the roles and functions of different government agencies, and the provision of equipment. In the second part of the decade, donors began to provide the same sort of assistance to civil society organizations, especially educational institutions, NGOs and some mass media.

Training – Training activities play a central role in many TC programmes. They include courses for government officials, on-site training, study tours, and support to young people's education in internationally recognized universities. This activity also includes establishing special educational institutions such as the Banking Training Centre.

Access to information – Considering the insufficient development of information infrastructure and the geographic barriers to the movement of people, a sizeable component of TC programming has focused on eliminating the information gap. The main forms of this assistance included establishing information centres providing free access to foreign mass media, social and political literature, as well as information about education and economic opportunities in developed countries. The Soros-Kyrgyzstan Foundation information centre and the IREX Resource Centre financed by the US Government are the best examples of such initiatives. Another important focus has been providing people with free access to the Internet, in particular by UNDP, the Soros Foundation and IREX. It is especially important that this kind of activity was targeted at youth and students.

Consulting – Consultancy services to government agencies and enterprises are the most expensive activities in the framework of TC projects. They are provided mainly by foreign experts with long- and short-term advisory missions. Their role consists of

TABLE 6.5: TECHNICAL COOPERATION BY SECTOR, 1992-2000 (US$ 000S)

Year	1992	1993	1994	1995	1996	1997	1998	1999	2000	Total
GRAND TOTAL	3,032	3,925	14,172	25,535	30,490	33,670	35,040	30,047	28,649	204,559
Economic Management	120	1,334	3,391	4,423	3,039	4,253	5,705	3,471	3,650	29,386
Development Administration	0	556	950	1,448	2,456	2,757	3,612	3,718	3,785	19,282
Natural Resources	0	0	267	1,090	2,330	1,451	1,962	1,664	1,311	10,075
Human Resources Development	2,912	1,416	3,122	4,974	5,035	4,069	7,813	5,255	3,273	37,869
Agriculture, Forestry and Fisheries	0	0	985	2,207	5,859	5,081	3,404	3,500	2,400	23,436
Area Development	0	0	36	245	178	178	983	1,458	946	4,024
Industry	0	0	200	1,400	2,848	3,592	2,659	1,953	200	12,852
Energy	0	45	126	704	342	413	82	87		1,799
International Trade	0	0	40	200	250	140	260	180	540	1,610
Domestic Trade	0	0	420	129	131	0	0	0	0	680
Transport	0	0	48	43	1147	809	871	990	600	4,508
Communications	0	16	1,620	3,499	2,352	946	620	533	235	9,821
Social Development	0	0	0	611	230	1,376	3,001	2,770	2,553	10,541
Health		350	1,915	2,584	2,969	5,654	2,491	2,741	6,761	25,465
Disaster Preparedness	0	0	0	0	0	0	93	93	93	279
Humanitarian Aid and Relief	0	0	0	0	350	319	123	152	615	1,559
Political Participation, NGO, civil support	0	0	0	308	391	425	276	433	627	2,460
Judicial reform	0	32	248	357	20	68	284	599	617	2,225
Banking system	0	155	569	495	1	0	0	0	0	1,220
Other	0	21	235	818	562	2,139	801	450	443	5,469

Source: UNDP

providing government agencies – and sometimes the private sector – with method-ological assistance in the preparation of legislative and normative documents and analytical tools. This training should help in developing consistent government policies.

Participation in international organizations – Another form of TC is enabling Kyrgyzstan to participate in international organizations and agreements. Technical cooperation in this area mainly consists of an explanation of the goals and forms of activity of these organizations. In some cases, international organizations provide money for membership fees.

Research and culture – A relatively small but important part of TC goes towards developing research and cultural potential. This means involving local specialists in international research projects, supporting environmental studies, and developing analytical capacity. The same assistance is provided in the cultural and arts spheres.

Preparation of investment projects – An essential component of TC projects is connected with implementing the most expensive type of external financial aid – investment projects. This includes sectoral research and feasibility studies for anticipated investment projects.

Figure 6.2 presents the expenditure structure of TC projects estimated on the basis of a UNDP database. It is notable that the salaries of foreign experts constitute the second biggest item.

During the last few years, significant changes have taken place in the sectoral structure of TC. The share of TC to industry, agriculture and communication in 1998-2000 was considerably reduced. At the same time, donors' attention to public administration and social and regional development increased. This demonstrates the change in priorities of both the Government and donors. To some extent, it is also a result of critical analysis of results from previous TC programmes.

The information on TC in Kyrgyzstan reveals some important trends that determine, to a large extent, how projects are implemented and how efficient aid programmes are.

Multiplicity of Donors

Dozens of different donor organizations are active in the country. At least 10 of them can be considered as large TC suppliers. On the one hand, donor multiplicity ensures considerable TC inflow into the country and potentially creates opportunities for faster development. On the other hand, this multiplicity generates numerous problems. There is a clear lack of coordination among donors, as well as duplication of activities originating from different agendas and discrepancies in methods and approaches. This leads to the conclusion that the large number of donors creates more problems than it solves.

Multiplicity of Sectors

As mentioned above, TC programmes affect many sectors. This is a reflection of the specific priorities of each donor and Kyrgyzstan's readiness to accept almost every TC proposal, which was especially characteristic of the first years of independence. Too often, this led to the dissipation of aid and insufficient focus for creating truly sustainable changes in the desired direction.

Government as the Largest TC Recipient

An important feature of TC programmes in Kyrgyzstan is the predominance of the Government as an aid recipient. Because many problems addressed by TC are related

FIGURE 6.2: TC STRUCTURE BY TYPE OF EXPENDITURE

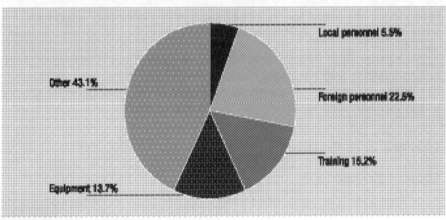

Local personnel 5.5%

Foreign personnel 22.5%

Training 15.2%

Equipment 13.7%

Other 43.1%

Source: UNDP

to the provision of public goods, this makes sense, at least theoretically. The abundance of TC projects focused on government structures, however, detracts from their individual effectiveness. This is because the Government's ability to absorb aid is low – much lower than that of civil society organizations. Also, concentrating TC resources within government does not help in delimiting and clarifying the roles and functions of government.

Uneven Territorial Distribution

Another peculiarity of TC programmes in Kyrgyzstan is their excessive concentration in the capital, Bishkek. This concentration reflects the fact that the majority of pro-grammes are focused on nation-wide issues. Another reason is the availability of much better infrastructure (communications, local staff, etc.) in Bishkek. Territorial concen-tration results in uneven development opportunities, especially for rural areas. At the same time, it is clear that a mechanical reallocation of TC projects to provinces will not solve the problem, because of the region's lack of absorptive capacity. Territorial reallo-cation requires a change in the design of TC programmes that would have to account for the specificity of needs and potential in different parts of the country.

TC Programmes and Conditionality

A specific feature of TC activities is their relationship with programme and investment loans and grants. Implementation of TC projects is often a prerequisite for the alloca-tion of such loans. This relationship is quite logical, but very often leads to a situation wherein recommendations produced in the framework of TC projects are perceived by beneficiaries as something thrust upon them, as an "unavoidable evil" they must accept. This practice is clearly antithetical to country ownership, even if the condition-ality associated with TC programmes is not very rigorous. Lack of success in implementing projects or the beneficiary's failure to comply with conditions does not lead to an immediate withdrawal of aid. This provokes insufficiently careful and real-istic design of TC projects by donors and TC providers, and ambiguous behaviour by beneficiaries, who almost always formally agree with project ideas and content, but rarely intend to implement the recommendations.

To sum up, while it is possible to note the impact of TC on a large number of sec-tors, its influence does not always result in the direction desired by stakeholders. In its current scale and form, TC greatly exceeds the absorptive capacity of the country, with an immediate and negative impact on its effectiveness.

Changes in TC Practices and Management

Strategic Documents

By the latter half of the last decade, there was consensus among the main donors and local policy makers that one of the reasons for low effectiveness of TC projects was the absence of a clear national development strategy. Technical cooperation projects were fragmented, uncoordinated and non-complementary. An overall operational and gov-ernance framework was needed to shift from a project- to a policy- and programme-based approach. With the strong support and assistance of international donors, local authorities developed the *National Strategy for Sustainable Human Development* and the *Comprehensive Development Framework* as umbrella frameworks. Their basic con-cepts are characterized below.

National Strategy for Sustainable Human Development – The NSSHD was initiat-ed in 1996-97 by UNDP and approved by a National Forum in 1997. The NSSHD is the country's long-term development strategy, leading up to the year 2015. It provides a conceptual foundation for national development in the 21st century, and a platform for overall coordination of development activities. The Strategy aims to achieve its devel-opment objectives based on domestic resources – human, social and environmental. The basic idea is to link national priorities and development programmes, and trans-form them into nation-wide policy.

Under the NSSHD, the country's commitment to social progress is reflected in seven components, with a system of objectives that are to be met by solving a range of medium- and short-term tasks. The main components are: (i) the integration of soci-ety, (ii) overcoming internal and external isolation, (iii) overcoming threats to human security, (iv) developing natural capacity, (v) developing human and social potential, (vi) promoting a competitive economy, and (vii) building democratic governance. Several thematic programmes have also been developed, including poverty allevia-tion, governance and environment.

A big disadvantage, however, is the lack of a built-in mechanism to implement tasks. As a result, many statements in the NSSHD have remained mere good inten-tions and many short-term strategy targets have been missed.

Comprehensive Development Framework (CDF) - In March 1999, Kyrgyzstan was selected as a pilot country for the World Bank-supported Comprehensive Development Framework. In this regard, the Government began to formulate a national development strategy for 2000-2010. The CDF is based on two important principles. The first focuses on public participation in the discussion, preparation and realization of CDF objectives. This involves bringing NGOs, academia, media, business, local and national government, and international organizations together to define development objectives and the means of attaining them.

The second principle is a comprehensive approach to the process of achieving CDF objectives, taking into consideration human and physical factors of development. The CDF document was finalized in 2001 and was also approved by the National Forum. The CDF clearly states national priorities and goals, highlighting three main interrelated areas for focused effort by government and society: good governance, social development and sustainable economic growth.

The CDF attempts to analyze and quantify all required and available resources for strategy implementation. While the final document is based on a number of assumptions that may seem optimistic, the attempt to achieve a balance between goals and means is a new and positive change. The country's visible ownership is another important feature of the CDF. Finally, one sign of a more responsible approach is the inclusion of a special chapter on monitoring and evaluation.

Government Initiatives

The Government has not traditionally given high priority to TC projects, focusing instead on resource-rich investment projects and budgetary aid. Recently however, the Government has taken steps to improve coordination of TC activities. In December 2000, the President dissolved the State Committee for Foreign Investment and Economic Development, a specialized body responsible for TC coordination, and transferred these functions to the Ministry of Finance. The decision reflected the Government's dissatisfaction with TC practices and the committee's failure to coordinate TC activities and attract foreign investment. The Ministry of Finance now coordinates all government-related TC and manages the relationship with donors. No TC projects with a government agency as a counterpart can begin without prior approval by the Ministry.

Measures to improve the financial transparency of projects have been undertaken as well. For example, new regulations governing remunerations of local project staff have been approved. Applying them to the managers and staff of TC projects could realize significant "savings". Much still remains to be done in the sphere of transparency. No attempt to integrate government-related TC projects into the government budget has been made. This obviously weakens the coordinating capabilities of the Ministry of Finance and does not allow for effective public control – in resources terms – of a very significant part of the activities of governmental agencies.

The lack of coordination is problematic. To date, the Government does not have any comprehensive database of projects. The first attempt to create one was undertaken by UNDP's Kyrgyzstan office, on the basis of the now-defunct Goskominvest's information. The Ministry of Finance is now compiling its own database with the help of the TACIS Coordinating Unit. Reflecting the priorities set in the CDF, more attention is now paid to attracting foreign investors: the Government considers the fostering of an attractive investment climate as one of the most important functions of TC. The newly-appointed Special Representative of the President for the Attraction of Foreign Investment has assumed an important role in TC project selection and aid coordination.

Donor Activities

In recognition of some of the underlying problems with the TC scenario, many donors, including UNDP, TACIS and the World Bank, have produced their own programme frameworks to drive their inputs.

Based on the UNDP Country Review for Kyrgyzstan, the UN Common Country Assessment and the National Sustainable Human Development Strategy, the latest UNDP Country Cooperation Framework was formulated in 1999 for the period 2000-2004. The core themes include the intensification and deepening of democratic governance reforms and the creation of conditions for market-based solutions for poverty alleviation. The objectives are to be achieved through: (i) changing the role and functions of the state and creating the infrastructure for democracy and accountability, (ii) poverty alleviation and social governance, and (iii) political reconciliation and preventive development. The document also has two cross-cutting themes: gender in development/promoting the economic and political empowerment of women during transition, and aid coordination.

Beyond programme framework documents, donors have also implemented changes in the way they organize projects, albeit sometimes with contrasting results. For example, UNDP has switched from a large number of relatively small, less accountable projects to fewer, larger programmes with clearly specified objectives and more transparent procedures. The transition to a programme, rather than a project approach has been the trend in donor policy. TACIS, however, has begun shifting from larger, less successful but ambitious projects, to smaller ones with very concrete and realistic objectives.

Both UNDP and TACIS claim these changes will improve results. Both organizations also agree on the desirability of reducing the number of Chief Technical Advisors (CTA), the most expensive components of projects. They are also gradually decreasing the use of short-term expatriate consultants who do not bear full responsibility for the project, relying more on local consultants.

Coordination of International NGOs

Although the activities of international NGOs in Kyrgyzstan only account for a small proportion of total TC, these organizations are important for national capacity building. Because their activities are more distant from government, coordination is difficult. UNDP is playing an intermediary role in gathering and distributing information on NGOs. An upcoming UNDP Development Cooperation Report that includes the results of a survey on donor TC activities will include those of international NGOs.

TC for FSU Countries

In the last several years, a number of international organizations and private donors have supported activities related to national capacity building, mainly through human capital development and support to civil society. The activities of the organizations described below were designed not only for Kyrgyzstan, but for all FSU countries. One of the most active and probably the most successful organizations is the Soros Foundation (see Box 6.1).

Other programmes that aim to increase national capacity for FSU countries are the Joint Vienna Institute (JVI) and the Economic Education and Research Consortium (EERC). Both of these organizations are located abroad and provide support to local staff. Both of them focus on human development, but JVI provides training mainly to policy makers while EERC provides support to researchers involved in economic policy research. After almost 10 years of activities, JVI has begun to assess the impact of its training on national capacity. Representatives are currently visiting countries involved with the programme in order to establish an alumni network (see Box 6.2).

Local NGOs

The importance of local non-governmental initiatives in national capacity development has been widely recognized. In Kyrgyzstan, the development of civil society organizations has been slow. Among the limited number is the Centre for Social and Economic Research (CASE-Kyrgyzstan).

CASE-Kyrgyzstan was established with the help of CASE-Poland and with the initial financial support of Soros Foundations' Open Society Institute. In the process of establishing the organization, the experience gained during the Polish transition and advice of Polish experts was utilized extensively. The founding of CASE-Kyrgyzstan can thus be considered a good example of horizontal (South-South) cooperation (see Box 6.3).

In sum, despite numerous problems with TC implementation, there have nevertheless been positive changes. First, Kyrgyzstan has developed strategic frameworks that provide for better targeting of TC activity and long-term development planning. Second, donors now have mid-term TC frameworks of their own, which can facilitate inter-donor coordination. Third, there is now a deeper understanding – even if more action is yet to materialize – on the part of the Government of the need for radical improvement in TC coordination. Fourth, there are valuable regional institutions of capacity development from which Kyrgyzstan can benefit, promising a strengthening of human potential and dissemination of best practices. And fifth, there is the increasing involvement of local research institutions, NGOs and individual specialists in TC activities.

BOX 6.1: Activities of the Soros Foundation-Kyrgyzstan

The Soros Foundation-Kyrgyzstan has operated since January 1993. The Foundation's mission is to create the necessary conditions for building an open society through support to public institutes and initiatives. Education, science and culture are priority fields of activity. The Foundation works towards achieving its goals through a number of programmes. They include:

- The Civic Education and Democracy Programme (familiarizing students with human rights concepts and the fundamentals of constitutional democracy; assisting educators in developing and disseminating methodological literature; introducing new subjects).

- Economic Reform Programme (the Soros Economics Olympiad; training programmes for economics teachers; a children's economics school).

- Higher Education Support Programme (established the School of Future Elite; seminars; exchange programmes; summer schools for students and professors; internships).

- Regional Student Exchange Programme.

- Mass Media Programme (consultations, seminars and internships).

- Publishing Programme (seminars for publishers; consulting on modern equipment; funds for publishing books and textbooks by local authors related to national culture, history and humanitarian subjects).

The Foundation's activities have not been limited to the programmes mentioned above. Projects have been successfully implemented in other fields such as gender, refugees and health. The Foundation's Open Society Institute also supports the American University in Kyrgyzstan and a number of local NGOs.

Profile of Stakeholders in TC

Kyrgyzstan hosts about 25 donor agencies, many foundations and a large number of international NGOs. Among them are powerful multilaterals (WB, IMF, UNDP, TACIS, ADB) and bilateral donors like the United States Agency for International Development (USAID), the German Technical Fund (GTZ), the Danish International Development Agency (DANIDA) and the Turkish Agency for International Development. Almost all of them exert pressure on Kyrgyz authorities to implement their proposals, and the abundance of actors brings forth a potentially chaotic array of projects derived from different cultures.

At the beginning of the transition, TC was entirely supply-driven. From the latter part of the 1990s, however, the relations between stakeholders have become more balanced, although the initiative in designing TC still resides with donors.

Self-perpetuation is a driving force. Technical cooperation provides jobs for those involved, and the effectiveness of TC is compromised by the continuation of projects even where no significant results have been achieved. For example, the lack of progress in reforming the state apparatus has not resulted in any marked changes of orientation. The absence of change may be partly justified by the inherent limitations

BOX 6.2: Regional TC Initiatives

The Joint Vienna Institute (JVI) was established in 1992 by a number of international organizations (including the International Monetary Fund, the World Bank, the World Trade Organization) and the Austrian Government. The Institute offers a variety of courses in the areas of economic and financial administration and management, primarily for public officials. JVI training has two components: the Seminar Programme and the Main Programme. The Seminar Programme consists of a series of stand-alone, specialized courses of short duration. The Main Programme includes Introductory and Applied Economics Policy courses. The JVI's Introductory Course in Market Economics and Financial Analysis is an 8- week course taught in three regional centres: Kiev, Moscow and Tashkent. Their purpose is to provide an intensive introduction to the principles of modern market economics and financial analysis. At the end of this course, selected participants are invited to Vienna attend the Applied Economics Policy Course. Since 1992, JVI has trained approximately 600 participants from 31 transition economies, including over 20 from Kyrgyzstan. In addition, hundreds of people have taken part in various JVI workshops and seminars.

The Economics Education and Research Consortium (EERC) was created with international funding in 1995 to strengthen economics education and research capabilities in CIS countries. The initial focus was on graduate-level education in Ukraine, and research in Russia. Since 2000, EERC-Russia has served as the regional representative of the Global Development Network (GDN) among CIS countries. With support from the GDN, Russian EERC activities have been extended to other FSU countries (including Kyrgyzstan), leading to the creation of a CIS-wide research network. The EERC mission is to promote a research culture, encourage economists to work at the frontiers of the discipline, and subject their research to international standards of excellence. The EERC puts special emphasis on capacity development and the formation of a CIS-wide professional network of economists engaged in policy-relevant studies. The EERC delivers funding for original research through a cycle of semi-annual grant competitions and special research projects. In addition to funding, network members are provided with many opportunities for professional growth through participation in international research workshops, conferences and seminars. The EERC also conducts a variety of training programmes aimed at developing the capacities of individual scholars throughout the region. One research development programme launched in 2000, the Transition Economics Research Network (TERN), is primarily targeted at younger scholars. In 2000, a TERN summer school session took place in Kyrgyzstan, with one-third of the participants from the country.

BOX 6.3: Centre for Social and Economic Research in Kyrgyzstan

The Centre for Social and Economic Research in Kyrgyzstan (CASE-Kyrgyzstan) is an independent, non-governmental research organization founded by the Centre for Social and Economic Research in Poland. Established in 1998, CASE-Kyrgyzstan's mission is to assist social and economic development through research, training and advisory activities. The Centre is one of the country's first think tanks. All activities are based on a principle of independence from government and non-engagement with political parties and organizations. All staff members are Kyrgyz citizens. CASE-Kyrgyzstan collaborates with the Kyrgyz Government and international development organizations, including the World Bank, ADB, UNDP, TACIS, the Open Society Institute and USAID. The Centre is active in research on a broad spectrum of topics including macroeconomic forecasting; fiscal, monetary and social policy; agricultural economics; foreign trade; privatization; and investment. CASE-Kyrgyzstan publishes the quarterly *Kyrgyz Economic Outlook*, which contains a detailed analysis of recent economic developments and provides a short-term forecast of basic macroeconomic indicators. Advisory activities are concentrated in TC to the Ministry of Finance, the Ministry of Agriculture, and other government agencies. An essential part of this assistance consists of quantifying the impact of various policy proposals; statistical analysis of the economic, social and budgetary context; and economic forecasting. The Centre provides training for government officials in microeconomics, macroeconomics, public finance, econometrics and information technologies.

of external aid. Donor agencies can formulate proposals for reform and provide TC, but in politically sensitive areas, only governments can take the difficult decisions.

Bilaterals – The TC decisions of individual donor countries are driven mostly by their respective policies (and sometimes geo-political) concerns. Following independence, Turkey focused on re-establishing cultural and political ties with the Turkish-speaking nations of Central Asia, and supported a number of projects aimed at human resource development, culture and institution building. From the middle of the 1990s, when it became Kyrgyzstan's main TC donor, Germany has focused on industrial investment projects as well as advice on governance policy and social service reform. Swiss assistance has concentrated on advisory and educational programmes in agriculture and business promotion. Japan has supported structural reforms, the development of cultural institutions and communications-related programmes. The Scandinavian countries have supported the reform of social services and ecology, whereas USAID's preferences have been wide-ranging: enterprise; trade; land, fiscal and local government reform; democratic culture; primary health care; and environmental management.

All bilateral donors have demonstrated a commitment to support reforms, backed by the necessary financial and human resources. But bilaterals have introduced their own distortions. Some have sought to "tie" their TC – directly through the acquisition of their equipment – or more indirectly, through cultural and political ties and the fostering of a conducive investment climates for their firms.

Bilateral donors have also differed in their choices of local partners. Some have cooperated closely, and worked with the Government. Others have preferred to operate more at arm's length, using intermediaries. Switzerland has concentrated more on development programmes at the local level, trying to combine the efforts of local authorities, NGOs and state agencies to support rural development.

International organizations – The contribution of international organizations is significant and is predominantly directed towards government institutions. UNDP focuses almost exclusively on policy advice at the central and local levels, while TACIS programmes are accompanied by technical equipment. Both organizations collaborate with the Government and participate in all stages of TC programming (planning, implementation, monitoring and evaluation). There is a certain degree of competition between UNDP and TACIS, which results in some duplication of effort.

Senior officials and the staff of international organizations like to make their own impact on the course of change in conformity with the goals and values of their organizations. Local publicity provides the incentive to do so, as well as the approbation of the authorities. Awards of merit are given by the Government to heads of international organizations at the end of their terms. Local staff and consultants of international organizations are motivated by high salaries, compared with pay rates in government.

Development banks – The Asian Development Bank and the World Bank have contributed most to TC programmes in Kyrgyzstan. The ADB focused first on education reform, and has gone on to finance a range of smaller programmes in agriculture, trade, industry, ecology and institution building (banking, Ministry of Economy, pension system reform).

The World Bank and other international financial institutions (such as the IMF) played a leading role in the Kyrgyz transition to a market economy. The World Bank was involved in privatizing industry and agriculture, reforming industry and the health sector, and various rural development projects.

The Bank has sometimes been criticized for development concepts that seem derived from a global cookbook rather than from local ingredients, as well as for insufficient efforts to build participation among local stakeholders. The latter accusation is perhaps only partly justified, as the country did not have a coherent concept of transition, and was thus ready to accept any and every donor proposal. In the second part of the 1990s, however, the Bank and other multilateral donors made substantial efforts to support national programmes in the social sphere, and involved all major local stakeholders in the preparation of the Comprehensive Development Framework.

The World Bank recently contributed to the state administration programme. Although its objectives are similar to those of earlier programmes supported by UNDP and TACIS, there is the expectation that the project will extend analytic work to other ministries and will monitor the implementation of previous recommendations. A continuation strategy was elaborated in cooperation with representatives of the UNDP and World Bank country missions.

Private foundations – Kyrgyzstan is a good example of a former Soviet republic where a private foundation, Soros-Kyrgyzstan, has played an important role in public life and the transition process. While other donors have concentrated on market reforms almost exclusively, Soros-Kyrgyzstan extended its work into other dimensions of transition – democracy, an open society and national identity building. The main incentive for establishing the Foundation in January 1993 was the image of the country then as an "island of democracy" in Central Asia.

The Foundation has benefited greatly from four interrelated factors: ample financial resources, independence from central authorities, powerful leadership and an impact on the intellectual elite. It has contributed to transparency of TC programmes and public work in general by publishing its annual financial reports, a jolting novelty in Kyrgyzstan. For all these reasons, Soros-Kyrgyzstan has become, on one hand, a quasi-opposition centre challenging the behavior of the political establishment, and on the other hand, the object of some envy.

A number of other organizations have recently started operations, including the Eurasia and the Friedrich Ebert foundations. They offer a set of educational programmes for Kyrgyz partners, although their activities are as yet much less visible.

International NGOs – Western NGOs have been central to the development of domestic NGOs. Both have focused mostly on education and training, and deliver the same set of educational services and programmes, which leads to an excess of supply over demand. Critics point out that the number of NGOs interested in training is decreasing and that the slogan "No more seminars" has become more vocal. Persistent concentration on training and development of organizational structures may hamper the growth of NGOs, because in a poor country, financial resources for primary missions are needed more than the endless mastering of organizational skills.

Religious organizations – The role of religious organizations in TC projects is negligible. The Dutch inter-church organization ACT works with pensioners and the elderly, and supports rural, community infrastructure projects. The Adventist Adra Foundation finances a system of home kitchens for the poor, accompanied by self-help training schemes for the elderly. Other religious organizations concentrate on pure charity.

Kyrgyz Authorities

As stated above, the Kyrgyz Government is the main recipient of TC. In the period immediately following independence, Kyrgyz authorities did not carry out any programming work connected with TC, acquiescing to every project submitted by donors. Technical cooperation programmes were mostly geared to restructuring the central organs of executive power. Only in 1998 did UNDP propose a decentralization programme prepared for local government, and a small-scale project on capacity building for Parliament.

The Kyrgyz authorities have benefited greatly from TC programmes. They helped to restructure the Government, create the State Property Fund, the State Investment Committee (or Goskominvest, the government agency responsible for privatization, foreign investment and aid, respectively), and the Tax and Customs offices. Technical cooperation programmes developed capacity in the Ministry of Foreign Affairs through language and other training, and also helped in restructuring the Ministry of Finance, which along with other state institutions, were supplied with modern technological equipment. Officials took advantage of numerous training programmes at home and abroad, and some went on to work on projects. These factors helped to develop an image of the ruling elite as reformers, and to engender self-confidence.

At the same time, the hierarchical structure of the strongly centralized state did not change and a number of poorly qualified civil servants retained key positions in the administration. Powerful politicians in central and local government committed themselves to hasty privatization, but did not tackle the moral hazards in the Government's involvement with banks, investment funds and corporations outside the financial sector. Lack of transparency and widespread corruption inhibited the process of change. Officials began to treat international assistance as a means to increase both power and income.

Programme coordinators, too, were pressured to treat the funds allocated to their respective programmes flexibly, in order to provide incentives for their Kyrgyz hosts. In a situation of donor competition, these pressures bore fruit. Typical incentives included equipment, jobs for relatives, paid lectures, foreign tours, payments for key information, and various other underhanded methods of "financing" officials. The "flexibility" shown by both sides reduced the effectiveness of aid. There was an impression that authorities desired TC to shore up the existing power structure, not to change it. Middle management expected financial and other returns from donors' interventions, and TC became a form of subsidy.

Local authorities are much more positive with respect to the decentralization programme, which helped build capacity among local government bodies through participatory planning. Communities also benefited from additional financial resources allocated by donors. The central authorities support the programme, and a growing number of donors are turning to projects focused on local government and development as a complementary and effective way of supporting change.

Ministries

To target external support more effectively, a number of specific sector programmes were drawn up in the mid-1990s. They included *Ayalzat* (a programme to improve women's position in society); *Jetkinchek* (a presidential initiative promoting access to education): *Emgek* (labour market and employment); and *Manas* (health). Donors contributed to the conception and implementation of reforms in health and education. Here, elements of partnership appeared; in the case of *Manas*, local NGOs were involved in the process of implementation and monitoring of TC programmes.

Despite significant successes, the programmes under consideration were not completed for a number of reasons. First, resources were insufficient. Another important factor was the rotation of top officials in the ministries, which resulted in a loss of institutional memory. One minister would sign the project, the next would oversee its implementation, and a third would receive the recommendations of evaluation missions. But nobody would take into account what had been done by predecessors. Competition among donors promoting models based on different principles advanced conflicting advice and complicated the strategic choices. Finally, corruption disrupted progress.

NGOs

Domestic NGOs have been playing a growing role in TC programmes. First, they are recipients of assistance and profit from it in many ways, such as institutional and skills development and technical equipment. Second, donors recognize them as important social actors, and their weight with respect to domestic authorities has been strengthened. Third, some of the more developed NGOs take part in TC implementation as providers of services or organizers of training. Fourth, NGOs have become the medium of mentality changes that are fundamental to the transition process.

NGOs benefit financially from TC that provides grants and creates jobs. NGOs have also created an important incentive for women to take a more active part in public life, in a context where men tend to monopolize politics. Finally, the NGO sector substitutes, in one way or another, for the political parties and free media that are absent in Kyrgyz public life.

At the same time, NGO programmes produce some ambiguous results. Many NGOs are primordially grant-seekers, switching from one kind of activity to another. Strong competition makes cooperation among existing organizations difficult, and discourages accountability. Finally, NGOs cannot solve many of the social and political problems they try to address. In many cases, a political solution or an intervention is needed from the state. This puts the dilemma of participation in politics at stake. The Government has made some efforts to invite "recognized" NGOs to join the Presidential Council of NGOs. But less known organizations still experience restrictions and harassment, resulting in a deepening of the divisions among NGOs.

Private Sector

The private sector has not been a principal beneficiary of TC, and Kyrgyz authorities have demonstrated a certain reluctance to promote this sector. UNIDO assistance to the Small and Medium Size Enterprise Development programme, for example, was located in the Ministry of Labour, not in the more strategic Ministry of Economy. The programme provided the training, expert services and financial resources to design and implement a private sector development strategy. Within the project (implemented over the period 1997-2000), some 3,500 representatives of small businesses received training. A number of "business incubators" were established and over 1,000 business plans prepared.

Recently, many more projects have aimed to support small business. The Swiss agency Helvetas provides assistance to enterprises in tourism and agriculture. Participants benefit from training, consulting services and access to data. In the case of the tourism enterprises, there has been a measurable impact on incomes. Agricultural firms have been hurt by three problems: lack of markets, low and variable profitability and the de-monetarization of the Kyrgyz rural economy.

Universities and Research Centres

As of the late 1990s, none of the Kyrgyz universities had delivered services or expertise for TC programmes as subcontractors. However, individual academics have been invited to take part in UNDP projects or have worked as trainers for various donors. Their experience has resulted in the creation of new centres that are aimed at providing services to international donors on a more regular basis.

The Centre of Human Development, for example, was established at the Kyrgyz-Russian-Slavonic University in 1998 to propagate ideas of human development. It focuses on monitoring social mobilization, the organization of social partnerships and advocacy. The Centre participates in research and educational projects dealing with human development.

A similar role is played by the Institute of Regional Studies, which takes part in UNDP's decentralization project, and monitors the national poverty alleviation programme (through studies administered by the World Bank and the ADB). The Centre of

Economic Research established at the National Academy of Sciences in 1998 is another potential partner that has not been part of the consultancy market.

A successful example of the potential of local expertise is given by the Centre for Public Opinion Studies and Forecasts. Established in 1998 with UNDP support, the Centre started its work on opinion polling research during the parliamentary and presidential elections in 2000, and publicized its results through the media. Thereafter, the Centre has conducted research on an assessment of UNDP services by its clients, a national survey on the quality of primary education, corruption in Kyrgyzstan and an analysis of Kyrgyz NGOs.

The Centre has built on its professionalism in many ways. It has received many requests for new research from the Presidential Administration, Parliament and donors. Staff members have been invited as consultants to Parliament. They have also started working as consultants in Tajikistan and Azerbaijan. Experience in collaboration with donor agencies and good relations with state structures and private business have contributed to its success.

At the same time, the findings of its *Monitoring Learning Achievements* study became the basis for discussion between donors and the administration concerning a common strategy in education. As a result, a five-year programme was drawn up, attracting support from UNICEF, UNESCO and other donors.

Local Consulting Firms

Technical cooperation programmes spawned nearly 30 local consulting firms that emerged in the second part of the 1990s. Many of them were established by former state officials or staff members of state agencies dealing with foreign aid (such as Goscominvest and the State Property Fund). Most consulting firms deliver narrowly specialized services such as internal audits for donors, or training in international standards of accounting for state agencies and private companies. Others offer advice and training for small business and state institutions. The most experienced firms have initiated work on wider programmes focusing on the country's utilization of international aid.

In this context, the KAPPA Group is worth noting. KAPPA is a consulting agency that sub-contracts to various projects. It is able to mobilize about 40 local consultants and takes part in most tenders announced by donor agencies. The head of the agency recently served as a voluntary advisor on international aid issues at the Ministry of Finance. He led the working group charged with preparing an institutional mechanism for more effective and transparent grant disbursement. KAPPA can be seen as an example of a new group of social actors capable of improving the process of planning, distribution and implementation of international aid.

Local consulting firms could lead to the emergence of more independent actors in TC relationships, and would provide for more competition. Until now, this option was limited by political and bureaucratic barriers, and lack of transparency in the selection process. In practice, winning a contract "costs" about 5%-10% of its value. Consulting firms are thus vitally interested in increasing the level of competition and transparency in the consulting market. For now, they are disadvantaged by a two-tier pricing system that remunerates the services of expatriate experts at higher rates than local consultants.

International Consulting Firms

International consulting firms service TC programmes as contractors or sub-contractors of donor agencies at commercial rates. Their overheads are high, usually amounting to 25% of direct costs. Some of them do not have permanent professional staff, but hire freelance consultants or local specialists when obtaining contracts. The consulting firms collaborate with the donor representatives in charge of financing project implementation, but do not provide for participation on the part of the Government. International consulting firms work for profit, and are not strongly committed to developing the capacity of local partners.

Apart from typical recruitment agencies, a number of more specialized foreign consulting firms also operate in Kyrgyzstan. They are strongly oriented towards local actors and their needs. An example is the Urban Institute (UI), which established its own office in Bishkek with USAID support to assist in the local government reform process. The UI dedicates itself to building local institutional capacity. Its work focuses on fostering strong partnerships with local counterparts to sustain reforms in municipal finance, and on improving effectiveness and accountability of local administrations. It is also involved in reviewing draft laws and training.

Finally, bilateral aid agencies contract specialized consulting firms to promote the skills of local partners in specific areas, such as agriculture. The absence of domestic specialists in areas like local government will ensure the presence of such firms for many years to come.

Lessons and Conclusions

Unlike Central and Eastern Europe, the Baltic states, Russia, Ukraine and even the Caucasus republics, Kyrgyzstan began its independent existence with a small political and intellectual elite that was able to address the challenges of state-building and a market economy. The country's real need was for TC related to both general strategic issues as well as a range of specific technical problems. As a relatively liberal country with a Government set on rapid modernization and market reform, Kyrgyzstan offered a much better climate for TC inflow than its neighbors.

The demand for TC led to a large supply of projects financed by multilateral and bilateral donors. Looking back over the last decade, there is little doubt that international TC helped Kyrgyzstan give momentum to its economic and institutional transition to a market economy, particularly between 1993 and 1996. Concrete results in individual sectors, however, have been mixed. Not all TC projects were effective in terms of addressing the priority needs of the country, or with respect to project design, sequencing, financing, internal organization and staffing, and so on.

A number of problems on both the recipient and donor sides reduced the overall effectiveness of TC. Oversupply, compared to the realistic absorptive capacity of the country, was probably the most important, at least in the early part of the decade. The oversupply was determined by motivations on the part of both donors and national authorities. Donors wanted to help a relatively poor and handicapped country that was committed to quickly reforming its economy and building a modern state. Kyrgyzstan was perceived as a significant political window of opportunity for many donors, especially considering the country's complicated geopolitical neighborhood – more evident now than 10 years ago.

On the recipient side, the will for reform and a determination augmented by the feeling of deep geopolitical isolation pushed the country's leadership towards seeking Western support and adopting Western patterns of economic life. Popular slogans about Kyrgyzstan as the "Switzerland of Central Asia", although somewhat fanciful, reflected the real political choice of the country's elite. The great openness to Western TC – much more than in most other post-communist countries – was just one manifestation. And because TC projects were provided to Kyrgyzstan almost entirely free of financial obligation on the country's part, there was no rational demand barrier.

As in other transition countries, Kyrgyzstan had little experience and institutional capacity to manage TC at the very beginning of the transition process, when it was most urgently needed. This posed a challenge that donors and suppliers of TC services were poorly equipped to meet. Nor did they have a good contextual understanding of the scale and nature of the transition process, particularly in the less developed republics of the former Soviet Union.

Bilateral donors were initially uncertain about how to respond to the changing needs of the former Soviet republics. There was no initial thought of providing aid along the pattern of developing countries. Bilateral donors were thus mostly motivated by the political agendas and interests of the development industries in their own countries. International financial organizations, particularly the IMF and the World Bank (whose operations had originally begun in Europe), had a much better and more comprehensive understanding of what should be done in transition economies, but their TC activities were usually subordinated to lending programmes and associated with conditionality. Private donors such as the Open Society Institute (Soros Foundation) were also better prepared to support the transition process, but their assistance – though very important – constituted only a small portion of the total TC on offer.

Partly for these reasons, donors did not put much effort into coordinating their actions and helping Kyrgyzstan manage the huge TC inflow in a rational way. The lack of coordination was hardly new, however. Even in developing countries with long-established aid programmes, there is insufficient cooperation among donors, whether they are multilateral organizations – many of which belong to the same UN system (UNDP, UNIDO) – or bilaterals, which are members and shareholders of the same multilateral organizations, and have closely aligned foreign policies.

Because of ignorance and lack of experience in the transition process, donors experienced difficulties with the sequencing of TC projects, with defining priorities, and with responding quickly and flexibly to changing needs. Many TC projects suffered from unclear formulation and were excessively broad in scope. Some TC initiatives were launched too early, before the specific problems had been perceived as important by the Kyrgyz authorities, or before the relevant institutional ground had been prepared. This was the case with most of the civil service-related projects. Other expertise came too late, as did the capacity to appraise public investment projects.

Providers of TC services were even less prepared than donors. Most of them did not have experience with post-communist economies and did not understand their problems and needs. Many had no command of Russian and therefore had problems in finding a common professional language. There was consequently a heavy reliance on foreign experts rather than on local staff. Many projects had excessively complex organizational schemes, bad prioritization and sequencing, inappropriate staffing and delays in implementation.

Inappropriate staffing was also caused by shortcomings in recruitment policies related both to individual experts and institutional providers. Very often, donors limited recruitment to home country individuals and firms. Alternatives were usually not actively sought, and when they were, recruitment and procurement were not open and transparent. The same short cuts applied to recruitment of local staff, where it occurred.

Some donors (such as UNDP) prefer to employ individuals rather than institutions, which involves two kinds of problems. First, there is the risk of selecting inappropriate candidates. Second, it sometimes requires an excessive amount of time to put teams together. These problems can be avoided by recruiting institutional providers where it is feasible to do so.

All parties have made management mistakes stemming from a lack of experience in TC in the specific context of transition. These mistakes were probably unavoidable, and it was better to take risks than wait for institutional and organizational conditions that might have been long in coming. This is the price of radical change.

With time, there has been a learning process by all parties, and some of the early shortcomings have been overcome. The gap between TC supply and country's absorptive capacity has narrowed. Local experts have become more involved in the implementation of projects, and even in their management. Increasingly, projects have become smaller and shorter, addressing more specific technical needs. Generally, more attention has been put on local capacity development instead of just the provision of policy advice. Foreign teams have been more appropriately staffed, and the pool of international experts familiar with transition economies and the region, and specifically with Kyrgyzstan, has increased substantially compared to the beginning of the 1990s.

Some changes have not materialized fast enough, however. The lessons of the early TC experience have not been adequately examined and learned. In the second half of the 1990s, the TC process was driven mainly by inertia and vested interests on both sides. There have been changes in the profile of TC, but only slowly. Too much emphasis has continued to be put on central government, with regional and local government and the non-governmental sectors lagging behind.

The early reform enthusiasm on the recipient side has dissipated, and anti-reform coalitions of vested interests have become stronger. The evolution of the constitutional model towards a presidential republic in effect weakened the young parliament, and did not help in developing a modern political system or active civil society. There were serious weaknesses in public administration, which undermined TC projects meant to strengthen the public sector, promote a civil society, and strengthen parliamentary institutions.

Many of the earlier irregularities also became more persistent and difficult to overcome. They included corruption and nepotism, the parasitic exploitation of TC projects for specific interests, and distorted incentives for project staff and the personnel of beneficiary agencies. The country as a whole has become heavily aid-dependent, not only in terms of TC, but also in terms of increased financial cushioning of fiscal and external imbalances. In sum, a decade of large-scale TC has been, in some ways, typical of many other country cases. For both donors and recipient, it has followed a cycle that began with reform enthusiasm and excessive expectations, followed by critical reflection and a certain sense of disappointment.

What are the immediate prospects? In spite of a drop in TC volumes during the last three years, Kyrgyzstan is expected to remain a key recipient during the present decade. The country's participation in the World Bank-initiated process of preparing the *Comprehensive Development Framework* is intended to create, apart from other potential uses, the long-term conceptual basis for large-scale foreign aid in its various forms. In addition, recent global political developments (including the war against terrorism) have increased the international importance of the entire Central Asia region, which will probably translate into a substantial and sustainable inflow of aid, including TC.

There are several lessons to be retained from experience. The continuation of the TC effort should be based on a more precise identification of the country's real needs and reform readiness. Appropriate conditionalities attached to financial aid packages would be helpful. Donors cannot, however, be substitutes for local leadership and will. When strong national leadership and determination are absent, donors should be cautious, since the probability of failure is high.

The issue of country ownership of the reform process is fundamental, as is ownership of associated TC projects. Ownership of the reform process depends very much on the political will and determination of national authorities to carry out concrete policy and institutional changes. Ownership is a quintessentially political phenomenon. In Kyrgyzstan, the political will was present in the first half of the 1990s, but diminished thereafter.

TABLE 6.6: TECHNICAL COOPERATION BY RECIPIENT ORGANIZATION, 1992-2000 (US$ THOUSANDS)

	1992	1993	1994	1995	1996	1997	1998	1999	2000	Total
GRAND TOTAL	3,031	3,925	14,171	25,532	30,491	33,671	35,041	30,048	28,649	204,559
Ministry of Health	0	0	1,534	2,391	2,389	4,796	1,959	972	5,820	19,861
Ministry of Agriculture and Water Resources	0	0	750	1,557	3,883	3,212	2,165	3,213	1,555	16,335
Ministry of Finance	0	225	415	425	825	1,623	2,407	1,653	1,718	16,246
Ministry of Education, Science & Culture	2,912	1,406	2,897	1,428	1,359	151	836	897	204	12,090
State Committee on Foreign Investments	0	1,095	1,268	2,083	901	1,076	695	784	1,364	9,416
Ministry of External Trade & Industry	0	0	0	460	2,100	1,650	304	0	0	7,628
Ministry of Labour & Social Protection	0	0	0	777	348	1,382	1,671	1,548	340	6,066
National Bank	0	0	484	900	610	1,100	1,400	234	400	5,128
Ministry of Transport & Communications	0	0	48	0	1,100	747	854	990	600	4,339
Ministry of Environmental Protection	0	0	117	30	720	280	1,019	789	356	3,311
SAGMR	0	0	150	600	1,000	600	650	200	0	3,200
National Broadcasting Company	0	0	1,200	1,649	247	66	6	0	0	3,168
Centre for Development of Private Sector	0	21	195	568	368	1,312	590	0	0	3,054
Joint-stock company "Kyrgyzenergo"	0	45	90	1,001	715	681	382	87	0	3,001
Kyrgyz-Turkish Manas University	0	0	0	0	0	0	3,000	0	0	3,000
Soros Foundation-Kyrgyzstan	0	0	0	708	769	548	495	226	252	2,998
Joint-stock company "Kyrgyztelekom"	0	0	0	1,300	950	480	0	0	0	2,730
State Forestry Agency	0	0	70	650	800	550	0	0	0	2,070
Gender in Development Bureau	0	0	0	0	0	0	211	648	742	1,601
Office of the President	0	0	0	8	17	0	114	631	761	1,531

	1992	1993	1994	1995	1996	1997	1998	1999	2000	Total
Ministry of Internal Affairs	0	11	6	0	15	492	380	325	213	1,442
NOKP	0	0	0	0	350	0	0	1,064	10	1,424
Financial Company for credit unions	0	0	0	0	0	0	150	324	910	1,384
State Property Fund	0	0	0	0	100	529	276	265		1,170
Ministry of Foreign Affairs	0	0	260	120	152	120	200	169	100	1,121
Other	120	3,779	8,594	13,266	14,535	14,164	17,863	17,164	24,476	10,3742

Source: UNDP

Apart from ownership of the reform process in general, it is important to rational-ize TC demand and ensure that the country takes responsibility for project definition and implementation. Project co-financing and the requirement to repay loans, as in the case of many World Bank projects, would help to better filter TC demand, and provide incentives for more effective use. Co-financing would not only increase national own-ership, but also the accountability of the Government and donors. The Kyrgyz Government could be required by donors to provide contributions in kind (office prem-ises, for example), and the salaries of local staff involved in the project.

Local ownership of TC projects would also be strengthened by more involvement in defining the TC agenda and setting priorities. Local stakeholders need to be part of the discussion on terms of references, the selection of suppliers, project management and staffing, and monitoring and evaluation. But a balance of responsibilities needs to be maintained. Donors still retain the right to determine where and how their money is spent. And there are no guarantees that the prerogatives of the recipient country will help to minimize observed flaws and irregularities. As international experience shows, if the recipient country does not have an efficient public procurement mechanism and an effective and well-paid civil service – neither condition prevailing in Kyrgyzstan – foreign aid can lead to new sources of corruption.

With the transition process in Kyrgyzstan already at an advanced stage, future efforts should focus on a narrower, but better-defined agenda. Smaller TC projects with simple management structures, staffed with Russian-speaking foreign experts familiar with transition economies, and supported by competitively-recruited local experts and administrative personnel, have a chance to achieve more than some of the larger, earlier programmes. Smaller projects can be more flexible and responsive to changing demand, and less bureaucratic and costly in their implementation.

Another change in TC priorities should involve a greater emphasis on strengthen-ing regional and local authorities, as well as non-government sectors. In the latter case, this means promoting independent media and supporting academic, cultural and research activities. Human rights and minorities' organizations, and policy research and cultural institutes also merit strong assistance. Civil society in Kyrgyzstan is ripe for external support in order to avoid an anti-democratic drift and forestall the ethnic or religious conflicts so often present in Central Asia.

Some lessons apply more broadly. Apart from closer cooperation with the recipient country, donors should seek to improve coordination and cooperation among themselves to avoid duplication and conflicting conditionalities and advice. Closer coordination will create opportunities for more comprehensive TC approaches. Donors should also encourage TC providers to employ local experts and organizations, as well as foreign experts who understand the local context and language.

Technical cooperation agencies could also separate donor functions from the process of providing, organizing and managing TC projects. Financing TC programmes and delivering professional services represent two different spheres, and combining both in one agency can lead to conflicts of interests and low efficiency.

Donors should concentrate on the overall TC agenda and in supervising its implementation, but should not be directly involved in project micro-management and staff recruitment. The latter should be delegated to professional TC providers (consulting firms, institutes, NGOs and other relevant organizations) working in a competitive environment that increasingly involves local suppliers and personnel. Donors can best contribute in this way to strengthening local think tanks and public policy institutes in developing and transition countries.

Finally, there are lessons to be drawn by the Kyrgyz authorities. Apart from a greater readiness to provide their own input to TC projects, they must create the proper incentives for those in public administration to use TC projects in the most effective way. Civil servants at all levels need to know that their active and creative engagement in TC projects will pay off in terms of their individual careers. The Government should also establish clear and transparent tendering procedures, which will help in selecting local TC providers and experts. Duplication and overlapping in TC often comes from contradictory messages from different government agencies, and lack of sufficient coordination between them. Although the Kyrgyz Government has now selected the agency formally in charge of aid coordination and monitoring (previously the Goscominvest, currently the Ministry of Finance), its functions cannot yet be considered adequately efficient.

References

Aslund A. 2000. "From Budget Crisis to Sustained Economic Growth and Welfare: A Vision for Kyrgyzstan." Bishkek: United Nations Development Programme.

Berg, E. and United Nations Development Programme (UNDP). 1993. *Rethinking Technical Cooperation: Reforms for Capacity Building in Africa.* New York.

Dabrowski, M., W. Jermakowicz, J. Pankow, K. Kloc, and R. Antczak.1995. "Economic Reforms in Kyrgyzstan." *Communist Economies & Economic Transformation*, Vol. 7.

Dabrowski, M. 1996. "Different Strategies of Transition to a Market Economy. How Do They Work in Practice?" Policy Research Working Paper for the World Bank.

―――. 1997. "The Reasons for the Collapse of the Ruble Zone" in *Trade and Payments in Central and Eastern Europe's Transforming Economies*, edited by L.T. Orlowski and D. Salvatore. Westport: Greenwood Press.

R. Mogilevsky. 1999. "Kyrgyzstan: Common Country Assessment." Bishkek: United Nations Development Programme.

Organisation for Economic Co-operation and Development/Development Assistance Committee (OECD/DAC). 1991. *Principles for New Orientations in Technical Co-operation*. Paris.

Slider, D. 1991. "Embattled Entrepreneurs: Soviet Cooperatives in a Unreformed Society." *Soviet Studies,* Vol. 43.

United Nations Children's Fund (UNICEF). 1999. "Definitions of Capacity Building and Implications for Monitoring and Evaluation." New York.

United Nations Development Programme (UNDP). 1998. "Capacity Assessment and Development in a Systems and Strategic Management Context." New York.

―――. 1999. Human Development Report 1999. New York: Oxford University Press.

―――. 2000. Human Development Report 2000. New York: Oxford University Press.

―――. 2000. The Kyrgyz Republic National Human Development Report 2000. Bishkek: UNDP

―――.2001. Human Development Report 2001. New York: Oxford University Press.

―――. 2001. "Problems and Future Prospects in Relations Between State and Civil Society of the Kyrgyz Republic: Preliminary Report." Bishkek.

Karatnycky A., A. Motyl, and A. Schnetzer (Eds.) 2001. *Kyrgyz Republic in Nations in Transit 2001: Civil Society, Democracy and Markets in East Central Europe and the Newly Independent States.* New York: Freedom House.

Government of the Kyrgzy Republic. 1999. "Strengthening the Ongoing Civil Service Reform in Kyrgyzstan." Final Report. Bishkek.

―――. 2000. "Empowering the Poor for Self-Reliance and Advancement." Evaluation Mission Report from the Gender in Development Bureau. Bishkek.

7 *Philippines*[1]

BRINGING CIVIL SOCIETY INTO CAPACITY DEVELOPMENT

Introduction

The present assessment of technical cooperation (TC) in the Philippines takes a broad reading of the term capacity development. It looks at capacity as the ability to achieve several aims, including analysing and setting goals, and identifying the tasks and functions to reach these goals. Capacity also includes the ability to establish effective processes and mechanisms for participation and accountability, and to institute norms and values, rules and incentive structures to improve performance or realize a goal. This study looks into the "whose capacity" issue, and recognizes that these capacities can be vested within individuals, groups, and institutions – all contributing to capacity at the national level. Finally, this study also looks at the "for what" issue, interpreting capacity development as either a means or an end, as improvement of abilities to perform tasks or functions, as well as creating an environment that aids the development of "national goal-seeking capacity" (UNDP/UNICEF 1999).

This chapter summarizes the modalities of technical cooperation practices in the Philippines and the impact of TC on capacity development. It also comments on the evolution of official development assistance (ODA) practices in relation to the Government and NGOs, addressing key areas of TC reforms and covering innovations

---

[1] This paper was prepared by Jeanne Frances I. Illo, Research Associate and Coordinator of the Women's Studies Programme at the Institute for Philippine Culture, Ateneo de Manila University. Contributing authors, also at the Institute for Philippine Culture include research associates Sylvia Bagadion-Engracia, Maria Concepcion L. Chan and Leland Joseph R. de la Cruz; and Mary Racelis, IPC Director.

and policy issues. The report closes with a reflection on the contributions of the Philippine case study to a better understanding, not only of how TC works at the country level, but more importantly, how certain elements have worked particularly well in the Philippines.

Background

The Philippines is composed of 7,107 islands, many of them mountainous. The geography and topography of the country account for its underdeveloped physical infrastructure and the high cost of transporting people and goods. With 78 million inhabitants in 2000, the Philippines is the most densely populated country in Southeast Asia: 263 people per square kilometre. Almost 59% of its people live in urban areas, 11 million of them in Manila. The population speaks a total of 111 languages and dialects, all of which belong to the Malayo-Polynesian family. Filipino, which is derived largely from Tagalog, a language spoken in Metro Manila and nearby areas, is the national language.

The Philippines has been the slowest-growing country among the members of the Association of Southeast Asian Nations (ASEAN). Between 1989 and 1998, its real GDP grew by 2.7% per year. The 10-year period was marked by a slowdown in the early 1990s, followed by a short-lived resurgence from 1993 to mid-1997. The annual growth rate peaked at 5.8% in 1996, just before the financial crisis that hit East Asia. In 1998, at the height of the crisis, GDP contracted by 0.6%. It has since grown by 3.4 to four percent a year (ADB 2001).

The Philippine economy has been plagued by weaknesses. They include comparatively low rates of domestic savings by Southeast and East Asian standards; stagnating agriculture; a "hollowing-out" of the industrial sector, with growth concentrated in non-tradables such as transport, construction, and real estate; and the concentration of exports in a narrow band of commodities (such as electronics and transport equipment) that use few domestic inputs and in which the Philippines is losing competitive advantage. The economy also suffers from a chronic current account deficit and high volatility resulting from an inflow of portfolio investments fuelled by the liberalization of the Philippine capital market. Ever-increasing foreign debt depletes the domestic resources used to service it (Illo 1999). All these weaknesses were unmasked by the financial crisis of the late 1990s, which provoked a new wave of poverty.

Income poverty consistently declined from 1985 to 1997, but increased again in 2000 (see Table 7.1). In rural areas where poverty levels are significantly higher, El Niño brought an additional setback. Three years after the beginning of the crisis, the proportion of poor rural families was higher than 1994.

In terms of capacity development, the country offers several important features. There is a well-educated work force, and an adult literacy rate of 95% for both men and women. There are also many deeply committed non-government organizations (NGOs) and a well-developed public bureaucracy. These institutional strengths, however, are undermined by excessive politics within the Government as well as the NGO community.

TABLE 7.1: POVERTY INCIDENCE, 1985-2000

	1985	1988	1991	1994	1997	2000
Number of poor families (in millions)	4.355	4.23	4.781	4.531	4.511	5.22
Poverty incidence among families (%)	44.2	40.2	39.9	35.5	31.8	34.2
Urban	33.6	30.1	31.1	24	17.9	20.4
Rural	50.7	46.3	48.6	47	44.4	47.4

Source: Family Income and Expenditures Survey, National Statistics Office

Public commitment to basic services such as health, housing and food still falls short. More needs to be done to improve the quality of education. Financial responsibility for training in a trade or occupation still falls largely on individuals or families, and is shaped as much by foreign job opportunities as by domestic labour market factors. Moreover, the Government promotes overseas employment as a source of foreign exchange remittances, thereby reducing the skills available to the domestic public and private sectors.

Addressing graft and corruption is an urgent priority as it contaminates the civil service, undermines the effectiveness of governance, and raises costs of doing business in the country. Additional capacity development issues for the Government include the need to rationalize the distribution of personnel and the compensation system. This includes the need to make civil service salaries competitive with those of the private sector, the need for more meritocracy, and ending the near-universal practice of patronage politics in the hiring and promotion of personnel. Devolution problems, including patronage politics and the share of local governments in tax revenues, must also be addressed. The Government also needs to rationalize the education sector, including its management, financing and incentives structures, and investments in school facilities. Finally, there is a need to improve the programme development and management capacity of government agencies.

There is likewise a need to address the high incidence of poverty, particularly in rural areas. In this connection, capacities are needed to help farmers improve the productivity of agriculture and other rural enterprises. These capacities would enable the Government's agriculture agencies, NGOs and communities to plan, design, manage and implement agricultural programmes and projects, help local governments access and negotiate TC, and facilitate cooperation between the Department of Agriculture and local government units (LGUs).

In view of the central role that they play in poverty alleviation and people empowerment, NGOs also need assistance in building various skills across management, advocacy and participation in public planning and decision making processes.

Aid and Technical Cooperation

Despite declining official development assistance (ODA) levels worldwide, donor interest in the Philippines remained high for the period 1989 to 1998. This attention stemmed from donor support to the return to democracy and the rule of law under the Corazon Aquino administration. It also illustrated the relatively good performance of the Philippine Government in its utilization of ODA resources. Rates of disbursement were high between 1989 and 1996 – at 79% – but fell to 74% in 1997 and 66% in 1998 (Gonzales 1998, 2000).

For 1989 to 1998, total ODA commitments to the Philippines totalled $20.9 billion, or an average of slightly over $2 billion a year. This amount was almost 14% of foreign exchange earnings from exports. It also supported 16.7% of the budget, and accounted for 3.5% of GDP.

During the period 1986-1999, ODA flows to the Philippines came from 28 donors. The largest sources of ODA were Japan (44%), the World Bank (22%), and the Asian Development Bank (18%). Other large donors were Australia, Canada, France, Germany and the United States. The United Nations system contributed 0.7% of the $27.81 billion that flowed into the country during the 13-year period.

Technical cooperation accounts for a relatively small percentage of the total aid – in most years less than 10% (see Table 7.2). Australia, the European Union, and UNDP are the largest contributors. For 1989 to 1998, their total TC contributions reached more than $1.3 billion. The TC funds generally supported capacity development under a governance facility such as the Australian Government's overseas aid programme (AusAID) and the Canadian International Development Agency (CIDA), as part of an integrated area development programme (EU), or as an integral part of capital assistance projects (ADB and World Bank).

From 1986 to 1996, the social sectors (mainly health and education) received 29% of total TC. The agri-industrial sector (composed of agriculture, agrarian reform, natural resources, industry and tourism, and science and technology) got 23%, and infrastructure, 15.7% (see Table 7.3). Substantial portions of the water resources and integrated area development projects, however, were in fact agricultural in nature and their capacity development components pertain to the building or strengthening of rural organizations and institutions, and training for livelihood and skills development.

Since its creation in the early 1970s, the National Economic and Development Authority (NEDA) has managed ODA in the Philippines. As the key planning agency, NEDA has to ensure two things: that projects which receive ODA loans, grants and other forms of external assistance are in line with the Government's economic programme; and that proposals which emanate from line agencies result from an investment plan supporting strategic medium-term goals in their respective sectors.

Projects approved by the NEDA board for funding are formally endorsed by the Government. The donor appraises the proposal and makes its funding decision. The

TABLE 7.2: TOTAL ODA AND TC, 1992-1998

Year	TC (US$ millions)	ODA (US$ millions)	TC as % of ODA	TC as % of GDP	TC as % of budget
1992	58	1,504	3.9	0.1	0.5
1993	161	1,186	8.8	0.3	1.3
1994	175	1,927	9.1	0.3	1.4
1995	293	2,370	12.4	0.4	1.9
1996	232	1,397	16.6	0.3	1.5
1997	173	2,654	6.5	0.2	1.0
1998	153	1,862	8.2	0.2	1.2
Totals	1,245	12,900	9.6	0.3	1.3

Sources: OECD/DAC website for TC; Gonzales (2000) for ODA; NSO Philippine Yearbook for the GDP and GOP budget raw data.

TABLE 7.3: SECTORAL DISTRIBUTION OF TC COMMITMENTS (IN GRANTS) FOR 1986-1996

Sector	Total grants (US$ millions)	Percent of total (%)
Agri-industrial development	774.6	23.0
Of which, agriculture and agrarian reform	(381.9)	(11.4)
Social sectors	987.0	29.4
Infrastructure development	527.6	15.7
Of which, water resources	(249.0)	(7.4)
Integrated area development	214.5	6.4
Development administration	180.8	5.4
Disaster mitigation, commodity aid, and others	676.6	20.1
Total	3,361.1	100.0

Source: Gonzales (1998).

donor then informs the Government through diplomatic channels of the projects that they have chosen to support, and the amount they are pledging. Negotiations follow. The Department of Finance holds loan discussions with the donor; in the case of grant agreements, NEDA usually takes the lead in representing the Government in negotiations. The loan or grant agreement is signed once the donor has approved funding for the project. The agreement stipulates the commitments made by both the donor and the Philippine Government.

Since 1992, the Government has conducted annual portfolio reviews to identify and address factors affecting the country's absorptive capacity for ODA. The process begins with individual project reviews between NEDA and the Department of Budget and Management on one hand, and project management offices (PMOs) on the other. The process ends with the presentation of the annual report to the NEDA Board, including recommended measures for improving implementation performance.

Although the Philippine Government has established policies, processes and procedures covering ODA and TC, it recognizes that each donor agency is also subject to those of their respective Governments and governing councils.

Donor Management Practices

The major aid donors to the Philippines maintain an office in the country. Most multilateral agencies have delegated management responsibilities to their country offices (the ADB, with its headquarters in Manila, opened a separate Philippine office in September 2000). Bilateral aid agencies, however, observe differing practices. The United States Agency for International Development (USAID) resident mission oversees all United States TC contracts, whereas, until very recently, AusAID contracts were managed in Canberra. The Japan International Cooperation Agency (JICA) and CIDA Philippine offices also have limited management control over projects.

Day-to-day management of TC projects again differs by donor. The varying degrees of involvement of government agencies are evident in the following project management modes.

- **Organic Project Management Offices** – Loans and very large TC projects are often run by a project management office that is composed of organic staff (or permanent agency personnel) and contractual consultants/staff. The PMO is usually headed by an agency official, with the assistance of a team of contractual staff.

- **Co-management** – In projects supported by JICA and the EU, a Japanese or European is named as co-coordinator or co-director of the project alongside an official designated by the Philippine implementing agency. The field staff, however, can consist of locally hired administrative staff (clerical and financial), fieldwork personnel, short-term local consultants, and short- and medium-term foreign consultants.

- **Expatriate executing or management firms** – In projects funded by CIDA or AusAID, a Canadian or Australian firm executes or manages the project. In CIDA projects, the PMO may be headed by either a Canadian or Filipino consultant, but the executing agency is represented in the Philippines by a Canadian. In AusAID projects, an Australian firm normally opens an office on site that is headed by an Australian consultant.

- **Direct and/or local administration** – Unlike many bilateral aid agencies, USAID manages its contracts or grants either directly or through project administration by a local agency which USAID monitors. The experience of USAID and other agencies with local executing agencies have proven this mode to be inefficient. Fund disbursement is slow as a layer of donor bureaucracy is superimposed on the local bureaucracy.

Where the local implementing agency does not manage the project, an opportunity is lost to build that agency's management capacity. This loss needs to be weighed against efficiency and ease of project administration, including smoother fund flows, timeliness of delivery of inputs and outputs, and similar benefits to both donors and the final beneficiaries of the project.

Co-management can help develop local project management capacity. The EU and its medium- to long-term projects provide the implementing agencies ample opportunities for on-the-job learning about project formulation, implementation, and monitoring and evaluation. In contrast, JICA's shorter-term TC activities are less appropriate for the institutional development of local agencies.

Regardless of the mode of project management and implementation, TC projects hire consultants for technical advice, to guide the implementing agency or group through activities such as training or organizing, or to conduct studies and craft project reports and documents.

Many – if not all – bilateral aid organizations are bound by their Governments' policies regarding procurement of equipment and materials and hiring consultants. This means that despite official commitment to untied ODA, much of TC is, in fact, tied aid. Except in very small TC contracts, bidding for consultancy services takes place in donor countries among firms that are qualified according to their rules (such as being listed in the Australian stock or securities exchange, in the case of AusAID). Winners of the bids usually contract part of the TC services to Filipino experts.

In sharp contrast to this practice by some bilateral agencies, multilateral agencies and USAID open the bidding of TC projects to all qualified firms, regardless of nationality. To strengthen their bids, foreign-based firms often pair with local consulting firms or invite local experts to join their roster of consultants.

The UN agencies follow a different system of contracting consultancy services. For projects generated locally, UNDP and other UN agencies generally hire local consultants, with inputs from the implementing agency. Technical cooperation coming out of headquarters usually involves expatriate consultants who partner with local consultants recommended by the Philippine office.

The fielding of nationals by bilateral aid agencies is purportedly based on the premise that the former have knowledge, skills and practices that they can share or of which they enjoy comparative advantages. This may be true in the Department of Budget and Management's e-procurement project with CIDA, and in AusAID's distance education or technical-vocational training projects. But there are fields wherein local expertise is already equal, if not superior, to that of expatriates. This includes gender, community organizing, institutional development and policy analysis.

Despite the comparative advantage and lower costs of hiring local consultants, the national policies of certain bilateral aid organizations compel these donors to continue fielding their citizens. Japanese firms or consultants doing development studies or TC-type projects, however, often hire local individuals or groups to conduct background research that requires local knowledge, or to do basic data gathering. Other funding agencies take advantage of the less expensive and more grounded local consultants to deliver training services, provide management and development advice, and undertake community organizing and institutional development activities on site.

Several factors are deemed to have contributed to the increasing employment of Filipino consultants by funding agencies. These include the shift by donors to area-based programming, which creates a demand for local (provincial or regional) consultants who know the area; greater contracting autonomy in the country offices; participation of local stakeholders in the selection of consultants; and increasing concern among some donors over cost-efficiency.

In addition, there are several local institutions that can provide capacity development services in specific areas. For governance, CIDA projects have tapped the Asian Institute of Management, the Ateneo de Manila University School of Government, the Development Academy of the Philippines, and the University of the Philippines. Agricultural and agrarian reform projects have collaborated with the University of the Philippines (Los Baños) and other universities with agricultural colleges. Urban poverty, gender and child labour projects draw on the Institute of Philippine Culture at the Ateneo de Manila University.

Policy Analysis

Part of TC from bilateral and multilateral donors is in support of policy analysis and reform. Some agencies have mechanisms for policy-oriented TC. Other agencies have programmed part of their TC for policy reform without creating a specific facility for it. UNDP funding for policy analysis and reform is a good example. Policy-related inputs can also be provided in the course of general project implementation. USAID support to the energy sector required building up enough capacity to craft the country's energy policy, and for Congress to formulate an energy or power bill. Another example is CIDA's project with the Bureau of Customs, which resulted in a policy of making customs regulations available online. This made information widely available and accessible to the public, thereby limiting misinformation and corruption. It also helped the Philippines to comply with World Trade Organization (WTO) requirements and support its anti-corruption drive.

At the sub-national level, UNDP worked with NEDA offices on regional development planning. CIDA, USAID and AusAid have assisted local governments in crafting local policies and legislation.

Working With NGOs

One of the major features of the Aquino administration's structural reforms addressed people's involvement in the decision making, planning and implementation of programmes, especially through community organizations and NGOs. This objective was enshrined in the 1987 Philippine Constitution and in various laws passed by the Philippine Congress.

Gonzales (1998) classifies NGO funding mechanisms from aid sources into *responsive funding,* or resources that support activities initiated by NGOs and participating communities; and *contractual funds,* which are provided by donors or government agencies to NGOs to carry out certain tasks pre-determined by the funds holder. This distinction is important. Under the first type of funding, the project belongs to, or is owned by the NGOs; in the second instance, the NGOs are treated as contractors and assume the role of a for-profit, private consulting firm.

Responsive funding systems are of several types. First and foremost are foreign NGO-to-Filipino NGO co-financing schemes, which is the traditional means of channelling ODA to NGOs. The second type consists of embassy funds, in the form of the ambassador's discretionary fund or small grants schemes. The third type is composed of donor-managed NGO funding mechanisms. This includes USAID's Private Voluntary Organizations Co-Financing Programme, AusAID's Philippines Australia Community Assistance Programme, and area-based funding mechanisms managed by a project management office (such as the Antique Integrated Area Development Programme in Antique Province). The fourth type pertains to NGO-managed funding mechanisms. CIDA provides numerous examples of this category of NGO financing. Of the four types of financing, the NGO-managed funding scheme provides the greatest opportunity for building the capacity of the NGO sector as a whole (Quizon 1997, cited in Gonzales 1998).

It is difficult to ascertain the exact amount of ODA funding for NGOs, given the sheer volume of transactions in co-financing schemes, and the mixture of private and public contributions. However, NGO co-financing schemes contribute the largest portion of responsive ODA funds (Gonzales 1998:93). These schemes alone generated over $50 million per annum during the first half of the 1990s (Gonzales 1998:90).

Drawing on the results of a survey of 35 NGO funding programmes conducted by the Association of Foundations, Gonzales (2000) reports that among 17 programme areas, gender received the highest priority (in 63% of programmes), followed by livelihood and enterprise (in 57%), agriculture and agrarian reform (in 51%), and health and indigenous peoples (43% each).

Why do donors fund NGOs? Donors interviewed for this study as well as those interviewed by Gonzales (2000) cite several reasons for working with NGOs. Strong grassroots links and long-term commitment to poor and marginalized groups make NGOs attractive to funding agencies with community-oriented and poverty reduction programmes. Another set of reasons often cited pertain to the nature of NGOs and NGO operations: flexibility, innovation, process orientation, and expertise in community organizing. The relatively small size of NGOs makes for less red tape and more cost-effective projects.

Funding agencies have also encountered a number of problems with NGOs. They find it hard to distinguish between "fly-by-night" and authentic NGOs. Bad experiences with the former have compelled donors to impose stringent reporting and accountability requirements. Other problems relate to a lack of institutional systems and mechanisms, their inability to provide counterpart funding, and long-term, heavy dependence on external funding. Finally, donors sometimes find NGOs too self-righteous, highly politi-cized, or unwilling to adapt to the management style of donors.

These problems notwithstanding, the involvement of NGOs in the development process, and the willingness of the donor community to assist NGOs, particularly in community-level TC activities, offer a good case study in TC practices. NGOs expand the potential sources of expertise that can be tapped for capacity development, particularly of communities. Meanwhile, the presence of highly respected training institutions and a large pool of actual and potential capacity development consultants create oppor-tunities for local support for national capacity development.

The more vibrant NGOs and training establishments have profited from previous TC projects that allowed them to develop their programmes and competencies. Scholarships and training opportunities helped make possible the large base of skilled men and women who can be tapped for TC work. Finally, innovative TC practices have generated changes in the way government works and in the way people and com-munities participate in issues that matter to them, including development.

TC and Public Sector Reform

The Philippine civil service comprised 1.4 million employees in 1997, or two percent of the total population. This translates to one civil servant per 51 Filipinos, which is slight-ly lower than in other ASEAN states such as Malaysia or Thailand.

Key public sector oversight agencies are the Department of Budget and Management (DBM), the Civil Service Commission (CSC) and the Department of Interior and Local Government (DILG). DBM is the lead agency in the task of promoting quality spending and pursuing fiscal and management reforms. Aside from budget management, it also administers compensation and classification systems and assesses the organizational effectiveness of the bureaucracy (DBM n.d.). DILG assists the President in the exercise of general supervision over local government.

The CSC is meant to play a key role in civil service reform, since one of its tasks is to develop capacity for efficient public service. Its training programmes concentrate on two areas: skills, including supervisory development; and values, such as ethics and accountability. The CSC focuses on piloting training programmes with service-wide applications. It does not undertake training directly, but accredits training service providers. Agencies are free to develop and conduct staff development programmes with the assistance of these service providers. Since most of the accredited training groups are located in Manila, however, government agencies have tapped non CSC-accredited institutions for training programmes in other regions.

Human Resource Management officers (HRMOs) are the links between the CSC and other government entities. Although HRMOs ensure that CSC policies are followed, the CSC itself has no say in the hiring of human resource personnel. Agencies simply have to adhere to the quality standards set by CSC for the position. HRM practitioners in the public sector have marginal influence in senior management decisions. They are reportedly identified more with clerical rather than technical roles. It seems unlikely that front-line CSC staff face demands for technical advice.

In practice, the Philippine bureaucracy has been judged to be over-politicized. This description applies at all levels and affects recruitment, promotion and performance evaluation. Currently, less than 40% of senior executive positions are filled by qualified career officers (World Bank, n.d.). In 1997, elective officials constituted 1.5% of the 1,378 million government personnel. They brought in about 19,000 officials and 153,000 "casual" or "contractual" workers. These political appointees accounted for 12.5% of the government work force (BLES 1998).

Political appointment is but one form of political patronage; the other, more insidious form appears through graft and corruption. These persist even as the Government pronounces its commitment to an honest and competent bureaucracy. The Medium Term Philippine Development Plan (MTPDP) for 1987-1992, for instance, vowed to shift away from "a system which provides incentives on the basis of accessibility to power to one which gives importance to efficiency and equity considerations". Its successor document stresses the need for an administrative framework that enables private enterprise to operate under a system of impartial and consistent rules, and that enforces contracts or resolves disputes fairly and quickly (MTPDP 1993-1998:5). Although observers have noted greater transparency, graft and corruption continue to flourish.

To protect public service from patronage politics, various presidents have attempted to create a permanent, apolitical civil service through the Career Executive Service Officer system. This requires individual civil servants to obtain qualifications, through examination and experience, prior to appointment to tenured posts. Higher-level appointments require candidates to complete training courses from institutions accredited by the Civil Service Commission. Among them are the Asian Institute of Management, the Ateneo de Manila University School of Government, the Development Academy of the Philippines, and the National College of Public Administration and Governance (NCPAG) of the University of the Philippines.

Related to the issue of patronage politics, graft and corruption have been the major challenges to good governance in the country. The Social Weather Station surveys from 1986 to 2001 listed the failure in fighting corruption as a major source of public dissatisfaction, second only to the failure to control inflation (Mangahas 2002). Transparency International, however, notes a decrease in the perception of graft and corruption from 1998 to 2001. This might be due to the removal from power of former President Joseph Estrada as well as the frequently reiterated promise of the current President, Gloria Macapagal-Arroyo, to promote governance based on improved moral standards.

The Government's procurement system has been identified as a key to reducing opportunities for graft and corruption. The current system is beset with problems including inconsistent and fragmented rules and regulations, non-transparent practices and abnormally long approval processes (World Bank, n.d.).

A positive development relevant to growing efficiency and transparency in public service is the increasing use of information technology. As of October 1997, more than 100 agencies were connected to the Internet. Administrative Order No. 332 was issued to promulgate the 'RPWeb' as the nucleus of the Philippine Information Infrastructure, and directed all government agencies down to field offices to interconnect through the web (MTPDP 1999-2004). Information ranging from drivers' licenses to tax records can now be more rapidly obtained from connected offices.

In addition to problems of corruption, there are other issues that are pertinent to capacity development:

- **Need to rationalize the distribution of personnel** – The bureaucracy is perceived to be bloated primarily because of poor deployment of personnel across regions and occupational groups. In 1997, 66% of the government workforce was employed by the national government. About 40% were teachers and police officers, with a majority of the remaining work force assigned to non-technical or administrative positions. Even at the national government level, the number of non-technical personnel has declined over the years (MTPDP 1999-2004).

- **Need to rationalize the compensation system** – Average wages in the civil service rose by over 75% between 1994 and 1998 as a result of the salary standardization process mandated by the 1987 Constitution to align public sector salaries to private sector levels. However, salaries of senior officials are typically 60% below market rates (World Bank, n.d.). This does not reward commitment to public service, and leads to low morale and lack of continuity in programmes.

  Several government institutions have also sought exemptions from the Salary Standardization Law (SSL), causing wide discrepancies between salaries of officials in these agencies and those in non-exempted ones. The Government Service Insurance System, for example, was exempted by Congress in 1997. It granted itself pay increases such that the salary of a senior GSIS official is now four times that of a Cabinet Secretary (World Bank, n.d.).

- **Need for meritocracy** – The near-universal practice of patronage politics in the hiring and promotion of workers has undermined efforts to institutionalize the Career Executive Service Officer system. Because of low salaries at the senior executive level, those who are induced to seek careers in the civil service may not be the most creative or efficient.

- **Need to address devolution problems** – One of the more important initiatives since the return to democracy in 1986 has been to bring public services into closer contact with users, for greater responsiveness to their needs. The enactment of the Local Government Code of 1991 vested local governments with substantial powers for self-governance. Although no systematic evaluation has been done of actual performance, the Galing Pook Foundation, administered by the Asian Institute of Management, has published case studies showing how devolution has pushed local authorities to improve service delivery.

A pressing problem is the internal revenue allocation to local governments. Its current formula is deemed to benefit richer areas, and is not related to the actual cost of delivering devolved services or to different needs across the various regions of the country. Patronage may also be a problem, considering that 25% of local employees are contractual workers. With local elections held every three years, lack of continuity can be an even greater problem at the local than at the national level (World Bank, n.d.).

- **Need to rationalize the education sector** – Reviews of the education and training sector have identified problematic issues ranging from management, financing and incentive structures, to investments in school facilities. Specifically, there have been instances of ill-advised official support and recognition of substandard universities. Further issues include inadequate incentive structures for teachers, particularly those in underserved areas and those handling science and technology subjects, and inadequate support for public elementary and secondary education. Moreover, considering that four out of five technical and vocational education and training providers are privately-owned, there is little support from the Government to these institutions (ADB/WB 1999).

Within the Government, key respondents interviewed for this study cite weak programme development and management capacity as a major problem. The World Bank identifies lack of capacity in procurement and financial management, particularly at the local government level, and extremely slow project preparation and implementation in the social sector as factors that increase costs for the Bank and the Government (World Bank, n.d.). Capacity development interventions to sustain and strengthen the devolution process remain critical (Brillantes 2001; World Bank, n.d.).

Considering the factors that influence governance, the Government's public sector reform plans have focused on the creation of a civil service based on merit. This includes the adoption of a more appropriate compensation scheme, improvements in management systems with a focus on its procurement system, and continuing capacity development, particularly for local government units. The frequent changes brought about by normal rotations in administration as well as through "people's power" revolts, however, have disrupted implementation of public sector reforms. Stability, continuity and sustainability in implementation must be present for these reforms to succeed (Brillantes 2001).

In public service reform, the main partners have been USAID, CIDA and AusAID, all of whom have provided assistance at both central government and local levels. GTZ has targeted the central institutions, and JICA funded an area development pro-gramme. The Civil Service Commission, Department of Budget and Management, the Department of Interior and Local Governance and the National Economic and Development Authority are among those that have benefited from these programmes.

The TC provided under these programmes has contributed to improving the com-petencies of civil servants and management systems at the national and local levels. Foreign-assisted project staff of three agencies (CSC, DBM, DILG) all agreed that skills had been enhanced among individuals in project management offices as a result of training programmes and study tours, as well as from the performance of work assign-ments within their respective projects. These skills included project development and management, and preparation of terms of references. For DBM, the experience of implementing TC has made staff realize that their financial policies and procedures are sometimes too cumbersome.

Retaining personnel trained under these projects, however, has been a problem, particularly at the local government level. Turnovers in key staff with every change of administration have exacerbated the problem, virtually guaranteeing almost no capacity retention despite the multiplicity of training programmes. Many municipal employees (particularly in poorer municipalities) leave the public service after completing the two years of service required by the training grant, because they find it difficult to build careers in local government. Meanwhile, with new competencies, it becomes much easier to find work outside the civil service. In the Visayas, for instance, project devel-opment and management trainees of local governments easily found employment in several local development banks.

The lack of clarity in the training priorities and needs of local government is also a concern. Training is currently supply-driven, as national agencies promote their sec-toral concerns instead of responding to needs identified by local government units. The governance facilities of aid agencies, however, are increasingly funding local gov-ernment initiatives. With the focus shifting from projects to sites, funding facilities are providing TC to help local governments in assessing their capacity development needs and designing programmes. This type of TC is reportedly improving local government performance as it builds real organizational capacity, and not just the capacity of politicians whose terms in office can be very limited.

NGOs and Public Sector Reform

With graft and corruption a critical issue in governance, the contributions of NGOs become vital. NGOs have played key roles in the political landscape, especially in exact-ing accountability from the Government, either directly or through the community groups they help organize. NGOs were instrumental in developing the strategic actions that led to the ouster of former President Estrada, and some NGO leaders have been appointed to key positions in the present Government. It is not surprising, therefore, that an increas-ing number of donors are now opening opportunities for engagement with civil society.

One such undertaking is the Philippine Governance Forum (PGF), a collaborative project of UNDP, the Ateneo School of Government and the Ateneo Center for Social Policy and Public Affairs. The Forum is undertaking several initiatives to promote transparency and good governance, including Government Watch, which monitors government projects; Budget Advocacy, which seeks to build up the budget literacy of NGOs and legislators; and the Transparency and Accountability Network, a coalition of 19 organizations engaged in good governance efforts.

Aid has clearly encouraged the growth of civil society organizations. With the return to democracy in 1986, several donors such as CIDA and AusAID created funding windows to help NGOs build their capacity to deliver services for poverty alleviation, as well as to advocate for reforms and provide a venue for the voices of marginalized sectors.

Fighting graft and corruption has increasingly become the focus of several donors (the World Bank and UNDP, among others). Most initiatives have incorporated civil society as watchdogs for good governance. Government Watch does "spot monitoring", focusing on actual accomplishments versus targets, outputs, costs and time frames. Results are discussed with agencies and commitments are secured in terms of their response to identified backlogs. Implementers plan to link up with Rotary Clubs across the country to ensure sustainability once UNDP funding ends.

Moreover, the opportunities for NGO-government partnership in service delivery that are offered by some foreign-assisted projects (such as AusAID's street children programme) have led to a better understanding of the Government's operational mechanisms. This can help NGOs in designing monitoring and evaluation tools for their roles as watchdogs.

There are complaints that TC to NGOs does not generally produce measurable outputs. Capacity development of the NGO is seen more as an end in itself, and this serves as a disincentive to donors. Most of the funds allegedly go to salaries and not to services for targeted clients. NGOs argue that it is the process of organizing communities to decide how best to take a series of actions and utilize local resources, that brings about people-led change.

TC Processes and Practices

Most respondents saw no problem with donors having their own TC agendas as long as these fit the priorities of the recipient agencies and organizations. In the area of governance and public sector reform, most donors approached the recipient agencies with offers of assistance. Priorities are defined by the domestic agencies and articulated in the Medium-Term Philippine Development Plan, and discussed with donors and civil society or private sector groups.

Donors are seen to have an increasingly open programming process, with UNDP credited by many as having set the example. Most donors, including the World Bank and the Asian Development Bank, now hold consultations about their country assistance strategies and specific programmes.

Many believe that the Government is now more in the "driver's seat" in the process of identifying and prioritizing projects to fund, even if the projects themselves are designed by donors with the active participation of agency staff. The counterpart agency has a principal role in needs identification, project selection and initiation, with the help of consultants (both foreign and local) provided by the donors. A major anti-poverty project currently under negotiation with the World Bank was prepared by the Department of Social Welfare and Development without a single foreign consultant.

In the efforts to strengthen decentralization, however, there have been instances where donors pushed their agendas when local governments were not ready. An example is the implementation of water and sanitation projects in the Autonomous Region of Muslim Mindanao. The project failed to consider lack of capacity in local government for financial management, and it is unclear how the funds were utilized. Local conflicts in the area also make auditing difficult.

Some also claim that the processes of consultation on projects are neither inclusive nor transparent enough. This concern is particularly strong when it comes to projects funded through loans, the share of which has been steadily increasing.

Decisions in staffing project management structures are normally left to the recipient agency. For the Civil Service Commission and the Department of Budget and Management, "organic" project management offices (those created from existing staff resources) usually handle project management. Evaluation is done both by consultants and internally by the PMO, while agency staff handles accounting and financial reporting if funds are involved.

Organic PMOs are seen to be more conducive to technology transfer and more efficient at records management. The problem, however, is providing adequate time for project concerns without neglecting other regular functions. "Inorganic" PMOs (with their own contractual staff) can concentrate fully on project management since staff members have no conflicting concerns. In both arrangements, there have been no problems with salary differentials, since agency personnel do not receive honoraria for work on the projects.

The use of organic PMOs was promoted through a DBM policy banning the hiring of contractual staff beyond the salary grade of division chiefs. All PMO managers are now organic personnel. Contractual personnel of some PMOs have the same salaries as regular personnel, since they are covered by the Government's social security scheme. Before the DBM policy, salaries of such personnel were 20% higher than those of regular staff.

Employment and Availability of Local Experts

The employment of foreign consultants from donor countries is often cited as an indication that development aid is "tied". Yet, as noted above, bilateral donors still employ significant numbers of expatriate experts. Foreign consultants provided by donors have been generally effective and culturally sensitive. Many of those interviewed, however, believe that foreign consultants should be hired only when there is no available local expertise, since the costs of foreign consultants are significantly higher than those of local experts.

Local expertise in the domain of governance can be found in academia and civil society. The Ateneo School of Government and Institute of Philippine Culture, the University of the Philippines' National College of Public Administration and Governance, the Development Academy of the Philippines and the Asian Institute of Management are some of the institutions that have provided expertise in capacity development for public sector reforms. A major problem lies in the lower rates set for national consultants – ceilings set by donors are sometimes too low to attract good local consultants. Local consultants also rarely become team leaders.

Project vs. Programme Approaches

Most donors are beginning to adopt a more programmatic approach, and many bilateral donors now agree to more "progressive" engagements. After a preliminary, diagnostic TC, they proceed into one that looks at change management before providing further assistance. This allows for a better idenitification of key problems and the design of interventions. Agency diagnosis is seen as critical. This progressive engagement also builds relationships of trust with recipient agency champions.

One of the agencies that has benefited from the programmatic approach is the Department of Interior and Local Government. Most of the agency's projects before the 1990s were related to capital assistance. Now, many include institutional development or capacity building components, and DILG staff have come to view capital assistance as a tool for capacity development. Most projects provide local and international training for DILG staff and local government officials.

Aid Management

Coordination with donors in ODA programming is undertaken by NEDA. A donors' meeting on the Medium-Term Philippine Development Plan is usually convened to inform them about government priorities and obtain feedback on donor concerns. NEDA has begun joint programming meetings with the World Bank and ADB, and ODA portfolio reviews with the World Bank, the ADB and the Japan Bank for International Cooperation. Multilateral donors currently hold multi-sectoral consultations previously convened on a per sector basis. More bilateral donors have also begun to consult with the Government on a regular basis regarding their country assistance strategies. CIDA holds annual consultations. Germany does so every two years, and Spain every three years. Likewise, there is more frequent coordination among donors' task managers, leading to greater focus and sharing of resources (as in twinning arrangements).

In the arena of ODA review, NEDA has an important role as the official social and economic development planning and policy coordinating body. One of its units, the Public

Investment Staff (PIS), provides support in the coordination and review of ODA flows to ensure consistency with national development priorities. Current project monitoring practice, however, focuses more on physical accomplishments and disbursements rather than outcomes. According to a former PIS head, NEDA needs to develop social assessment as well as project monitoring skills. A recent World Bank-funded project enabled a multi-disciplinary team from the Ateneo de Manila University's Institute of Philippine Culture to partly address this need.

Institutions involved in the capacity development of local and national government officials have strong interests in TC initiatives, since the latter provide revenues for these organizations. Government agencies involved in capacity development include the Development Academy of the Philippines, the Civil Service Commission and the National College of Public Administration and Governance. Private institutions include consulting firms and various universities with schools for government, public administration and the social sciences.

Local consulting firms are naturally in favor of strictly enforcing a requirement giving preference to Filipino firms and consultants in the implementation of ODA projects, as prescribed under the Official Development Act of 1996. They acknowledge, however, that bilateral donors must also consider their respective countries' policies regarding ODA. Establishing linkages with donor country consulting groups is one strategy often adopted to improve chances in competitive bidding.

Technical Cooperation in Agriculture

Agriculture has always been a major sector in the Philippines. It continues to account for more than a fifth of the country's GDP, and until recently, absorbed more than half of the employed population.

The Philippine rural sector has long been plagued by several interrelated problems. Flawed policies and chronic neglect were the result of post-war development strategies that preferred industrialization over agriculture.[2] Defective incentive structures for farmers and other rural producers created by the concentration of land ownership among a few families and institutions (including the Catholic Church) remain structural issues. Soil erosion brought about by deforestation and the destruction of watersheds; periodic typhoons and droughts; inadequate marketing support for agricultural commodities; the massive conversion of agricultural land to residential subdivisions or industrial estates; and the retreat of government support to agriculture, compound the sector's problems (De Guzman 1999, Gordoncillo and others 1998,

---

[2] The pursuit of import-substitution and/or export-oriented industrialization tended to favour overvalued currencies that placed agricultural exports at a disadvantage. Credit was rationed and industrial enterprises were prioritized in credit allocation. More resources went to infrastructure for urban centers, leading to the neglect of rural infrastructure. Thus, rural areas are sorely lacking in reliable farm-to-market roads, and post-harvest facilities and irrigated land area declined in the 1990s (Habito and others 2001). At times the emphasis on industrialization led to the systematic exploitation of agriculture. The devaluation of 1962 and the progressive devaluations in the 1970s were accompanied by the imposition of export taxes. Increased earnings from exports due to the devaluation were reallocated to industrial enterprises. Taxes were also imposed on agricultural imports.

Paunlagui 1999). Despite attempts at change such as agrarian reform, dismantling monopolies and deregulation, these problems persist.

The agricultural sector has also suffered from issues related to capacity at the institutional, personnel and community levels. At the institutional level, failures to produce results have been traced to mismanagement (MTPDP 1987-1992), politicized bureaucracy (Tolentino 2001b) and weaknesses in the institutional structure of government (David, Ponce and Intal 1993). Inadequate research and development infrastructures and a low ratio of extension workers to total rural population also contributed (MTPDP 1987-1992). The sector faced major constraints in planning, implementation, monitoring and evaluation (ADB 1996a). Key stumbling blocks cited were the absence of integrated agricultural development plans at the regional and local government levels, and a long-term agricultural strategy. Other important constraints included inadequate database and information systems, and no clearly defined linkages and mechanisms for policy and programme formulation and implementation between the Department of Agriculture and local governments (ADB 1996a).

Problems at the personnel level are associated with high turnovers of managers and technical staff because of the instability of leadership at the Department of Agriculture, and recruitment by the private sector and aid agencies. Contributing to the problem is the inadequate in-house capacity to conduct policy studies and craft policies (ADB 1996a), or to design and deliver agricultural support services. Ineffective agricultural extension services is identified among the main causes of low productivity among Filipino farmers.

At the community level, institutional capacity development has become an important issue as post-Marcos administrations sought to bring about "the transformation of the poor into self-reliant and productive citizens capable of actively participating in the total development effort" (MTPDP 1987-1992:3). Considering the lack of budgetary support to agriculture and the low ratio of agricultural extension workers to the growing rural population, the need for organizations of farmers and other rural producers as well as other members of the rural sector has a practical rationale.

Weighed against these challenges are at least three positive factors. First, the Philippines has an excellent public agricultural university (the University of the Philippines Los Baños) and several private universities with respected agricultural colleges. For the past three decades at least, students from Asian and African countries have attended these institutions on scholarships from their own Governments, international foundations or aid agencies. The Philippines also has a network of state agricultural schools, training institutions and research facilities throughout the country. In addition, the International Rice Research Institute, which has trained hundreds of Filipino researchers over the years, has its headquarters close to the Los Baños campus.

Second, the Philippine educational system is turning out an average of 12,000 agricultural graduates per year. Many seek employment in Government or the private sector rather than farming. In the past two decades, a significant number of Ph.D. holders from foreign and local universities served as advisers or consultants, or occupied top leadership positions at the Department of Agriculture and other departments. This may no longer hold considering that fewer young professionals seem to be going into postgraduate training. This trend may undermine the staffing of agricultural colleges and universities; the supply of consultants and technical staff; and the number of reflective analysts, commentators and critics.

A third source of support for the country's agricultural capacity development agenda is civil society, notably NGOs. Their considerable expertise and experience in community organizing has helped the Government establish agrarian reform communities and various groups of rural producers. In many instances, however, general community organizing skills are not sufficient, as the organizers have to be knowledgeable about technical issues, including, for example, irrigation construction and management, or credit sourcing and financial management. Grassroots organizations, like farmers' cooperatives and rural women's groups, also contribute significantly to local capacity development.

Plans and Strategies

The Medium-Term Philippine Development Plan articulates broad policy directions and national and sector development strategies. The plan generally treats agriculture as part of the broader rural, agrarian and natural resources sector. In consultation with NGOs, the private sector and other stakeholders, the Department of Agriculture crafts the sub-sector plan for agriculture and fisheries; The Department of Environment and Natural Resources for forestry, natural resources and the environment; and the Department of Agrarian Reform for reform entailing land title transfers and support to agricultural production. The three departments also provide leadership in the preparation of the investment plans (listing of prospective projects and possible funding sources) for their respective sub-sectors.

In 1997, the Philippine Congress passed the Agriculture and Fisheries Modernization Act (AFMA), which serves as the framework developing both sectors. The law provides for reform and reorientation in the provision of public production and marketing services. Key among these reforms is the creation of Strategic Agriculture and Fisheries Development Zones (SAFDZ) based on the natural resource characteristics of particular areas, rather than political boundaries. Each SAFDZ is mandated to craft an integrated development plan that maximizes natural resources.

The MTPDP identifies general capacity building areas under "human resource development" (education, health and nutrition) and cites sectoral training and capacity development needs as part of the broad strategies for the sector. For 1999-2004, agriculture and fisheries used AFMA as its framework for needed institutional reforms, the provision of various support services and for capacity development in the agricultural sector. Two areas that pertain directly to capacity development are the rationalization and strengthening of the National Agriculture and Fisheries Education System (NAFES) for quality agriculture and fisheries education; and the promotion of a dynamic, client-responsive National Research and Development System in Agriculture and Fisheries under the Department of Agriculture.

In the MTPDP 2001-2004, these and other capacity building concerns are integrated as part of the broader strategy for modernizing agriculture and fisheries. A few examples of capacity development components include:

- Improvement of support service delivery and the promotion of demand-driven capacity development through extensive use of information and communication technologies (access to information, extension services, procurement and regulatory systems).

- Continued rationalization of the research, development and extension systems into "one system - one programme".

- Protection of the most vulnerable from the adjustment shocks of modernization and globalization by expansion of non-farm livelihood training.

- Development of the capabilities of partner institutions and ensuring the continued full participation of stakeholders in the implementation of AFMA. This includes facilitation of technology transfer from research institutes to local government units, cooperatives and peoples' organizations; and the delegation of responsibilities for project formulation, implementation, monitoring and evaluation to cooperatives and peoples' organizations.

NGO Participation

In line with the participatory and consultative approaches of the Aquino and Ramos administrations, the Government sought the assistance of NGOs to organize community groups and to help in the delivery of agricultural services. During the Ramos Presidency, however, the opportunities for Government-NGO collaboration declined. At this time, the Department of Agriculture focused on agribusiness and the promotion of globally competitive crops, while NGOs concentrated on traditional crops and food security.

On their own, NGOs play an active role in Philippine agriculture. During the Marcos regime and the early years of the Aquino administration, many NGOs prioritized policy advocacy and dedicated a large part of their efforts to the pursuit of a genuine agrarian reform programme. Foreign funding agencies financed these activities in order to promote human rights and social justice. In the 1990s, the passage of a watered-down agrarian reform law, the shift of ODA funds to newly-independent Eastern European countries and the imperatives of globalization pushed most NGOs to devote their energies to sustainable livelihood projects that aimed at increasing incomes of small farmers. Early NGO strategies featured integrated rural development approaches, but with resource constraints, many NGOs moved to less costly and more specialized interventions.

According to a leader of a national farmers' organization, NGOs working on sustainable agriculture differ in their understanding of issues or approaches. Some view sustainable agriculture in terms of sustainability of sources of income, while others are biased against any form of modernization.

Role of Local Government

Apart from the Department of Agriculture, local government plays an important role in TC for agriculture. Before the passage of the Local Government Code in 1991, the Department of Agriculture had provincial and municipal offices with their complement of technical and administrative staff. Since 1991, these offices were turned over to local government units that are now mandated to plan and implement agricultural programmes. The devolution of functions and personnel, however, was not accompanied by commensurate devolution of resources. In many instances, this meant the allocation of a large portion of the local agricultural services budget to personnel costs, leaving little for the purchase of equipment or transport. Not surprisingly, the post-devolution performance of most LGUs in terms of agricultural extension has been spotty at best. The few LGUs that have been able to deliver significant agricultural services are those with more resources at their disposal and/or strong leadership.

Tensions between the Department of Agriculture and local government persist. There is much that still needs to be done in order to improve cooperation between national and local government, even in the area of maximizing the utilization of TC for agriculture. One initiative that is currently being implemented is the appointment of provincial and municipal coordinators among the regional Department of Agriculture staff.

The Role of TC

The major sources of TC grant assistance are the EU, Japan and China, although Japan, the ADB and the World Bank are also major sources of loan assistance (with and without TC components). A significant proportion of TC is channelled through the Department of Agriculture and its constituent offices and agencies.

Technical cooperation for the agricultural sector has improved research and development capacities of several agricultural agencies through the upgrading of facilities and training of local researchers. It has also built competencies in project management, monitoring and evaluation within agricultural agencies and among the development industry.

At the personnel level, capacity development occurred as a result of formal training and/or scholarships, or as people did their jobs. Many of the local consultants and professors in agriculture received their doctorates on TC scholarships, and a number of officials at the Department of Agriculture received training at Philippine institutions or overseas. Too many scholars and trainees, however, either never returned to their home institution, or left soon after they completed their service period.

At the field or community level, TC projects have supported community-organizing efforts that established farmers', fishers', and rural women's organizations. The institutional development component of irrigation projects is a good example of capacity development outcomes of capital assistance to the agricultural sector. However, partly as a result of the devolution of responsibilities for farmer-owned communal irrigation systems in 1991, confusion reigned and support for communal systems declined. So did the functionality and performance of these systems and the irrigation associations.

There are, however, three ways in which TC can diminish capacity development:

- Technical cooperation projects often fail to take into consideration local government development plans and therefore undermine them. Local governments, on the other hand, accept any form of assistance that comes their way, even if the assistance is out of line with local needs. The long-standing differences between the Department of Agriculture and LGUs also hinder the national agency from adequately providing assistance to its local counterparts.

- The attractive salaries and work environment of the funding agencies often lead to personnel leaving the public sector to join foreign funding agencies or research institutions. This is especially true for younger and more qualified personnel at the Department of Agriculture. Personnel sent abroad for higher degrees on TC grants return only to complete their service contracts before moving on to better-paying jobs.

- Donors continue to rely on expensive foreign consultants more than is justified by available local expertise.

This survey points to the following elements as necessary for ensuring that TC leads to capacity development:

- A framework for development and/or capacity development, whether at the national, sectoral or local level.

- Institutional mechanisms for ensuring that proposed TC projects are in line with the development framework and that they build capacity.

- Adequate and experienced personnel.

These points can be demonstrated by contrasting the experience of local government and the Department of Agriculture. The latter has all of the above elements in place, so it can ensure that TC projects are aligned with the priorities of the administration and that they do build capacity. Local government units, on the other hand, lack some of the elements above. While most local governments have development plans, approved TC projects often diverge from these plans because local authorities are not part of the TC planning process.

Two other elements have been found to help bring about capacity development through TC projects. One is the presence of mechanisms and processes for selecting and designing projects independently of the priorities of foreign aid agencies. The Department of Agriculture's practice of hiring local consultants for project development has created a market for expertise. Another element pertains to the increased sensitivity of donors to domestic priorities and processes. This enhances institutional capacity and supports efforts to install transparency and accountability into TC projects.

Lessons and Conclusions

The review of policies, processes and practices of TC in the Philippines indicates the importance of preparing a national development agenda, and the process by which this is done. The Government agenda includes the broad outlines of national capacities that are required for achieving national goals. It actively seeks the participation of various sectors of society, notably NGOs and people's organizations, in planning as well as implementation. It also generates processes of consultation with funding agencies for performance reviews of aid portfolios, programming and negotiating for ODA (including TC). Donors, for their part, generally harmonize their country assistance plans with Philippine priorities while pushing for global considerations and their own areas of concern.

Persistent poverty, slow growth, inequitable distribution of income, law/order problems, and corruption in Government impede progress in the Philippines. Official development assistance, including TC, has supported Government and non-government initiatives to address these issues. Moreover, donors have gone into joint programming and multi-donor ODA and TC in specific regions (such as Mindanao) or issues (safe motherhood, HIV/AIDS and agrarian reform).

Following Philippine rules, bilateral and multilateral aid agencies fund the programmes and projects not only of central government but also those of NGOs and local government. The establishment of special funding facilities by donors such as CIDA and AusAID, area-based programming by the EU and AusAID, and other innovations have enabled development aid to respond to broad national concerns and to immediate needs within specified areas. Despite the difficulties donors encounter in dealing with NGOs, the latter are still perceived as easier to deal with than the Government, especially since NGO agendas reflect grassroots concerns.

The commonest forms of TC continue to be technical advice from consultants hired either by the donor or by the project, support for research and development, and various training and institution building activities. While donors are increasingly utilizing the services of local institutions and experts for TC, most funding agencies continue to hire expatriates despite the availability of expertise in the Philippines. A large portion of TC is in kind and involves the importation of equipment or materials from donor countries. Furthermore, TC projects often require the creation of project management offices, although several of these are "organic" or staffed and run by regular staff of implementing agencies. Some projects are managed by firms from donor countries or co-managed by an official from the Philippine agency and a national of the donor country. In all cases, these PMOs are staffed with locally contracted administrative and technical personnel.

In many funding agencies, governance is a recurrent theme. It has also influenced the ways donors manage their aid programmes. Funding facilities and other programmes and projects have steering or management teams/committees that draw their membership from the donor agency, the Government and NGOs.

Impact of TC on Capacity Development

The links between TC and national capacity development are by no means systematic or comprehensive, but there are some important exceptions. Technical cooperation for public sector reform has yielded at least two positive general outcomes. These are improved government competencies and systems, and increased capacity of NGOs to advocate for, and monitor public sector reforms. The first has resulted in better performance (such as increased rates of collection), while the second has produced a vigilant monitor eager to stop corruption.

At the local government level, some TC projects have created a multiplier effect, albeit limited, of good practices in local governance. A local-level outcome in Naga City has seen greater transparency in local governance through the provision of computer access to information.

At the field or community level, a number of TC projects or have supported efforts that made possible the formation of farmer, fisher, women and youth groups. While a number of these organizations have become moribund at the end of the project, some have persisted. The countless stories of irrigation associations that have helped the National Irrigation Administration (NIA) design more workable irrigation systems, or have taken on the operation and maintenance of irrigation facilities – with or without official guidance – provide good examples of capacity development outcomes related to the TC component of capital assistance to the agricultural sector (Korten and Siy 1989, De los Reyes and Jopillo 1986).

Some of the positive examples of TC-supported innovations and best practices in the field are captured in manuals. The process of selecting best practices forms part of a culture of learning.

At the individual level, capacity development occurs as a result of formal training and/or scholarships, or on-the-job learning. Scholarships and study tours have yielded both unfavourable and favourable results. A number of scholars and trainees never returned to the country or to their home agency or institution. Many, however, did come back, some to serve in Government in elective or appointed positions, and others to return to their NGOs or academic institutions.

Yet there are various factors inhibiting the impact of TC on capacity development. Bureaucratic inertia is one, and is applied to both the Government and donors. With respect to the Government, red tape prevents speedier implementation of projects, fund disbursements and the commitment of counterpart funds to projects. Moreover, government agencies do not always show their commitment to TC or are resistant to greater donor harmonization.

At the local government level, problems include overhauls in key staff with every change of administration and the lack of clarity in priorities for training. Except in a few places, training at local government level is supply-driven, as national government agencies advocate their own sectoral concerns instead of responding to the priority needs of local governments. Capacity retention remains an obstacle: the difficulty of building careers in government service, particularly at the local level, drive civil service officers to the private sector or international aid agencies.

On the donor side, several factors have been identified as actually or potentially hindering capacity development, although some pertain to ODA in general.

- Policies can be so rigid and decisions so centralized that local donor offices cannot take advantage of opportunities to respond to emerging TC issues or to enter into partnership with other donors.

- The nature and responsiveness of funding is affected when personnel of funding agencies are generalist bureaucrats rather than development practitioners.

- Field operations and TC project commitments are adversely affected by political decisions (made at headquarters or in donor countries) to divert previously committed funds to more strategically expedient areas.

- Different planning cycles constrain possibilities for joint programming and multi-donor assistance initiatives.

- Lack of transparency in the selection of TC consultants or contractors persists. In some instances, the consultant/contractor is selected even before bidding begins.

This survey also revealed a number of positive factors that enhance the impact of TC on capacity development. Technical cooperation works better when:

- It is lodged in existing units that are responsible for the relevant functions, and training is focused and customized to agency needs.

- It is approached sectorally, with donors selecting parts of the whole programme of intervention to support.

- Inputs of expatriate experts are maximized only when they possess knowledge and/or skills that are not available locally, and when they are culturally sensitive and can communicate effectively.

- The selection of TC providers is transparent.

- Use is made of the contacts of national or regional consultants to determine capacity development and other beneficiary needs.

Ownership

The Philippine study indicates that the concept is complex and multidimensional. Technical cooperation projects and/or donors that promote a certain notion or level of ownership may have mechanisms that undermine it, or fail to identify the strategic partner or "owner" of the TC project.

- **Priorities and counterparts** – The Government and its TC donors claim to have instituted processes and mechanisms that would encourage ownership of the TC agenda by the Philippine Government and other relevant organizations. They point to the donors' use of the MTPDP and results of consultations with various groups as bases for the donors' country programming. However, this is tempered by the fact that the Philippine agenda is but one of the many inputs to a donor's country strategy. In the case of NGO funding, the NGO agenda is upheld only in cases where the funding mechanism allows this. Another indicator of ownership that donors and Philippine proponents mention is the latter's counterpart to the TC. Donor requirements differ, however, and it is difficult to say whether projects that require counterparts are truly "owned" by the implementing agencies.

- **TC conceptualization and design** – Another dimension of the ownership issue pertains to the origin of the TC request, and inputs to project planning and design. In the Philippines, donors vary in the amount of control they wield regarding the content of projects. In some instances, donors offer TC and local groups accept it, sometimes reluctantly. In others, donors send consultants to develop the project. Some donors seek the inputs of the beneficiary agency or group on the scope of work and selection of consultants that will deliver the TC, while other donors fund TC as requested by the Government or NGOs. A number of donors, however, require TC to be provided by their nationals and that equipment be brought in from the donor country.

- **Project execution** – Yet another issue related to ownership concerns project management or execution. Using this yardstick, the different modes operating in the country denote varying degrees of control (or ownership) of the project by the implementing agency. At one end are TC donors that encourage organic project management offices, and at the other are donors that leave project management to firms based in their own countries. In between are donors that set up co-management systems. However, even when PMOs are organic or co-management is in force, the TC may be supplied almost exclusively by expatriate consultants or experts – with the Philippine co-director or manager a mere figurehead.

- **Identity of the strategic partner** – The last issue relates to the question: Whose ownership? Until the mid-1990s, consultations meant meeting with central government agencies and their senior officials, although a few donors were already seeking the inputs and commitments of local governments and NGOs. By the late 1990s, several donors had area-based or sub-national programmes or projects in addition to TC to national government agencies. Their interest was to foster the commitment of the TC beneficiary group, be they local governments, communities or a national government agency.

Making the Philippine partner institution or group feel committed to the capacity development initiative often involves a time-consuming process. Donor agencies that truly want to engage in this process often find themselves in a quandary, as they also have to meet deadlines and keep project costs within approved budgets.

Donor Coordination

The Philippines has more than 20 ODA sources that provide TC, but Japan accounts for more than half of ODA, especially if its contribution through ADB-initiated projects is included. The Government periodically meets with donors separately or in groups for country programming and joint programming exercises, and the NGO community also invites donors to discuss prospective and current programmes.

As funding agencies respond to the priority needs identified in the current MTPDP, they are likely to formulate programmes around similar themes. Since the late 1990s, these have been poverty, governance, the Mindanao situation and economic growth. Many donors did channel funds to address these issues. Fortunately, other large TC donors continued to pursue area-based programming outside Mindanao, good governance work in the provinces considered among the poorest in the country, and to support policy research in a wide variety of sectors.

Donors also confer among themselves, particularly when they plan to allocate TC and other ODA funds to a particular region (such as Mindanao), or to address a particular issue. Joint programming or multi-agency assistance initiatives can reportedly minimize the red tape that each donor must contend with. The decision on whether or not to participate in these initiatives is hampered by different programming cycles and the degree of autonomy each donor can exercise.

Over the past six to seven years, more and more funding agencies have begun to move toward programme-based assistance. Japan is the most recent. Programme-based assistance requires that a certain amount of decision making take place in the local office of the donor, and it can only work with a greater delegation of responsibility. Some donors are moving towards operating local funding facilities, a model spearheaded by CIDA. Funding facilities can help local offices become more responsive to addressing the emerging needs of recipients.

Many of the donor representatives interviewed believe that TC can fill gaps in various areas. It can help usher in new structures, new ways of thinking and new practices. What it does, therefore, is make available to recipient countries expert services in areas that have been deemed important. The expertise can come from within the agency, from the recipient country or from another country.

As aid budgets get tighter, bilateral donors have found it necessary to become more accountable to taxpayers. While cost-effectiveness should favor the hiring of more local expertise, it is also politically important to continue dispatching donor country experts and maintaining a high level of visibility in recipient countries.

However, all the donor agency officials interviewed for this study claimed that their agencies have been hiring more Filipino consultants and contracting local universities and training institutions for capacity development. The recourse to local expertise has been facilitated by at least two factors: a large and highly diversified pool of professionals and institutions, and relatively lower costs. While donors are hiring university-based professionals, NGO workers, or independent consultants for short- or medium-term TC services, they have also been tapping the public sector for longer-term assignments or posts. A job with a donor agency is highly coveted as it pays at least four times the salary of a technical staff member or a senior government official.

Sustainability

To ensure sustainability, funding agencies often require the Government to provide counterpart funding. Because of chronic budget deficits or cutbacks, this has not always happened. When it has, there have been delays or reductions in the release of the funds. The problem is compounded in the case of foreign-assisted local government projects. As JICA has discovered, local government budgets are often inadequate to sustain the project or activity. There are also no guarantees that succeeding governments will support projects their predecessors (who may be political rivals) have endorsed.

In any project, the core staff should be supported by the host agency. The project should also provide for additional (contractual) staff for project management or short-term technical inputs, but who would be phased out. This way, project-related costs do not burden the institution by way of expanding staff. A question related to sustainability arises when capacities developed among contractual PMO staff are not transferred to the staff of the implementing agency.

The Importance of Change Management

The design of TC must pay attention to the need for managing the change process, meaning the change introduced while TC is ongoing, as well as the change that is expected after the life of the project. The importance of building in mechanisms for institutionalizing TC outputs cannot be overemphasized. Recommendations must always include follow-through activities that should consider the environment in which such recommendations would be implemented. Recommendations should also include plans to enhance management's commitment and capacity to drive the change process. Impact evaluations should be factored in.

The process for implementing TC must also be adequately discussed among all parties involved. Real partnerships must be in force for significant capacity development to occur. Early in the process, a champion from within the agency should be identified. S/he must occupy a position high enough to be able to initiate changes and mobilize resources to sustain TC outputs. In cases where a change in management is foreseen, potential second-generation champions must be identified and cultivated.

To develop an overall framework for reform or capacity development initiatives, it is important to know where the agency is headed in the next five years. As such, it is better to have a "diagnostic initiative" first before developing or implementing specific projects. This progressive engagement is more manageable and less expensive, since losses when the agency is not up to par are kept low.

Sustainability of outputs is a common concern among all stakeholders of TC initiatives. Characteristics of sustainable TC include the following:

- Sustainable TC projects respond to the mainstream functions of agencies, and more generally, the beneficiary groups (communities, NGOs and local governments). If the focus is on mainstream functions, budgets for follow-through activities are more likely to be included in regular appropriation. Since they concern core functions, such TC is not isolated. With greater ownership, significant commitments in resources are more likely.

- Sustainable TC is usually lodged in existing units that are responsible for such functions. Artificial PMOs are not created. This allows for greater capacity development of the institution.

- Sustainable TC initiatives usually approach problems sectorally. A more holistic approach that looks at change incentives and sanctions, plus technology needs, is essential. Large sector studies have been helpful, and have allowed donors to fund parts so as to complete the entire programme of intervention.

- Training provided in TC projects should be more focused and customized to the needs of the agency or beneficiary group. It is best for training programmes to be anchored on the change process in an agency.

This country study has highlighted several features of the Philippines that make it an interesting case study. First, the country has a large and diversified pool of professionals and local expertise that can be tapped for various capacity development TC: public sector reform, sectoral TC (agriculture, health, education), and thematic issues (gender and environment). Foreign donors, however, seem to be tapping the same experts.

Second, the country institutionalized participation of the private sector, NGOs and people's organizations in governance matters, including ODA and TC processes. The country study, however, shows the contentious nature of government-NGO relations, as NGOs still view themselves more as watchdogs than as partners (despite the incorporation of NGO agendas and former NGO leaders in high-level offical positions).

Third, there have been several innovations in TC for capacity development. One example is the creation by donors of funding facilities that afford them greater flexibility within specified programme areas. Another is the increasing transparency of a number of funding facilities and TC projects. Donors consult with various stakeholders – weaving the donor agenda with the Government's priorities and other stakeholders' interests – and collectively select the consultants or providers of capacity development services. Yet another innovation is the conduct of joint or multi-donor assistance initiatives that allow donors to support respective parts of large sectoral TC projects.

Finally, mechanisms governing NGO participation in ODA and TC respect the autonomy of NGOs, reflect the Government's confidence in the capacity of NGOs to police their ranks, and allow NGOs to seek their own funding. Funding windows or facilities for NGOs allow them to pursue their developmental and change agenda, unlike sub-contracting components of government or donor projects and programmes.

References

Abad, Ricardo G. 1974. "Migration Expectations of Filipino Medical Graduates: An Overview." Paper prepared for the Conference on International Migration from the Philippines, sponsored by the East-West Population Institute. Honolulu.

Agriculture Policy and Strategy Team. 1986. "Agenda for Action for the Philippine Rural Sector." Agricultural Policy Research Program, Philippine Institute for Development Studies. Makati.

Asian Development Bank (ADB). 1995. "Fourteenth Report of Post-Evaluation Abstracts (from 1994 Reports). Manila.

———. 1996. *Key Indicators of Developing Asian and Pacific Countries 1996.* New York: Oxford University Press.

———. 1996a. "Technical Assistance to the Republic of the Philippines for Institutional Capacity Building for Policy Formulation, Planning, Monitoring and Evaluation for the Agriculture Sector."

———. 1997. "Country Operational Strategy, Philippines." http://www.adb.org.

———. 1997a. "From Project Financier to Broad-Based Development Institution." In *Annual Report 1997.* Manila.

———. 2000. "Philippine Country Assistance Plan 2000-2002." http://www.adb.org.

———. 2001. *Key Indicators 2001: Growth and Change in Asia and the Pacific.* New York: Oxford University Press.

———. 2001a. "Special Evaluation Study on Sustainability of Policy Reforms through Selected Advisory Technical Assistance." Manila.

———. and World Bank (ADB/WB). 1999. *Philippine Education for the 21st Century: The Philippines Education Sector Survey.* A joint study in collaboration with the Government of the Philippines. Manila.

Bagadion, Benjamin U. 1989. "The Evolution of the Policy Context: An Historical Overview." In *Transforming a Bureaucracy: The Experience of the Philippine National Irrigation Administration,* edited by Korten, F. and Robert Y. Siy, Jr. Quezon City: Ateneo de Manila University Press.

Balisacan, Arsenio 1999. "Poverty Profile in the Philippines: An Update and Reexamination of Evidence in the Wake of the Asian Crisis." Unpublished paper.

Bello, Walden F., Frank Lynch, and Perla Q. Makil. 1969. "Brain Drain in the Philippines." In *Modernization: Its Impact in the Philippines IV IPC Papers, No. 7.* Quezon City: Institute of Philippine Culture, Ateneo de Manila University.

Brigham, Susan and Emma S. Castillo 1999. "Language Policy for Education in the Philippines." Background Paper for *Philippine Education for the 21st Century: The 1998 Philippines Education Sector Study.* Manila: Asian Development Bank.

Brillantes, Alex B. Jr. 2001. "Public Sector Reform and Poverty Reduction." A paper delivered at the Conference on Poverty, Growth, and the Role of Institutions at the Asian Development Bank.

Cabanilla, Liborio S., and Merlyne M. Paunlagui. 1999. *Food Security in the Philippines.* Los Baños and Quezon City: Institute of Strategic Planning and Policy Studies, University of the Philippines-Los Baños, in cooperation with the UP Center for Integrative and Development Studies.

Cari_o, Ledevina V. 1990. "An Assessment of Public Administration in the Philippines, 1986-1988." *Working Paper Series No. 90-03.* Makati: Philippine Institute for Development Studies.

Clark, John. 1991. *Democratizing Development: The Role of Voluntary Organizations.* West Hartford, Conn.: Kumarian Press.

Constantino-David, Karina. 1998. "From the Present Looking Back: A History of Philippine NGOs." In *Organizing for Democracy: NGOs, Civil Society, and the Philippine State,* edited by Sidney and Noble. Quezon City: Ateneo de Manila University Press.

David, Cristina C., Eliseo R. Ponce, and Ponciano S. Intal, Jr. 1993. "Organizing for Results: The Philippine Agricultural Sector." In *Poverty, Growth and the Fiscal Crisis,* by Emmanuel S. de Dios et al. Makati and Ottawa: Philippine Institute for Development Studies and the International Development Research Centre.

De Guzman, Panfilo. 1999. "Land Conversion Issue Revisited: Where Have All the Rice Fields Gone." *Policy Forum.*

De los Reyes, Romana P., and Ma. Sylvia G. Jopillo. 1986. *An Evaluation of the Philippine Participatory Communal Irrigation Program.* Quezon City: Institute of Philippine Culture, Ateneo de Manila University.

Fernandez, Ederlinda M., Maisie Faith Dagapioso, and Emerita T. Basilio 1984. "Women, Development and Aid: Case Studies Assessing Official Development-Assisted Projects on Women in Zamboanga City." A report submitted to the Group of Ten Lakas Kababaihan, Inc.

Fikree, Fariyal, Riet Groenen, Nilda Lambo, Ietje H. Reerink, and Francisco H. Roque. 1999. "Final Evaluation of Strengthening the Management and Field Implementation of FP/RH Programme PHI/94/PO5-PO7)." United Nations Population Fund.

Foronda, Marcelino A. 1978. "America is in the Heart: Ilocano Immigration to the United States, 1906-1930." *The Journal of History.*

Gonzales, Raul. 1998. *Official Development Assistance in the Philippines, 1986-1996.* Quezon City: Caucus of Development NGOs, with the Sasakawa Peace Foundation, Japan.

————. 2000. "Trends in Official Development Assistance ODA) for Phlippine NGOs: A Follow-Up Study." Caucus of Development NGO Networks, in cooperation with the Sasakawa Peace Foundation, Japan.

Gordoncillo, P., Aragon C., Llorito M. Trinidad, Espanto, L., Laquinon, M. and Bagundol, E. 1998. "A Study on the Implication of Land Use Conversion on CARP." Institute of Agrarian and Rural Development Studies and the College of Economics and Management, University of the Philippines Los Baños.

Habito, C., Briones, R., and Paterno, Elizabeth M. 2001. "Investment Productivity and Land Markets Impacts of the Comprehensive Agrarian Reform Program." Department of Agrarian Reform.

Illo, Jeanne Frances I. 1994. "Working and Living for the Family: Gender, Work and Education." *Indian Journal of Gender Studies.*

————. 1997. *Women in the Philippines.* Country Briefing Paper for the Asian Development Bank.

————. 1999. "Gender Dimension of the Economic Crisis in the Philippines." *Philippine Labor Review.*

————. and Frank Lynch, S.J. 1974. "Who Gets the Job: The Old or the Educated? Education and Employment in the Bicol River Basin." *SSRU Research Report Series.* Social Survey Research Unit, Bicol River Basin Development Program.

Jeanne Frances I. Illo and Rosalinda Pineda Ofreneo (eds.) 1999. *Carrying the Burden of the World: Women Reflecting on the Effects of the Crisis on Women and Children.* Quezon City: Center for Integrative and Development Studies, University of the Philippines.

Illo, Jeanne Frances I., and Jaime B. Polo 1990. *Fishers, Traders, Farmers, Wives: Life Stories of Ten Women in a Fishing Village.* Quezon City: Institute of Philippine Culture, Ateneo de Manila University.

Illo, Jeanne Frances I., Carolyn I. Sobritchea and Ma. Cecilia G. Conaco. 2000. "Gender-Responsive Quality Reproductive Health Care Services in Selected NGOs." Final evaluation report of the Ted Turner Project by the Institute of Philippine Culture, Ateneo de Manila University.

Johanson, Richard K. 1999. "Higher Education in the Philippines." Background Paper for *Philippine Education for the 21st Century: The 1998 Philippines Education Sector Study.* Manila: Asian Development Bank.

Korten, Frances and Robert Siy (eds.) 1989. *Transforming a Bureaucracy: The Experience of the Philippine National Irrigation Administration.* Quezon City: Ateneo de Manila University Press.

Lynch, Frank. 1973. "Perspectives on Filipino Clannishness." *Philippine Sociological Review.*

Mangahas, Mahar. 1995. "Public Opinion about Officials." Paper presented to the National Academy of Science and Technology.

———. 2000. "Public Satisfaction with Governance in the Philippines, 1986-99." Paper presented to the Joint meeting of the World Association for Public Opinion Research and the American Association for Public Opinion Research. Quezon City: Social Weather Stations.

———. 2002. "Update on Surveys Concerning Corruption: A report submitted to the World Bank/Manila Office." http://www.sws.org.ph.

Mojares, Resil. 1983. "Cebuano Perceptions of the Hawaii Migration, 1909-1934." *Philippine Quarterly of Culture and Society.*

Monroe, Paul. 1925. *A Survey of the Educational System of the Philippine Islands.* Manila: Bureau of Printing.

Government of the Philippines / Bureau of Labor and Employment Statistics (BLES). 1998. *Yearbook of Labor Statistics.* Manila.

Government of the Philippines. *Medium-Term Development Plans* 1987-1992, 1993-1998, 1999-2004.

Republic of the Philippines / National Economic and Development Authority (NEDA). 1998. *The Philippine National Development Plan: Directions for the 21st Century.* Makati: NEDA.

Government of the Philippines. 2001. "State of the Nation Address by President Gloria Macapagal-Arroyo" with draft of the MTPDP 2001-2004.

Racelis, Mary. 1994. "From the Fringes to the Mainstream." *Intersect.*

———. 2000. "New Visions and Strong Actions: Civil Society in the Philippines." In *Funding Virtue: Civil Society Aid and Democracy Promotion,* edited by Marina Ottaway and Thomas Carothers. Washington, DC: Carnegie Endowment for International Peace.

Rodriguez, Luz Lopez, and Diosa Labiste. 1995. "Women and Development Aid: Case Studies Assessing Official Development-Assisted Projects on Women in Panay." A report submitted to the Group of Ten Lakas ng Kababaihan.

Silliman, G. Sidney and Lela Garner Noble (eds.) 1998. *Organizing for Democracy: NGOs, Civil Society, and the Philippine State.* Quezon City: Ateneo de Manila University Press. (Also published by the University of Hawaii Press.)

Smith, Peter G. 1981. "Population Pressure and Social Response on the Ilocos Coast in the Philippines." Working paper for the East West Institute. Honolulu.

Sobhan, Rehman. 1994. "Aid Versus Markets in the Institutionalization of Consultancy Services: Some Asian Contrasts." *Asia Pacific Development Journal.*

Tadeo-Pingol, Alice. 2000. "Changing Family Structures: When Gender Identities is a Matter of Choice." A paper presented during the Women's Studies in Asia 2000 Conference.

Tolentino, V. Bruce J. 2001a. "Discontinuous Sector Leadership and Stagnation in Philippine Agriculture." Paper presented at the Annual Conference of the Philippine Agricultural Economics and Development Association.

———. 2001b. "Can We Feed Ourselves? Rapid Population Growth and Rice Policy in the Philippines." A presentation at the Conference Towards a Better Understanding of Population in Philippine Economic Development.

United Nations Development Programme.1998. *Human Development Report 1998*. New York: Oxford University Press.

———. 2000, *Human Development Report 2000*. New York: Oxford University Press.

———. 2001. "Preliminary Report on Country Level Impact Assessment of the Philippines." New York / Manila.

———. / United Nations Children's Fund. 1999. "Capacity Development: An Analysis and Synthesis of Its Current Conceptualisation and Implications for Practice." Background paper.

World Bank. 2001. "Fighting Poverty for Lasting Results: Projects in Progress/Projects in the Pipeline as of 30 September 2001." Pasig City.

———. n.d. "Philippines Growth with Equity: The Remaining Agenda." Pasig City.

8 Uganda[1]

DRIVING TECHNICAL COOPERATION FOR NATIONAL CAPACITY DEVELOPMENT

Introduction

Eight years after the adoption of the OECD/DAC principles for technical cooperation (TC) in 1994, there is still a widespread perception that TC has changed little, remaining donor-driven and failing to address the priority needs of recipient countries. At its worst, TC is perceived to detract from, and even erode capacity development. In Uganda, a May 2001 government study found that: "(t)echnical cooperation has two significant drawbacks: It is a very expensive input and can sometimes substitute for, rather than complement the development of local capacity. It is almost entirely funded through the development budget and mostly by donors, which has reduced Government's control over its allocation." The report continues: "In some cases the employment of technical cooperation on donor-funded projects is motivated by the donor's need for accountability rather than the absence of local capacity."

This chapter attempts to address the following questions: How have the nature, policies, practices and modalities of TC in Uganda changed since the early 1990s? To what extent have they changed? What brought about, and what resisted change? What

[1] This paper was prepared by Arsene M. Balihuta, Senior Lecturer and Associate Director, Institute of Economics, Makerere University; Kenneth Mugambe, Assistant Commissioner, Economic Development Policy and Research Department, Ministry of Finance, Planning, and Economic Development, Government of Uganda; Augustus Nuwagaba, Senior Lecturer and Consultant, Faculty of Social Sciences, Makerere University; and Warren Nyamugasira, Executive Director, Uganda National NGO Forum.

has been the impact of TC on capacity development? How have various TC modalities affected impact?

Background

Uganda was one of the more developmentally-advanced countries in Sub-Saharan Africa until 1970. From 1971 until 1986, political instability and economic mismanagement plagued the country, reducing it to one of the region's most impoverished. Its infrastructure was devastated and its stock of human resources seriously depleted. Institutions that had been internationally recognized, such as Makarere University, stagnated and declined. The capacities available in the country in 1970 were largely diminished during this period.

The country changed course in 1987, signalling an end to its political and economic isolation. Economic reforms were initiated that year, with structural adjustment facilities from the World Bank and International Monetary Fund (IMF). The country began to rebuild infrastructure and develop its human resources. A market-oriented economy has rapidly re-established itself; GDP growth averaged about five percent in the 1990s. Macroeconomic stability is being pursued with greater control of the fiscal deficit. Inflation is under control. External debt is being reduced through the Heavily Indebted Poor Country initiative, with the savings channelled to primary education, basic health care, agricultural extension, rural feeder roads, HIV/AIDS, etc., through a Poverty Action Fund. The Government launched the Poverty Eradication Action Plan (PEAP) in 1997, offering a comprehensive framework for the eradication of poverty by 2017.

At 150th place out of 173 countries ranked on the 2002 Human Development Index, Uganda falls in the low human development category, sandwiched between Djibouti at one notch above, and Tanzania at one below. Trends in Uganda's HDI values have progressively risen from 0.384 in 1985 to 0.444 in 2000, just slightly below the regional aggregate of 0.471 for Sub-Saharan Africa that year. Uganda's life expectancy of 44 years is again below the regional aggregate of 48.7 years, but outperforms the aggregate in adult literacy (67.1% against 61.5%) and combined gross enrolment rates (45% to 42%). Finally, GDP per capita (PPP US) in Uganda was $1,208 in 2000, about a quarter below the regional average of $1,690.

There are important dimensions to Uganda's political development that are relevant to the country's efforts in capacity development. Dominated by the National Resistance Movement, the political system is an attempt to include varying political factions, allowing for the representation of people at all levels of Government. Political parties are not part of the system, which has worked well under a charismatic President. There is pressure now, however, for the opening of political space to enable a future exchange of power. Uganda has also undertaken an extensive process of decentralization, empowering districts to take responsibility for programmes and projects, and to raise revenue and plan expenditures. Finally, the Government has undertaken a major exercise in civil service reform.

Capacity Development

In this chapter, capacity is understood to mean the ability of individual Ugandans, their institutions and Government to effectively and sustainably develop the country. Capacity development (the acquisition of the ability, over time, to perform functions, solve problems, set and achieve objectives) therefore means both individual and societal development. So that TC and its impact are seen within a wider perspective, the following presents an assessment of past capacity development efforts.

In the belief that education is the primary avenue for developing capacity and empowering people, Uganda has first and foremost developed capacity through formal education and training. Religious missionaries, parents and teachers have been at the forefront of this form of capacity development. Their efforts endured even during very austere times, such as during the Idi Amin regime. As a result, the education system in Uganda has consistently produced human resource capacity in the form of educated and trained people.

Figure 8.1 illustrates the level of professional capacity produced by Uganda's education system between 1990 and 1999. Figure 8.2 shows the longer-run result of human resource capacity development in terms of gross enrolment at all levels of education. A close look at Figure 8.2 shows that there has been a large increase in school enrolment since 1997, the year the Universal Primary Education Programme was launched.

The second important mode of capacity development in Uganda was the "professionalization" of the Ugandan workforce. There are currently a sizeable number of chartered or certified accountants, insurers, surveyors, secretaries, administrators and other professionals who have acquired British and American professional qualifications. This form of capacity development is made possible by individual workers and organizations in both private and public sectors.

The literature on capacity development appears to assume that there can be no internal institutional capacity development without external assistance. This assumption ignores the historical fact that within each country there is an incessant historical, sociological and dialectical struggle that gives rise to slow and long-term institution building. Thus, notwithstanding other forms of external assistance, there has been a sociological process of institution-building in Uganda. The political system, decentralization, the Uganda Peoples' Defence Forces and the 1995 Constitution are examples of capacity building processes that developed as a result of dialectical sociological forces fermenting since independence. And there is no doubt that these processes constituted considerable institutional capacity. These examples illustrate the third mode of capacity development that has taken place regardless of external assistance.

The fourth avenue of capacity development in Uganda is technical cooperation. This mode of capacity development has largely consisted in the deployment of long- and short-term technical experts and consultants, mainly for organizational and institutional capacity development. Technical cooperation has been targeted largely at building

FIGURE 8.1: TRENDS IN THE NUMBER OF MAKERERE UNIVERSITY GRADUANDS IN SELECTED FIELDS

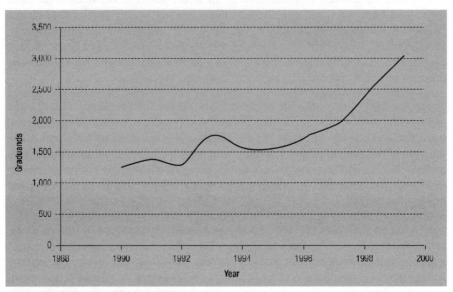

Source: GOU, Statistical Abstract, 1996, 2000.

FIGURE 8.2: SCHOOL ENROLMENT TRENDS (1950-1999)

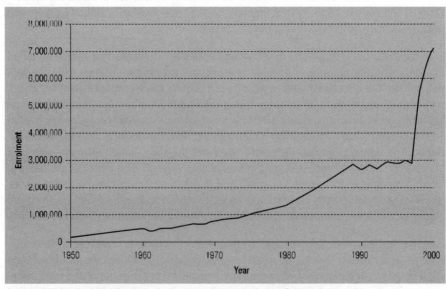

Source: UNESCO, Statistical Yearbook, (1963-1997); Background to the Budget, (1996-97).

central Government's capacity in designing and implementing structural reforms. The focus of this study is an assessment of the impact of this mode of capacity development.

A consideration of the foregoing suggests the following: that capacity development has been on-going at all levels since the turn of the nineteenth century, resulting in considerable individual, organizational and national capacity; that TC is just one, and perhaps not the most important, means of capacity development; and that new capacity development efforts should build on what already exists. The impact of TC on capacity development will be optimal if it occurs within the wider historical context of a country's capacity development process.

While it is now widely accepted that any capacity development effort should begin with an assessment of existing levels of capacity, no comprehensive and up-to-date information is actually available. The last manpower survey, which includes information on the number of specialists such as engineers, accountant, surveyors, etc., was conducted in 1989. It appears, therefore, that most capacity development projects in Uganda were based on the uninformed assumption that capacity was inexistent in particular areas.

Technical Cooperation in Uganda

The semantic advantage of the term technical cooperation is that it conveys the notion of a partnership between donors and recipients, whereas technical assistance connotes a giver-taker relationship (Berg/UNDP 1993). In this study, TC is understood to be the relationship between the Government and its donors, which in the case of Uganda, has by and large been cordial. In this relationship, the donors give, and Uganda receives, resources defined by the OECD/DAC as "aimed at developing human resources through the improvement in the level of skills, knowledge, technical know-how and productive aptitudes of the population in a developing country" (OECD/DAC, 1995). These resources have been aimed at institution building, particularly for better policy reform design, implementation and management. Although the TC relationship between Uganda and donors may be regarded as a cordial partnership, it has nevertheless been one between unequals in terms of resources, level of development and power.

The donors give Uganda two types of resources: free-standing technical cooperation (FTC) and investment-related technical cooperation (ITC). A 1999 report by the Government and UNDP defines FTC as *"the provision of resources aimed at the transfer of technical and managerial skills and know-how or of technology for the purpose of building national capacity to undertake development activities, without reference to the implementation of any specific investment projects."* ITC is *"the provision resources aimed at strengthening the capacity of the recipient country to execute specific investment projects."* FTC and ITC resource flows into Uganda between 1989 and 1999 are presented in Table 8.1.

Technical cooperation resources have increased since 1989, and as a proportion of official development assistance (ODA). Uganda receives the TC largely in the form of technical personnel and facilitation hardware such as computers and vehicles. A significant proportion of TC resources returns to donor countries in the form of remuneration to technical experts. Donors are increasingly providing resources through budget support, which places governance issues at the heart of aid management.

Table 8.2 shows the distribution of TC resources among sectors, with health and public services heavily favoured. Other sectors include economic management, natural resources, industry, energy, trade, disaster preparedness and humanitarian relief.

Table 8.3 presents the contributions of major TC donors between 1989 and 1999. In 1989, UNICEF and UNDP contributed the largest portion of technical cooperation. UNICEF and UNDP contributions later declined, while those of donors such as Sweden and the International Development Association (IDA) increased.

Forms and Practices of Technical Cooperation

Technical cooperation has taken various forms in Uganda. These include:

Institutional twinning – A donor country or institution sends technical experts to a national ministry or other institution. Examples of such arrangements include British Overseas Development Institute advisors sent to the Ministry of Finance, Planning and Economic Development and the Bank of Uganda. One Central Bank official suggested in an interview that in arrangements of this nature, would-be advisors have sometimes acted like interns attempting to gain experience in Uganda.

Foreign experts employed on specific donor projects – Under this modality, donors staff projects with their own nationals, regardless of whether local expertise is available. In such circumstances, the experts left when the projects closed. This resulted in duplication and substitution of national capacity in terms of human resources, with experts largely acting as sentries for donors.

Equipment with technical experts – Under this arrangement, donors supply their own nationals to handle TC equipment. Again, these experts act as custodians for donors during project implementation.

Long-term foreign advisors attached to government institutions or ministries – Most advisors come to the country accompanying multilateral and bilateral loans and/or grants. Technical advisors who accompany World Bank loans that are often co-financed by bilateral donors provide an example. Bilateral donors may also place advisors within a ministry or sector to which aid has been provided.

Short-term foreign experts and consultants – Shorter-term consultants are usually employed by donors to write feasibility studies for proposed projects. The World Bank and International Monetary Fund have used such consultants to take stock of national conditions before committing resources to development or balance of payment loans.

South-South technical experts – The Food and Agriculture Organization has employed many experts from Southern countries. This TC modality has been relatively cost-effective.

TABLE 8.1: TECHNICAL COOPERATION RESOURCE INFLOWS, 1989-99 (US$ THOUSANDS)

Year	FTC	ITC	Total TC	ODA	TC/ODA	TC/GDP	TC/GR	TC/GE	TC/Exports
1989	85,917	9,471	95,388	638,274	15.2	1.89	4.1	21.0	32.32
1990	143,634	26,240	169,874	658,940	25.0	6.31	8.5	42.6	88.74
1991	94,942	10,399	105,341	615,315	17.5	2.97	20.6	13.5	54.26
1992	149,195	22,358	171,553	610,652	67.6	3.95	21.7	18.3	66.98
1993	179,609	27,261	206,870	556,433	38.1	5.17	32.3	24.7	79.18
1994	195,370	14,780	210,150	610,449	37.8	2.32	14.6	12.4	25.19
1995	145,041	15,346	160,387	658,262	26.5	2.93	17.8	15.4	28.67
1996	190,269	24,568	214,837	681,490	71.4	3.07	16.9	16.7	25.91
1997	240,356	37,265	277,621	803,550	64.9	4.39	26.0	25.5	62.85
1998	270,596	37,529	308,125	759,918	72.6	5.12	29.3	27.7	59.87
1999	230,136	63,112	293,248	756,190	59.8	4.93	27.0	24.0	65.10

Source: GOU/UNDP Development Cooperation Report (1999).

TABLE 8.2: DISTRIBUTION OF TECHNICAL COOPERATION BY SECTOR, 1989-99 (US$ THOUSANDS AND %)

Year	1989	1990	1991	1992	1993	1994	1995	1996	1997	1998	1999
Agriculture	14,284	41,314	24,759	32,756	21,807	30,059	19,314	22,477	20,348	26,890	19,269
(%)	15.0	24.3	23.5	19.1	10.5	14.3	12.0	10.5	7.3	8.7	6.6
Education	13,997	15,310	9,400	3,825	13,802	7,429	16,798	17,527	17,632	20,145	63,440
(%)	14.7	9.0	8.9	2.2	6.7	3.5	10.5	8.2	6.4	6.5	21.6
Health	32,675	61,581	33,329	35,186	43,421	31,244	30,729	42,175	75,574	80,556	77,521
(%)	34.3	36.3	31.6	20.5	21.0	14.9	19.2	19.6	27.2	26.1	26.4
Public Serv.	8,379	16,869	12,276	20,300	24,179	36,227	26,036	29,240	38,279	45,593	35,989
(%)	8.8	9.9	11.7	11.8	11.7	17.2	16.2	13.6	13.8	14.8	12.3
Social Serv	1,092	1,359	448	40,135	34,844	24,882	13,018	11,450	13,357	22,674	30,600
(%)	1.1	0.8	0.4	23.4	16.8	11.8	8.1	5.3	4.8	7.4	10.4
Other	24,961	33,441	25,129	39,351	68,817	80,309	54,492	91,968	112,431	112,267	66,429
(%)	26.2	19.7	23.9	22.9	33.3	38.2	34.0	42.8	40.5	36.4	22.7
Total	95,388	169,874	105,341	171,553	206,870	210,150	160,387	214,837	277,621	308,125	293,248

Source: GOU/UNDP Development Co-operation Report (1999).

Scholarships – For many years, donors have granted scholarships to individual Ugandans. Many government officials are beneficiaries of this form of TC. There are those that point to this method as the most effective in terms of human resource capacity development.

TABLE 8.3: CONTRIBUTION OF MAJOR DONORS TO TECHNICAL COOPERATION, 1989-99 (%)

Donor	1989	1990	1991	1992	1993	1994	1995	1996	1997	1998	1999
Denmark	0.00	0.00	0.00	2.32	26.48	15.04	14.66	11.88	8.52	8.26	6.19
Germany	5.13	5.46	8.77	6.97	1.45	0.68	5.69	1.03	2.74	1.83	1.07
Italy	6.13	9.04	8.39	12.05	7.13	4.23	3.58	3.38	1.26	1.73	2.26
Sweden	0.67	0.24	0.29	0.26	0.54	0.20	0.00	0.61	2.51	5.13	5.57
UK	8.41	1.83	2.90	2.23	4.53	2.40	6.27	4.30	4.30	4.30	5.10
USA	9.65	19.69	14.65	24.62	19.01	17.56	21.76	19.12	13.26	13.52	16.16
IDA	7.07	7.15	4.56	3.43	10.23	36.12	19.55	26.39	34.87	36.96	29.36
EEC	2.00	4.61	2.58	2.27	2.50	2.09	2.86	2.69	2.77	1.98	2.01
UNDP	10.59	8.09	18.13	13.26	5.53	4.07	4.21	5.61	6.36	3.56	3.52
UNFPA	2.82	3.27	3.48	2.79	1.06	2.28	1.38	1.89	0.97	2.60	1.66
UNICEF	10.86	8.88	12.44	14.75	6.67	7.16	9.13	11.79	6.18	6.87	7.24
WFP	8.41	4.72	5.38	0.93	0.85	0.57	0.25	0.16	0.00	0.00	0.00

Source: GOU/UNDP Development Cooperation Report (1999).

The Government has recently begun to determine, coordinate and monitor more explicitly the type of TC it needs. The manner in which TC is practiced by donors has been slower to change over the last decade, however, and is still characterized by the following practices.

Use of foreign experts – There is still considerable reliance on the foreign expert modality of TC delivery, although there has been a substantial reduction since 1989. This is because in some cases there is genuine need for exceptional technical skills.

Bilateral donors insist on using their own national technical experts, claiming the need for accountability as well as visibility. For example, in its support for the Decentralization Programme, the Danish agency for development assistance (DANIDA) insisted on using Danish experts as financial management advisors at district level. Given existing weaknesses in financial management in most public sectors, the insistence on the use of Danish experts may have been warranted. This example, however, poses the question of the extent to which foreign experts may unduly influence national policy.

There are, moreover, numerous cases of foreign consultants who have been less skilled than their Ugandan counterparts. Interviews at the Ministry of Health, for example, revealed that in many cases, foreign experts built up their own capacities rather than those of their equally-skilled Ugandan counterparts. Long-stay foreign experts seem to be either gap-fillers or substitutes for local personnel.

Remuneration – Salaries paid to expatriate staff are very high compared to local personnel. This leads to strained relations between foreign experts and their counterparts, as well as loss of morale among local personnel. Projects may also be distorted through the subjective considerations of counterparts. There have been instances of government officials obtaining personal benefits (such as the use of vehicles) through TC projects.

Ill-matched projects – Many donor-funded projects with a TC component are overly ambitious, complex and reflect only a partial understanding of the local environment. This is partly due to the fact that donors do not seem to appreciate local experiences and insights, and partly due to the donor's desire to achieve different objectives simultaneously.

In many instances, little time is given to preparation of TC projects because donor deadlines must be met regardless of the reality on the ground. The training component in TC tends to be less innovative, and more supply-determined, with limited focus on sustainability. Project preparations sometimes fail to account for reforms that have already taken place, or of changes in information technology. In certain cases, capacities developed by earlier TC projects are not taken into consideration in the design of new ones.

In the past, individual projects predominated. The country has slowly but surely been moving towards the programme approach, pushed along by the development of sector wide approaches (SWAps) and reinforced by the budget support funding modality. But there are also TC-supported projects sometimes introduced in an ad hoc manner. Project Implementation Units staffed by foreign technical experts both within and outside of ministries also implement a number of projects.

Quality control – Foreign experts are not sufficiently primed in their development tasks. The scope of work of TC personnel is often drawn up with inadequate care – job descriptions are either too broadly or too loosely defined. The descriptions provide little guidance to incoming personnel, and rarely include measures of performance or output that would allow for effective monitoring and evaluation. Terms of references are not always explicit enough on priorities to orient or constrain behaviour of expatriate personnel. Even more important, the capacity building and institutional development objectives of projects are often muted and rarely given high priority.

Most technical experts, whether foreign or national, are accountable to the donors that pay their salaries. In principle, the experts' primary loyalty should be to the Government and its development cause. This presents difficulties for most technical cooperation personnel, because their careers are dependent on evaluations from the donor agency, consulting firm or non-governmental organization (NGO) that hired them. The potential for conflict exists due to such ambiguities in lines of authority, which complicate the task of a local manager seeking to impose coordination and control. According to respondents at interviews, there were instances whereby foreign technical experts working in the public sector ended their assignments without ministry staff ever having been apprised of their terms of references or reporting arrangements.

Donor visibility – The push for donor visibility works against coordination. Although there is increased coordination among donors, and between donors and Government, there still exists considerable competition among donors in the sense that each donor appears to want niches in particular sectors as a way to gain visibility. This has been watered down considerably through the PEAP/PRSP processes, and in particular through the partnership principles developed by the Government and donors in the PEAP. The strongest critics regard the insistence on visibility as characteristic of "late colonisers."

Lack of transparency – A number of technical cooperation projects are characterised by a lack of transparency – the real amounts of TC may never be known in some cases. Procurement procedures for some multilateral projects are also so complex and demanding that they often exclude participation by recipient country firms.

Aid practices began to change since 1997, with a growing emphasis on budget support and pooling. Multilaterals are increasingly complying with the Government's request to channel assistance through budget support. There is also increased discussion between Government and donors, particularly at the sector level, regarding the need, type and relevance of TC resources and modalities. There remain, however, a number of bilateral donors that continue to resist these changes for three main reasons: inhibitory laws in the donor country that do not allow for direct budget support, concern about the fungibility of aid and corruption.

The first of these reasons highlights the donor-driven nature of some bilateral aid. Technical cooperation practices and resources are derived from the laws, policies and objectives of the donor country, and these tend to prevail in decision making.

The second reason for resisting change reinforces the first. This is because in TC, the donor and the recipient each have their own, and at times contradictory objectives. Donor objectives include compassion, international obligations as defined by international conventions, historical obligation and long-run economic gains in terms of increased trade and production.

Even where objectives are in reasonable consonance, donors still believe that the use of aid resources should be aligned with the expectations of their taxpayers. This may lead to political objections – a number of donors will not agree to budget support, for example, as long as they consider spending on security excessive. In Uganda, there is an agreement between the Government and donors, re-emphasized in Consultative Group meetings, that Uganda's defence expenditures not exceed two percent of GDP. The Government has never exceeded this mutually-agreed limit.

The third reason for donor resistance to budget support and pooling derives from the country's reputation with respect to corruption. This places good governance considerations central to more cohesive aid management.

Technical Cooperation Policies

Technical cooperation is not a new phenomenon in Uganda. During the colonial period, the country's capacity was built through TC coming primarily from Britain, but also from other countries in the form of religious missionary assistance. After independence in 1962, the sources of TC expanded, with the Cold War adding a strategic dimension. Technical cooperation during this period consisted of Grants in Aid from the UK (the

TABLE 8.4: TECHNICAL COOPERATION EXPERTS BY ORIGIN, 1990-1999

Year	1990	1991	1992	1993	1994	1995	1996	1997	1998	1999
LONG-TERM EXPERTS										
Foreign	130	174	156	126	70	78	44	34	13	6
National	66	56	59	77	53	60	33	35	25	16
Total	196	230	215	203	123	138	77	69	38	22
VOLUNTEERS										
Foreign	17	19	7	8	6	8	2	n/a	n/a	n/a
National	n/a	n/a	n/a	n/a	n/a	n/a	n/a	n/a	n/a	n/a
Total	17	19	7	8	6	8	2	n/a	n/a	n/a
SHORT-TERM CONSULTANTS										
International	189	111	242	90	32	44	46	n/a	n/a	n/a
National	63	78	26	48	77	84	108	n/a	n/a	n/a
Total	152	189	268	138	109	128	154	n/a	n/a	n/a
Total TC Experts	365	438	490	349	238	274	233	n/a	n/a	n/a

Source: GOU/UNDP Development Cooperation Report (1999).

equivalent of today's budget support), technical experts, and material assistance, particularly for capacity building projects. Although several "white elephant" projects were initiated during this period, the Government's TC policy at the time was that any donor who could assist in fulfilling the objectives of its development plan was welcome to make contributions. From 1971 to 1980, however, TC to Uganda was reduced to insignificant levels due to political instability.

Donor support increased between 1980 and 1983, but slowed again when the security situation deteriorated between 1983 and 1985. Substantial TC inflows into Uganda resumed in 1986, but until 1993, there was no clear TC policy due to substantial institutional weaknesses on the part of the Government. During this period, donors designed and implemented projects in sectors of their choice, and recruited both foreign and local personnel to run projects more or less at will.

This situation created budgetary, administrative and credibility problems for the Government. Employees of line ministries, for example, would sign project agreements with donors that committed the Government to bearing a certain percentage of the project costs. As a result of these problems, the Government strove to design a TC policy beginning in 1990, and Uganda's Policy on Technical Assistance was finalized by the Ministry of Finance and Economic Planning in 1993. Its main provisions stipulated the precedence of the Government in identifying TC priorities, formulating projects and managing resources.

In 1997 the Government launched the Poverty Eradication Action Plan (PEAP), its comprehensive, long-term development strategy. As well as being the principal framework for external assistance, it spells out in some detail a set of principles, policies and practices governing TC, as well as the relationship between the Government and its development partners. The PEAP was revised in 2001 as part of efforts to meet HIPC/PRSP requirements.

Under the PEAP, the Ministry of Finance, Planning and Economic Development coordinates all TC needs and resources. A Government Standing Committee originally known as Technical Cooperation Committee and re-named the Development Committee, was established to ensure "horizontal coordination of TC activities".

As stipulated by the framework, the Government determines priorities, including TC needs, within the context of the PEAP. Donors participate as partners and stake-holders in establishing these priorities, which are constantly refined through national forums such as Sector Wide Groups.

The Aid Liaison Department, in consultation with the Ministry of Public Services and Ministry of Local Government, manages the allocation of TC in collaboration with donors, relevant sectors and local governments. This process is guided by sectoral needs, local governments, donor capacity, and restrictions donors impose on the sectoral allocation of their assistance. The sector and particular institution receiving the TC should be involved in the recruitment of the TC experts.

As far as possible, TC resources are reported as contributions towards the overall resource envelope available to the Government for development and recurrent expen-ditures. Technical cooperation is considered, like any other input, part of SWAps.

The use of TC for projects is scrutinized as part of the Development Committee's appraisal of proposed projects. The committee approves TC if it considers the project the cheapest way of achieving targeted objectives, including capacity development. In time, Project Management Units will be phased out.

Technical Cooperation and Capacity Development in Uganda

Where TC has targeted short or long-term training, it has had a significant impact on capacity development at the level of individuals, and indirectly at institutional, orga-nizational and national levels.

Until quite recently, when Makerere University began its Masters-level pro-grammes, most Ugandans who hold post-graduate degrees had been trained on TC grants in the form of scholarships from bilateral and multilateral donors. Some bene-ficiaries of these scholarships now run the country's tertiary institutions and public sector offices, while others are successfully engaged in the private sector.

A number of donors also assisted in the establishment of post-graduate programmes. The World Health Organization has been instrumental in building the Institute of Public Health at Makerere University. The African Capacity-Building Foundation and UNDP have been active in supporting graduate programmes in economics at Makerere University. United Nations organizations have been involved in on-the-job training of medical workers and communities, while the British Council and the Ford, Rockefeller and other foundations have given numerous scholarships for post-graduate training abroad and within the country. They have also supported capacity development and research in various fields.

Many professional Ugandans have been trained at short courses conducted by experts from donor countries through on-the-job training or in a professional training centre such as the Uganda Management Institute. Technical cooperation arrangements with educational and training institutions also includes the supply of computers, research and other equipment. This modality of capacity development, however, has been least emphasized by donors.

Since the late 1980s, technical experts have assisted the country in policy design and implementation, particularly at the central Government level. A 1999 World Bank-funded study on the impact of aid suggests that TC in the form of foreign consultants could have been the most effective mode of capacity development in designing and implementing economic reform policies, particularly where conditionalities were imposed. World Bank Technical Assistance Loans (TALs) have been instrumental in institutional development for economic policy design, implementation and management, particularly in the Ministry of Finance, Planning and Economic Development.

Technical cooperation has been effective in the reform and establishment of various organizations from the early 1990s. The Uganda Revenue Authority, for example, was successfully established mainly with the assistance of the United Kingdom, enabling the Government to raise more revenue. The Uganda Investment Authority was likewise established with TC support. The Economic Policy Research Centre at Makerere University was established with TC from the World Bank through the African Capacity-Building Foundation.

Technical cooperation has also been instrumental in developing a number of reform processes. These include liberalizing the domestic goods and services markets; dismantling the Marketing Boards; privatizing many government enterprises; floating the exchange rate; legalizing Forex bureaux; restructuring and opening the budget process; easing government licensing procedures; and decentralization. In the latter, United Nations Volunteers were placed as financial management advisors in districts such as Tororo, Busia, Pallisa, Bugiri, Sembabule, Masindi, Luwero, Nakasongola and others. Officials interviewed in the Decentralization Secretariat acknowledged the contribution of the UNV experts.

In most other cases where TC has taken the form of long-term foreign experts, its impact on capacity development appears to have been limited. Long-term experts usually operated in relative isolation, and on departure, left the gap they came to fill. While the existence of such gaps is explained partly by the bias of formal education towards earlier years, TC has not done enough to compensate for the absence of certain skills.

This failure of TC highlights the critical importance of the "counterpart problem". Public sector employees, including counterparts to foreign technical experts, are poorly remunerated. Low salaries undermine motivation. And where counterpart salaries are topped-up while projects are ongoing, there are additional incentives to leave posts once projects end.

More generally, the public sector suffers from poor management and inefficiency. Poor remuneration goes some way towards explaining poor governance, over-staffing, laxity of standards, bureaucracy, corruption and nepotism.

Technical Cooperation and Civil Service Reform

A Civil Service Review and Re-organization Commission was established prior to the implementation of the Civil Service Reform programme. The Commission's report and recommendations formed the basis for implementing the reform programme, whose mission was "to develop a public service which delivers timely, high quality, and appropriate services, at the least cost to the nation, supports national development and facilitates the growth of a wealth-creating private sector".

Ongoing since 1991, the programme has the following components: programme management, efficiency and effectiveness; management information and control systems; human resources development; time management and organizational discipline; and good governance. The programme's TC components include the provision of both foreign and national technical experts, training (mainly conducted within the country, to a lesser extent abroad), financial assistance, and equipment (such as computers and vehicles). The Civil Service Reform Secretariat, under the Ministry of Public Service and Cabinet Affairs, has responsibility for managing and coordinating the entire programme.

Table 8.5 gives a summary of the components of the reform programme and the actors involved in implementation.

With the absence of a TC policy framework in the initial phases of the programme, there was a lack of coordination among donors and line ministries. This resulted in duplication of effort, competition among donors and confusion among line ministries. The Government thus initiated the Civil Service Reform Programme, and UNDP was the first donor to assist in this effort. An influx of donors then ensued, with most vying for control of the programme. The World Bank emerged the dominant donor because, according to officials interviewed at the Ministry of Public Service, the Bank had more money, experience and information.

The high level of compensation paid to expatriate staff, when compared to local salaries, led to strained relations between the foreign experts and their counterparts. Poor remuneration did not allow for hiring and retention of skilled local personnel. As a result, foreign experts sometimes found themselves assuming executive functions within the Ministry. Procedures for recruitment did not take full advantage of local expertise, while those for procurement greatly minimized the role of the Government in deciding equipment to be ordered.

Since the Government has moved to take charge of the overall programme and TC policies in particular, the situation has changed significantly. There is improved horizontal

TABLE 8.5: PARTNERS IN THE CIVIL SERVICE REFORM PROGRAMME

COMPONENT	ACTIVITY	ACTORS
MANAGEMENT	• Management, coordination, monitoring, evaluation • Marketing the reform	Government of Uganda, Reform Secretariat, Ministry of Public Service
ENHANCING EFFICIENCY & EFFECTIVENESS	• Restructuring of local government • Result-Oriented Management training • Right-sizing, retrenchment • Compensation payments • Management of retrenchment	The Netherlands, the United Kingdom, World Bank, International Development Association, Government of Uganda
MANAGEMENT INFORMATION & CONTROL SYSTEMS	• Divestiture of non-core functions • Personnel & payroll systems • Budgeting & financial management systems • Pension management system • Records management • Audit & inspection • Assets management • Physical records management	The United Kingdom, the Netherlands, World Bank, International Development Association, Denmark, Government of Uganda
DEVELOPING HUMAN RESOURCES	• Payroll performance appraisal • Code of conduct • Implementing of job evaluation in districts • Training and development / plan implementation	The Netherlands, Austria, UNDP
TIME MANAGEMENT	• Time management	The Netherlands
GOOD GOVERNANCE AND PRIVATE SECTOR DEVELOPMENT	• Review of Standing Orders and Public Service Act • National service delivery survey	The Netherlands, Norway

Source: Compiled by the authors, 2002

coordination, collaboration and prioritization of TC needs. Sectors and institutions receiving TC have increasingly become involved in the selection process of experts. By and large, particularly since the formulation and launch of the PEAP in 1997 (and its 2001 revision), Government now sets TC priorities.

According to Ministry officials, there is still the feeling among donors that to fund a programme, external consultants must design it. The reality is that even where external consultants are involved in the design of programmes, Ugandans do the groundwork because of the need for local knowledge. This implies that much capacity has been built, most of it from internal resources, and suggests that the need for TC is diminishing.

Technical cooperation has had a positive impact on capacity development in Uganda's Civil Service in the following ways:

- **Upgrading competence through training** – All ministries and districts such as Moroto, Kotido, Kitgum and Bundibugyo, for example, were given training in Results-Oriented Management.

- **Payroll management** –The Ministry of Public Service can now track public service employees, and there have been increases in both remuneration and efficiency. The payroll system has been streamlined to ensure that staffmembers receive their salaries on schedule.

- **Regional office support** – A number of ministries received vehicles and other assistance in establishing regional offices. Examples include the Auditor General's Office, the Uganda Human Rights Commission, the Ministry of Lands and Minerals and the Inspectorate General of Government.

- **Local budget management** – Local authorities have been trained to manage the budgetary process to better handle finances at the local level.

Partly as a result of this positive impact of TC on capacity building, performance in the public service has shown some improvement. According to one respondent, the public service of today is considerably different from that of the early 1980s. There is also a sense that a good number of civil servants are committed to doing their work effectively and efficiently.

Given the volume of resources that have been disbursed, however, TC has not had its expected impact on capacity development in the civil service. This "limited" impact could be due to at least two reasons. In the first place, the period for evaluating impact was too short. Programme managers expected the civil service to fulfil certain conditions within an unrealistic time span established by donors. Second, the programme provided incentives only to those civil servants most directly involved, and not to others, who were discouraged from actively participating.

Technical Cooperation and the Health Sector

Uganda made the health sector a priority in the early 1990s. By 1995 it had designed a national health policy with the following objectives: ensuring quality health care with equitable access, strengthening partnerships between the public and private sectors in health care delivery, ensuring gender sensitivity, and promoting a sustainable financing system.

In recognition of the problems faced by the sector, its importance, and the Government's commitment to improvement, donors have responded with strong support. Health has been the major recipient of TC since the early 1990s.

Discussions with donors involved in the health sector brought to light a convergence of their TC objectives and the international development goals. There was emphasis on reducing poverty, addressing the AIDS scourge, reducing infant mortality and improving household welfare and productivity. Uganda's traditional donors have responded well both to decisions taken by the Government and the instruments already in place, such as the PEAP and the Health Sector Strategic Plan (HSSP).

The Government has gradually established appropriate mechanisms to ensure that both it and the donors are accountable for TC resources and the services provided to the health sector. The SWAps strategy is one of the instruments being utilized to harmonize and coordinate Government and donor activities.

Before 1997, TC in the health sector was characterized by a number of standard weaknesses. Donors were committing resources unevenly, and according to their own whims. Some districts were beneficiaries at the expense of others. Foreign technical experts were numerous, and the Government had no say in their selection. Many experts did not have adequate knowledge or skills, and few were familiar with Uganda. Many came to learn rather than teach. High differentials in pay between foreign experts and local staff led to serious distortions and resentment. With growing donor dependency came greater urgency for new practices.

The major change in TC practice has been a shift from project funding to budget support by major donors such as the United Kingdom, Sweden, Ireland, Belgium, the World Health Organization and the World Bank. The project approach, which usually results in donors doing the designing and implementing, is yielding to a process that ensures that resources are more closely aligned to national programmes for the health sector. Donors earmark funds for the health sector and put them into a central pool (common basket) under the HSSP. A Health Policy Advisory Committee was formed to enhance communications between donors and Government, and regularly reviews progress.

Donors that have not yet adopted the SWAps strategy are not opposed to its intentions per se. Indeed many of them, including DANIDA and USAID, base their interventions in the health sector on the HSSP, the PEAP and the National Health Policy, in line with sector-wide approaches. These donors, however, have not assented to the idea of putting their resources into the common basket and their interventions are consequently still project-oriented.

In either case, there is a significant level of collaboration between the Government and donors. The Ministry of Health, for example, often participates in the formulation of donor-funded projects. Even in the case of donors that strongly support funding their own projects, such as Denmark, personnel from the Ministry of Health are always invited to participate in design, monitoring and review. This process has been facilitated where the donor-funded projects are identified in the health plan.

The Ministry has also increasingly participated in the annual review of donor-funded projects, which enhances the Government's leverage on technical experts even when projects operate outside budget support. While the recipient sector initiates its own programmes and presents them for support, partners also propose certain projects to Government for approval. There is no record of any instance where the Government has rejected a proposal, although some donors have interests that at times take precedence over government priorities. However, as more partners adopt the SWAps strategy, there will be more participation in, and ownership of programmes by the Government.

Donors such as Denmark, Japan and the United States that continue to have reservations about budget support are concerned about financial prudence and corruption. They also cite military ventures as distorting government priorities. They continue to support projects that are sometimes run by personnel outside line departments, which can detract from capacity development. These concerns place the onus on the Government to improve financial management and to demonstrate commitment to the improvement of welfare.

Table 8.6 lists the public and private partners involved in the health sector, the basis of the relationship and the nature of the support that they provide. What is striking is the large number of partners and the range of different types of relationships. It provides an interesting snapshot of the challenge of managing and coordinating capacity development in a key sector.

Capacity development in the health sector has tended to focus on human resource and institutional development. In the case of human resource development, professional skills have improved through training. However, knowledge transfer has been insufficient with respect to handling hospital equipment procured under donor projects. This has sometimes resulted in needed equipment being under-utilized. Another concern is brain drain. Most technical personnel in the sector have been trained through TC, but a significant number of them continue to migrate to Western Europe, largely for economic reasons.

Capacity development has included infrastructure development, including the renovation of health centres and critical facilities such as operating theatres in various sub-districts. But districts lack the capacity to construct facilities and manage the new infrastructure themselves. Another problem is that the model rules of procedure for local councils (MOLG 1998) and the Local Government Act (1997) require that the tendering process be executed at the district level, and this may result in contracts being awarded to incompetent local contractors.

Capacity development in the health sector has also consisted of institutional strengthening, including organizational management and information systems, and supervision and accountability processes. The results have mostly been successful. Weaknesses remain in organizational management, which does not lend itself merely to technical solutions, and needs to be addressed in the appropriate cultural context over a longer period of time.

Recent Technical Cooperation Innovations

The environment within which TC operates in Uganda is a dynamic one, with continuing innovations by the Government, donors and civil society. The Government continues to consolidate its policy of ensuring that all TC coming into the country is matched to need and managed by the new Aid Liaison Department. This department

TABLE 8.6: TECHNICAL COOPERATION PARTNERSHIPS AND APPROACHES

PARTNER	RELATIONSHIP	APPROACH TO TC
Multilateral and UN system		
UNICEF	partnership	project/programme
UNDP	partnership	programme
UNFPA	partnership	project
WHO	partnership	project
Multilateral, Non-UN system		
EU	partnership	budget support
OPEC	donor-driven	budget support
The World Bank	partnership	budget support
Bilateral		
Denmark	donor-driven	project
USA	donor-driven	project
Japan	donor-driven	project
Austria	partnership	budget support
Netherlands	partnership	budget support
Sweden	partnership	budget support
Germany	partnership	budget support
Ireland	partnership	budget support
Italy	partnership	budget support
Development Banks		
WB/IDA	creditor	budget support /loans
African Development Bank	creditor	loans
Non-governmental sector		
Not-for-profit (NGOs)	service provider	social service delivery
For-profit	service provider	social service delivery
	• private practitioners	
	• pharmacists	
	• traditional healers	
	• informal sector	
a) University	service provider	social service delivery
	• Makerere University	
b) Research Institutes	service provider	social service delivery
	• Makerere Institute of Social Research	
c) Consulting firms	service provider	profit-oriented

Source: Compiled by the authors, 2002

ensures constant consultation among donors and between donors and the Government. The Government now makes inputs into the design of TC projects, as well as in the recruitment of technical experts. Civil society, represented by NGOs, is also gaining more access to these consultations within various forums.

As pointed out under the civil service reform sector analysis above, programme managers have gained experience and confidence in managing the TC process, and are now better able to defend the Government's position vis-à-vis the donors. Managers themselves feel more empowered through the capacities that many of them have acquired, for example, through private sponsorships for graduate degrees at Makerere University. The university itself has become more proactive in attempting to produce graduates with skills that are relevant to the needs of both private and public sectors.

Financing In the health sector has been compatible with the Medium Term Budgetary Framework (MTBF) since 1997. Available and projected funds are factored in the MTBF, which operates for a period of three years. Government and donor resources are all projected in the MTBF, which potentially facilitates the process of planning, on the assumption that donor commitments materialize. When they do not, the Government must top-up required resources while trying to maintain equity in budget allocations among districts.

On the donor side, a number of partners have contracted out TC activities to their national NGOs. An example is the Netherlands, which has entrusted most of its TC activities to the national development agency SNZ. Others, particularly the multilaterals, are focusing more on central and sectoral budget support as well as basket funding. Examples here include the World Bank and UNDP. Still others, such as the German development agency GTZ, have adopted a participatory approach and the use of local experts as their main modality for technical cooperation.

Lessons and Conclusions

Uganda is enjoying political stability and improved respect for human rights, particularly compared with the previous period, which was characterized by political turmoil. Political stability has been instrumental in the rehabilitation of the economy and has led to a great improvement in the country's international profile. This stability has encouraged the international community to provide significant TC resources.

Technical cooperation policies and practices began to change considerably in the late 1990s. Whereas during the earlier part of the decade there was minimal consultation regarding the nature and design of assistance, a national Aid Liaison Department now coordinates all TC. There are thus wider and more intensive consultations between donors and the Government on all aspects of TC programming. Some donors now provide TC through budget support, while others have shifted to the use of local experts as the predominant TC modality.

The Government was at the forefront of efforts to change TC practices as a result of its desire to have more control and coordination over donor activity and its impact on development and recurrent budgets. Critical to the Government's drive for change has been its growing capacity to analyze development problems, design appropriate policies and set priorities – and with this capacity, increased confidence in dealing with donors. There are nevertheless some donors, particularly bilaterals, who continue to resist efforts to change TC practices. This resistance stems from laws and procedures in the donor countries that inhibit the provision of direct budget support because of perceptions that aid may be mis-directed, or from concerns about corruption. It is also true to say that a number of public officials resist change, primarily because they have been beneficiaries of the status quo.

Technical cooperation's impact on capacity development can be seen in the design and implementation of economic and other reforms, and in individual human resource development through scholarships and short courses both within the country and abroad. The effectiveness of economic reform, undertaken mainly by the Ministry of Finance, Planning and Economic Development, is attributable to strong country leadership and commitment. At the individual level, most of the highly-skilled public servants in Uganda have benefited from TC scholarships. In other areas, TC has acted more as a gap-filler, particularly in public sector management and the industrialization process.

This analysis suggests a number of factors that explain TC's limited success in developing capacity. First, TC was not mainstreamed into established capacity development institutions, including and especially within education. Second, a number of crucial factors were missing: a commitment to the common good by those implementing TC projects, strong leadership and governance, and basic institutional and financial capacity. Third, corruption rendered TC less effective. Fourth, low salaries and limited prospects within public service skewed incentives. Fifth, there was a lack of coordination among donors in the design and implementation of TC projects. Sixth, procurement requirements and procedures for TC projects hindered project implementation and reduced contribution to capacity development. Finally, donors and Government focused more on technical cooperation inputs, and not enough on identifying existing capacity and building on it.

References

Bacha, E. L. 1990. "A Three-Gap Model of Foreign Transfers and the GDP Growth Rate in Developing Countries." *Journal of Development Economics,* Volume 32, pgs. 279-296.

Balihuta, A. M. 1999. "Education Provision and Outcomes in Uganda: 1895-1997." *Uganda Journal,* Vol. 45.

Berg, E. and the United Nations Development Programme (UNDP). 1993. *Rethinking Technical Cooperation: Reforms for Capacity Building in Africa.* New York.

Enge, E. 2000. "Poverty, inequality and aid: rhetoric and reality." Edited by Judith Randel, Tony German and Deborah Ewing. The Reality of Aid Project. http://www.rcp.net.pe/cti/documentos/Roa-Project.pdf

Dewey, J. 1916. *Democracy and Education: An Introduction to the Philosophy of Education.* New York: Free Press.

Easterlin, R. A. 1981. "Why Isn't the Whole World Developed?" *The Journal of Economic History,* Vol. XLI, No. 1.

Furley, O. 1988. "Education in Post-Independence Uganda: Change Amidst Strife" in *Uganda Now: Between Decay and Development,* edited by Holger B. Hansen and Michael Twaddle. London: James Currey.

Grindle M. and Hilderbrand M.E. 1994. "Building Sustainable Capacity: Challenges for the Public Sector." Pilot Study of Capacity Building prepared for the United Nations Development Programme.

Haddad, W. D., M. Carnoy, R. Rinaldi, and O. Regel. 1990. "Education and Development: Evidence for New Priorities." A World Bank Discussion Paper.

Helleiner, G. 2000. "Towards Balance in Aid Relationships: External Conditionality, Local Ownership and Development." Produced for the 2000 Reality of Aid International Advisory Meeting in Costa Rica. http://www.devinit.org/jpdfs/jhelleiner.pdf

Heyneman, S. T. 1983. "Education during a Period of Austerity: Uganda, 1971-1981." *Comparative Education Review,* Vol. 27, No. 3.

Holmgren, T., L. Kasekende, M. Ating-Ego, D. Ddamulira. 1999. "Aid and Reform in Uganda." A country case study. World Bank.

Jepma, C. J. 1988. "The Impact of Untying Aid of the European Community Countries." *World Development,* Vol. 16. pgs. 797-805.

Lancaster, C. 1999. *Aid to Africa, So Much To Do, So Little Done.* Chicago: University of Chicago Press.

Milen, A. 2001. "What do we know about capacity building?" Paper prepared for the World Health Organization.

Musanyana, E. J. W. 1972. "Uganda Education, 1925 to the Present." MA Ed, University of Calgary

Nzapayeke, A. and Denis Osborne. 2001. "Impact Evaluation of Support by the United Nations System to Capacity Building in Uganda: 1980-1995." In *Capacity Building Supported by the United Nations: Some evaluations and some lessons.* New York: The United Nations.

Nsibambi, A. R. 1976. "The Politics of Education in Uganda, 1964-1970." *Uganda Journal,* Vol. 38.

Organisation for Economic Co-operation and Development/Development Assistance Committee (OECD/DAC). 1991. *Principles for New Orientations in Technical Co-operation.* Paris.

Opeskin, B. R. 1996. "The Moral Foundations of Foreign Aid." *World Development,* Vol. 24. pgs. 21-44.

Psacharopoulos, G. 1988. "Education and Development: A Review." World Bank.

Republic of Uganda. 1993. "Uganda's Policy on Technical Assistance." Kampala.

———. 1994. "Capacity Building Plan." With the Ministry of Finance and Economic Planning. Kampala.

———. 1997. "Local Government Act 1997." Kampala.

———. 1997. "Report on Workshop on National Capacity Development." With the Ministry of Planning and Economic Development. Kampala.

———. 1997. "Poverty Eradication Action Plan (Vols. I & 3)." With the Ministry of Finance and Economic Planning. Kampala.

———. 1999. "Annual Report on Development Co-operation." Kampala.

———. 2000. "National Health Strategic Plan 2001/2002-2004/5." With the Ministry of Health. Kampala.

———. 2000. "Model Rules and Regulations for Operations of Local Councils." With the Decentralization Secretariat and the Ministry of Local Government. Kampala.

———. 2000. "Guide to Development Planning by Local Governments." With the Decentralization Secretariat and the Ministry of Local Government. Kampala.

———. 2000. "Development Cooperation in Uganda." Kampala.

Todaro, M. P. 1996. *Economic Development.* New York: Addison-Wesley.

United Nations Development Programme (UNDP). 2001. *Human Development Report 2001.* New York: Oxford University Press.

———. 1997. *Annual Report.* New York.

———. 1998. "Capacity Assessment and Development in a Systems and Strategic Management Context." New York.

———. 1995 "Joint Mission to Review Priorities and Proposals for Technical Co-operation programming." A UNDP/FAO/UNESCO Report on a Mission to Uganda.

United Nations Children's Fund (UNICEF). 1999. "Definitions of Capacity Building and Implications for Monitoring and Evaluation." New York.

World Bank. 1998. *Assessing Aid, What Works, What Doesn't, and Why.* Washington, DC.

Whitehead, Alfred N. 1929. *The Aims of Education and Other Essays.* New York: The MacMillan Company.

Statistical Annex

A REVIEW OF STATISTICAL EVIDENCE (1969 - 1999)[1]
EXECUTIVE SUMMARY

Preliminary Remarks

This assessment is primarily based on OECD Development Assistance Committee (DAC) statistics. The DAC has collected data on development assistance for more than 30 years, providing good coverage on a global level. However, the DAC database only allows for a global and particularly financial approach to technical cooperation (TC). The definition of TC[2] used by the DAC poses problems, and some data categories (such as TC provided by multilateral donors and information on human resources) are not well covered.

The DAC database is therefore not ideally tailored to the challenges of measuring TC and, in particular, adaptation to the new objectives and modalities of aid. The database remains overall a budgetary tool, which cannot respond to key questions on the impact of aid and TC in developing countries.

---

[1] A Review of Statistical Evidence was prepared by Pierre Baris and Jean Zaslavsky.
[2] Technical Cooperation: Includes both (a) grants to nationals of aid recipient countries receiving education or training at home or abroad, and (b) payments to consultants, advisers and similar personnel as well as teachers and administrators serving in recipient countries, (including the cost of associated equipment). Assistance of this kind provided specifically to facilitate the implementation of a capital project is included indistinguishably among bilateral project and programme expenditures, and not separately identified as technical cooperation in statistics of aggregate flows.

In order to analyse the complexities of TC, it is therefore necessary to explore in addition to the DAC database, other more qualitative, more fragmentary and less homogeneous data sources.

Evolution of Technical Cooperation

1) The drop in development aid since 1990 has primarily affected the poorest countries

In 1999, development assistance was valued at $59 billion (constant 1998 US$), of which $51.3 billion was disbursed to developing countries (87%) and $7.6 billion to the richer transition countries (13%). After an almost continuous rise for more than 20[3] years, official development assistance (ODA) has experienced a significant decline since 1992, falling back to levels achieved at the end of the 1970s. Although ODA climbed slightly after 1997, it is still too early to speak of a recovery. The fall in development assistance is alarming because it has primarily impacted the poorest countries, especially in Sub-Saharan Africa. ODA to Sub-Saharan Africa grew sharply until 1990, but has since experienced a severe decline. A substantial reduction of the debt of the poorest countries will be needed to rectify the situation.

2) Trends in TC have largely followed shifts in ODA, but with some deviations

From 1969 to 1977, TC stagnated despite the rise in ODA. TC then rose continuously until 1994, when it began a small decline, two years after the general drop in ODA. However, this decline seems to be controlled and TC has remained at about $13 - $14 billion for the last 5 years (corresponding to the 1990 level).

The fall in TC has particularly affected Sub-Saharan Africa (where TC is below $3 billion), and to a lesser extent the Far East. Other regions have been little affected by changes in TC, with the exception of Central and South America where TC has very slowly but continuously grown over the last 30 years.

The drop in TC first became apparent in the poorest countries. For high-income and upper middle-income countries, TC has remained stable or risen slightly. Lower middle-income countries have been very sensitive to the general drop in TC, losing one-quarter of their TC since 1994.

3) TC per capita, while stable overall, has declined for Sub-Saharan Africa and the LDCs

Over the last 30 years, per capita TC has averaged about $3.5 (constant 1998 US$) for all countries, with a small increase in the 1980s followed by a small decline since 1994. TC to transition countries and the former Soviet States is currently measured at about $8 per head, more than twice the average.

---

3 From 1969 to 1991, ODA increased from $30 to $67 billion constant 1998 US$.

ODA TRENDS (1998 US$ MILLIONS)

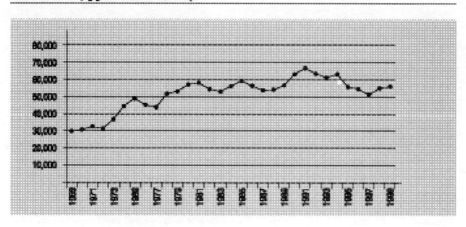

ODA BY REGION (1998 US$ MILLIONS)

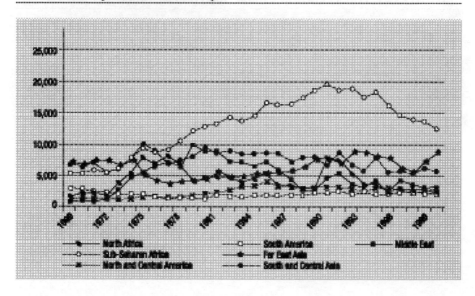

A regional analysis of the data shows a strong stability in TC per head in Asia (around $1) and in America (around $4). The Middle East and Europe have experienced strong fluctuations, which are partly related to oscillations in American assistance. Per capita TC to Sub-Saharan Africa has continued to decline since the 1980s, and is currently about $4 - $5 per head (half the level of the 1970s). The Sahel region, which includes many of the world's poorest countries, has experienced a severe TC decline — from $22 per head from 1980-1987 to $9 per head in 1999.

TECHNICAL COOPERATION TRENDS (1998 US$ MILLIONS)

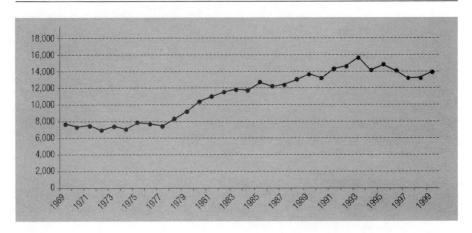

TOTAL TECHNICAL COOPERATION BY REGION (1998 US$ MILLIONS)

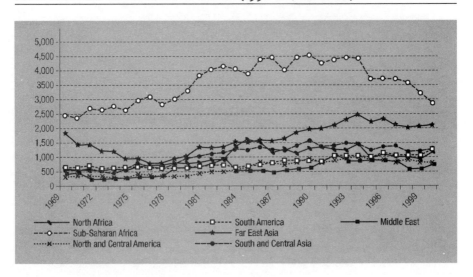

TC to LDCs fell from more than $8 per head at the beginning of the 1980s to about $4 in 1999. The only groups of countries where TC per capita has shown a tendency to grow over the last 30 years, are the high income countries (where TC increased from $6 to $13 per head) and the transition countries.

In general, TC disbursements correlate poorly to different indicators of economic and human development. Many countries that rank weakly on the Human Development Index (HDI) receive little TC, and vice versa[4].

[4] Of the 10 countries with the lowest HDI ranks, only two are among the countries that receive the most TC in comparison to GDP.

PER CAPITA TECHNICAL COOPERATION BY INCOME CATEGORY (1998 US $)

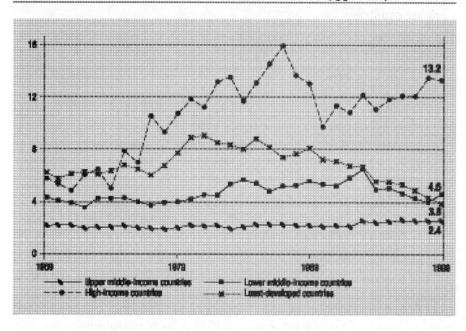

PER CAPITA TECHNICAL COOPERATION BY REGION (1998 US$)

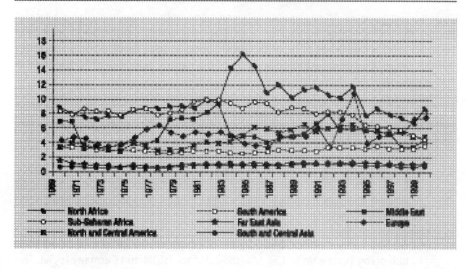

4) The share of development assistance devoted to TC is highest in the richer countries

The overall share of TC in ODA has remained surprisingly stable over the last 30 years, and has averaged 26% since 1985. This stability is even more surprising given that the relative importance of TC varies greatly by donor, region and type of countries considered:

- For the major providers of TC, two groups of donors can be distinguished. The first consists of Germany, the United States and France, which currently devote 40-50% of their assistance to TC. In the second group, Japan, the United Kingdom and the Netherlands provide 20-30% of their assistance as TC. This has not always been the case however. The share of TC provided by each nor has varied greatly over the last 30 years.

- It is the richer countries that receive the greatest portion of assistance as TC, and that tendency has accentuated. In 1969, the relative share of TC in assistance was 9% for high-income countries, but by 1999 it reached 88%. For the LDCS, the relative share of TC fell from 49% in 1969 to 21% in 1999.

The summary approach used here simply focuses on the percentage of TC in development assistance. It is assumed that the less TC a country receives, the more it could profit from investment. However the reality is more complex. A weak rate of TC is not necessarily a "good sign", especially since it tends to characterise the least developed countries.

5) TC is concentrated around a small number of donors

Over the last 30 years, TC has gradually become concentrated around 4 large bilateral donors, the United States, Japan, France and Germany, which together since 1990 have financed at least two-thirds of TC. Multilateral donors in 1999 provided only 11% of TC, but this figure is an underestimate because of the narrow definition of TC used in the DAC database.

The importance of particular donors in each region shows the global reach of major donors, and their political and economic priorities, which relate to historical ties (in particular former colonies) or geographic proximity:

- For North Africa, TC is dominated by the United States (56%) and France (23%). The relative importance of the United States was boosted in 1999 when it doubled TC to Egypt (from $336 million in 1998 to $645 million the following year);

- For Sub-Saharan Africa, three donors of equivalent weight provide more than half of the TC: the United States (18%), France (18%) and Germany (15%). The G7 countries account for only 68% of TC to Sub-Saharan Africa, a sign of the strong diversity of donors active in the region;

TECHNICAL COOPERATION AS A PERCENT OF ODA, BY DONOR

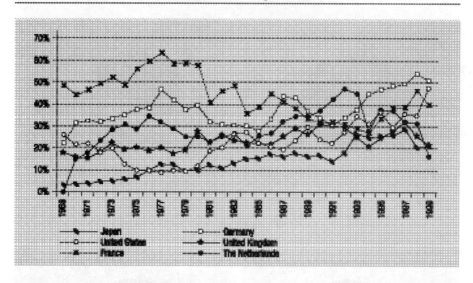

TECHNICAL COOPERATION AS A PERCENT OF ODA RECEIPTS, BY INCOME CATEGORY

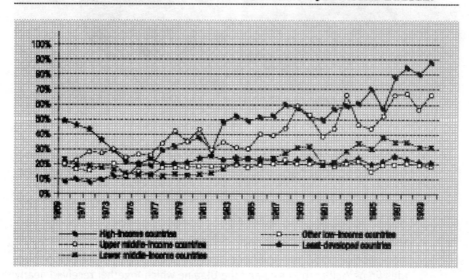

- For America, the United States provides 42% of TC. Overall, the European countries provide 31% of TC, with an emphasis on South America;

- For Asia, 3 countries provide two-thirds of TC: Japan (30%), the US (20%) and Germany (15%). Japan leads in the Far East (48%), followed by the US and Australia (8%);

NORTH AFRICA

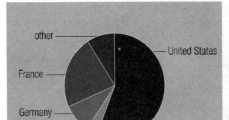

SUB-SAHARAN AFRICA

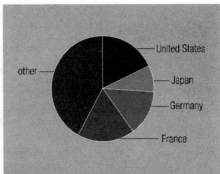

ASIA

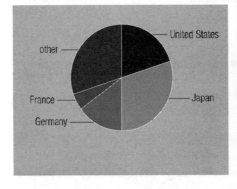

EUROPE

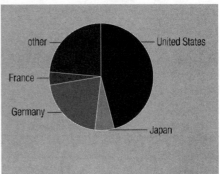

- In Europe, TC is dominated by the United States (46%) and Germany (20%). The United States (41%) and Germany (22%) also dominate in the Middle East.

The analysis is further clarified when one considers the regions and countries in which donors concentrated their TC in 1999:

- The United States disbursed one-third of its TC to the African continent (Egypt alone received 17%), one-quarter to America, and 28% to the transition countries (in particular to Russia and the Ukraine which together received nearly 20% of American TC). One of the particular characteristics of American TC is its mobility from one year to the next and capacity to respond to political concerns by avoiding dispersion;

- 60% of Japanese TC in 1999 was directed towards Asia — primarily China (17%), Indonesia, Thailand, Korea and the Philippines (5-6% each);

- France devotes 42% of its TC to Africa (two-thirds of which goes to Sub-Saharan Africa). French TC tends to concentrate on a small number of countries, almost all francophone: Morocco (6%), Algeria (4%), Tunisia and Senegal (3%), Côte d'Ivoire, Cameroon and Brazil (2%).

- German TC is more globally balanced, with an emphasis on Asia (33%) — in particular the Far East, and Africa (28%), mostly south of the Sahara.

It should be noted that Germany and Japan are the only large bilateral donors to have significantly and continuously increased their TC over the 30 last years. Starting from a relatively low base (especially in the case of Japan), they had caught up with France by 1990. This rise indicates a strategic investment in aid, which aims at restoring the political weight of these two economic powers in the international arena.

6) TC remains concentrated in the social sector — higher education for the richest countries, health and basic education for the poorest

Over the 10 last years, there has been a strong stability in the allocation of TC by sector, with a focusing of production in "cross-cutting" issues that correspond to the new priorities of assistance, such as gender and development or environmental protection. In 1999, two-thirds of TC went to the social sector, 9% to economic infrastructure, 11% to the productive sector and 13% to "cross-cutting" themes. Education had the most significant share (27%), followed by health (8%), agriculture (8%), support to the private sector (6 %), governance (5%), and the environment (4%).

Certain donors dominate in particular sub-sectors. The United States provides 80% of TC for the population sector, 75% to private sector support, 51% to the environment and 44% to governance. Japan dominates in the transport sector (58%), communications (54%) and in mines and industries (69%). France dominates in the construction industry (65%), and Germany in secondary education (48%) and trade (46%).

The richer a country, the more TC is concentrated in the social sector, and in particular higher education. On the other hand, the poorer a country, the more TC is directed towards health and basic education. For example, health absorbs 13% of TC to LDCs, but almost nothing for high-income countries. In the same way there are differences according to region: teaching absorbs almost two-thirds of TC in North Africa, infrastructure absorbs 40% of TC in Europe and "crosscutting" themes absorb 40% of TC in America.

7) Personnel and training costs are now equivalent

The share of personnel costs has remained stable at around 30%, while training, which represented less than 20% of TC 10 years ago, now accounts for 26% of costs. The shares devoted to personnel and training have become quite similar today.

However, the situation varies according to donor. For example, Japan has strongly increased its spending on both training and personnel, to $800 million and $1 billion respectively. On the other hand, France has reduced personnel costs to the benefit of training.

ALLOCATION AS TECHNICAL COOPERATION BY SECTOR (1999)

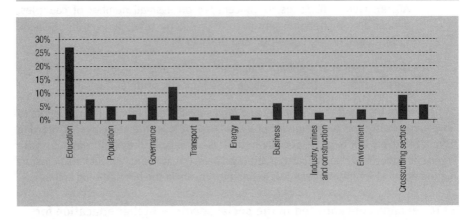

TECHNICAL COOPERATION BY SECTOR, MAJOR DONORS (1999 US$ MILLIONS)

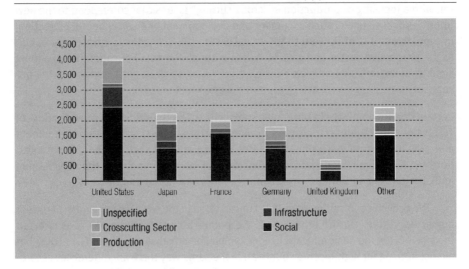

ABOUT THE AUTHORS

Bangladesh

Rehman Sobhan is Executive Chairman and Debapriya Bhattacharya is Executive Director, at the Centre for Policy Dialogue in Dhaka.

Professor Sobhan was a Member of the Panel of Economists of the Third and Fourth Five Year Plans of Pakistan, and served as Envoy Extraordinary with for Economic Affairs for the Government of Bangladesh. He was Director General at the Bangladesh Institute of Development Studies, and Chairman of the Board of Grameen Bank. He has published extensively. Professor Sobhan was educated at Aitichison College and Cambridge University, and was a Visiting Fellow at Queen Elizabeth House, Oxford University.

Debapriya Bhattacharya is a Senior Research Fellow (on leave) at the Bangladesh Institute for Development Studies. He participates in a number of consultative bodies for the Government of Bangladesh. His research interests include reform economis and strategic policy issues, investment and finance, enterprise development and technology, and foreign aid and the global trade regime. Debapriya Bhattacharya has a Ph.D. in Economics from the Plekhanov Institute of National Economy in Moscow and was a Visiting Fellow at Queen Elizabeth House.

The larger research team includes: Fouzul Kabir Khan, Chief Executive Officer, Infrastructure Development Company Ltd.; Sayed Alamgir Farrouk Chowdhury, Former Secretary, Ministry of Health and Family Welfare, Bangladesh; and Riffat Zaman, Assistant Professor, Department of Economics, University of Dhaka.

Bolivia

George Gray Molina is Director, Masters of Public Policy and Management, and Gonzalo Chávez, is Professor of Economics, both at Maestrías para el Desarrollo, at the Universidad Católica Boliviana in La Paz.

Professor Gray has conducted research on social policy, institutional development, and political economy in Bolivia, with a particular focus on popular participation. He has a Master's Degree in Public Policy from the Kennedy School of Government at Harvard University and is completing a Ph.D. in Politics from Oxford University.

Professor Chávez has served in Government and has written extensively on Bolivian economic policy. He holds masters degrees from the Kennedy School of Government (Public Administration) and Columbia University (Economic Policy), and is completing a Ph.D. in Economics at Manchester University.

Egypt

Faika El-Refaie is a Member of Parliament and the National Council for Women. She formerly served as Sub-Governor of the Central Bank of Egypt and previously worked in the United Arab Emirates as Head of Research at the Arab Monetary Fund. Her experience lies mainly in macroeconomic policy and planning. She holds a Ph.D. in Economics from Colorado University and a Master's Degree in Economics from Yale University.

Contributing researchers include Omneia Amin Helmy, Associate Professor of Economics at Cairo University and Senior Economist at the Egyptian Center for Economic Studies; Rawia Atef Mokhtar, Economist and Business Development Manager at Allied Corporation Egypt; Ihab Ibrahim El Dissouki, Lecturer in the Economics Department at the Sadat Academy for Management Sciences; Maha El Essawy, Undersecretary for US Grants at the Ministry of International Cooperation; and Naglaa Abdulfatah Nozahie, Assistant Manager, Economic Research Department, Central Bank of Egypt.

Kyrgyz Republic

Jacek Cukrowski is the Senior Expert at the Center for Social and Economic Research (CASE) and a Professor at the University of Finance and Management in Poland. Professor Cukrowski has conducted research and served as a policy adviser and consultant on economic reforms in a number of Eastern European and CIS countries. Professor Cukrowski received his Ph.D in Economics from Charles University in Prague and the Academy of Sciences of the Czech Republic.

Other primary researchers include Roman Mogilevsky, Executive Director and Senior Economist, CASE Kyrgyzstan; Radzislawa Gortat, Collaborator at CASE Warsaw, and Senior Lecturer at the Institute of Political Science in Warsaw University; and Marek Dabrowski, Chairman of the Council for CASE-Warsaw and a member of Poland's Monetary Policy Board.

Philippines

Jeanne Frances I. Illo is a Research Associate and Coordinator of the Women's Studies Program of the Philippines at the Institute for Philippine Culture, Ateneo de Manila University. She served as President of the Women's Studies Association of the Philippines and Secretary General of the Gender Studies Association of Southeast Asia. She has published extensively on gender in economic development and social dimension of irrigation development, and is on the editorial boards of Feminist Economics and Australian Feminist Studies. She received her Ph.D. is in Economics from the University of the Philippines.

The larger study team, also affiliated with the Institute for Philippine Culture, includes research associates Sylvia Bagadion-Engracia, Maria Concepcion L. Chan and Leland Joseph R. de la Cruz; and IPC Director Mary Racelis.

Uganda

Arsene M. Balihuta is Senior Lecturer and Associate Director at the Institute of Economics in Makarere University. His research focuses on education, poverty and general development issues, including the capacity of urban local governments in Uganda. As a consultant for a number of international organizations and government agencies, he evaluated structural adjustment loans, public expenditure reviews, poverty and income distribution, the impact of trade on the environment, and participated in the preparation of the Programme Support Document for the current CCP. Professor Balihuta holds a Ph.D. in Economics from the University of Notre Dame.

Other primary researchers include: Kenneth Mugambe, Assistant Commissioner, Economic Development Policy and Research Department, Ministry of Finance, Planning and Economic Development, Government of Uganda; Augustus Nuwagaba, Senior Lecturer and Consultant, Faculty of Social Sciences, Makerere University; and Warren Nyamugasira, Executive Director, Uganda National NGO Forum.